Incantations
and
Enchantments

About the Author

Donald Tyson is an occult scholar and the author of the popular, critically acclaimed Necronomicon series. He has written more than a dozen books on Western esoteric traditions, including *Tarot Magic*, and edited and annotated Agrippa's *Three Books of Occult Philosophy*. Donald lives in Nova Scotia, Canada.

DONALD TYSON

Incantations

and

Enchantments

THE POWER OF THE
VOICE and the BREATH
IN MAGIC

Llewellyn Publications | Woodbury, Minnesota

First Edition
First Printing, 2024

Book design by Samantha Peterson
Cover design by Verlynda Pinckney

Library of Congress Cataloging-in-Publication Data
Names: Tyson, Donald, author.
Title: Incantations and enchantments : the power of the voice and the
  breath in magic / by Donald Tyson.
Description: First edition. | Woodbury, Minnesota : Llewellyn Publications,
  [2024] | Includes bibliographical references and index. | Summary:
  "Esteemed magician Donald Tyson presents an advanced look at how to
  compose spoken charms and spells, enchant objects, use words and names
  of power, control the living breath, and more"— Provided by publisher.
Identifiers: LCCN 2024010838 (print) | LCCN 2024010839 (ebook) | ISBN
  9780738777191 (paperback) | ISBN 9780738777320 (ebook)
Subjects: LCSH: Incantations. | Magic. | Voice—Religious aspects. |
  Respiration—Religious aspects.
Classification: LCC BF1558 .T97 2024 (print) | LCC BF1558 (ebook) | DDC
  133.4/4—dc23/eng/20240516
LC record available at https://lccn.loc.gov/2024010838
LC ebook record available at https://lccn.loc.gov/2024010839

Llewellyn Publications
A Division of Llewellyn Worldwide Ltd.
2143 Wooddale Drive
Woodbury, MN 55125-2989
www.llewellyn.com

Printed in the United States of America

Also by Donald Tyson

Essential Tarot Writings (2020)

Kinesic Magic (2020)

Tarot Magic (2018)

Serpent of Wisdom (2013)

The Demonology of King James I (2011)

The Dream World of H. P. Lovecraft (2010)

The 13 Gates of the Necronomicon (2010)

The Fourth Book of Occult Philosophy (2009)

Runic Astrology (2009)

Grimoire of the Necronomicon (2008)

Necronomicon Tarot (with Anne Stokes) (2007)

Soul Flight (2007)

Alhazred (2006)

Portable Magic (2006)

Familiar Spirits (2004)

Necronomicon (2004)

1-2-3 Tarot (2004)

The Power of the Word (2004)

Enochian Magic for Beginners (2002)

Tetragrammaton (2002)

The Magician's Workbook (2001)

Sexual Alchemy (2000)

Disclaimer

The contents in this book are historical references used for teaching purposes only. The publisher and the author assume no liability for any injuries caused to the reader that may result from the reader's use of content contained in this publication and recommend common sense when contemplating the practices described in the work.

Contents

Introduction

I have enchanted by means of your words
which you created by means of the magic
which is in your mouth.
*—Inscription on a wooden statue
of the Egyptian god Horus*[1]

The most ancient and potent tool of magic is the human voice. In pre-historic times shamans danced around a fire, chanting or singing to the spirits of the natural world. We know they danced because they are shown dancing in paintings on the walls of caves, some of which are more than fifty thousand years old. We have no record of their singing, but shamanism has come down through history very much unchanged, and the shamans of recent centuries used singing and chanting in time with the beat of a drum or shake of a rattle. It is almost certain that Ice Age shamans used much the same kind of chants and songs.[2]

---

1. Owen Davies, ed., *The Oxford Illustrated History of Witchcraft and Magic* (Oxford: Oxford University Press, 2017), 10.
2. The word "shamanism" is based on the Manchu-Tungus word *šaman*, from the verb *ša*, "to know." A shaman is thus "one who knows."

In ancient times humans sang to honor the gods. Singing was not just an amusement or an entertainment; it was a sacred act. Similarly, poetry was recited primarily for the gods, not for other mortals. The Druids were literate but considered their songs too holy to be written down. The earliest Greek dramas, which involved singing and chanting, were enacted on a stage, not for the benefit of a human audience, but as an offering to the gods. Later, the custom devolved into decadence, and drama became a form of entertainment. But we still see the holy side of song in Gregorian chants and the singing of hymns in Christian churches. Chanting is used in Jewish synagogues and Muslim mosques. The repetitions of the Hail Mary on a rosary are a type of holy chant.

Of all human activities, magic is probably the most conservative. By that, I mean the practice of magic has not changed in any significant way for many thousands of years. What we know of magic in the dawn of human history is still being worked today by living magicians. The outward forms change to suit the times and customs, but the essential practices do not change. The ritual patterns used by our distant ancestors are still being used today. There is no real difference, in its essence, between the magic of the ancient Egyptians and the magic of modern Americans.

What is true of magic as a whole is also true of that aspect of magic that employs the human voice. The chants, spells, and prayers spoken and sung by modern magicians are not very different from those used by prehistoric magicians. They have the same structure, the same purpose, the same general forms of expression.

In this book we will take a look at the use of the voice in both ancient and modern magic. Use of the voice involves the breath, which is set into vibration to produce vowel and consonant sounds, for the formation of words that are used to express intentions in prose, poetry, and song. All these components of the voice play their part in magic. We are not interested in the present work with forms of magic that do not involve the use of the voice. Our focus here is on what may be broadly called incantation, although there are many other names for its various aspects, such as spells, charms, chants, curses, conjures, invocations, evocations, and so on.

Two terms that will be used frequently in the following pages are "incantation" and "enchantment." Both terms derive from the same Latin root: *incan-*

tare (to sing against). It is necessary that you have a clear understanding of their relationship. Incantation is the act of working magic by means of the voice. An enchantment is the product of that magic, what it was designed to achieve. People, places, or things are enchanted with incantations. An enchantress is a woman who works magic by means of incantations. An enchanted sword is a blade that has had an incantation chanted or sung over it.

Christianus Pazig, in his work *A Treatyse of Magic Incantations*, very well sums up what will be the main focus of our investigations:

> Incantation…we describe to be an act of Magic, wherein either by words alone, or also by the introduction of certain things and ceremonies they labour to produce some marvellous effect. From this we at once learn that in every Incantation, words whether few or many, are required to be uttered (*verba prophorica*), and hence in these pages we discard without further notice amulets with words inscribed on them, marks, ceremonies and other superstitious acts of this kind performed in silence, as is often the case.[3]

Pazig's scope is a little narrower than mine. I will not entirely ignore in this book written charms, on the consideration that written words, even when not spoken aloud, are uttered in the mind when they are read. Writing is only a kind of silent speech frozen in time. Most written charms were uttered aloud at the time of their creation to give them power on the living breath. Even when this was not the case, when we read them long after they were written, the sounds of the words echo in our heads, for how else could we understand what they mean? But our primary concern will be with incantations designed by their makers to be spoken aloud.

The topics we will examine include the composition of spoken charms, chants, and spells; the enchantment of objects; the use of words and names of power, in particular the use of the Ineffable Name of God known as the Tetragrammaton; the power and control of the living breath and the correct

---

3. Christianus Pazig, *A Treatyse of Magic Incantations*, ed. Edmund Goldsmid (Edinburgh, Scotland, 1886), 12.

way to vibrate vowel sounds; and the silent mental sounding of words. The general principles we derive will be expressed in the composition and use of incantations for healing, drawing a lover, binding and loosing, summoning spirits, protection, and malediction, with examples of each class of voice magic drawn from historical texts.

The specific external components of incantation are the breath with its inherent creative power, which is liberated by extended vowel tones and the correct vibration of words. Important considerations are the choice of specific words to vibrate and the manner of casting those words into poetic form by the use of such things as rhyme, alliteration, rhythm, and poetic meter. The incantations may be recited, chanted, or sung, and they may or may not include the use of sacred names or barbarous words of power.

Prayer is a particular type of incantation that we will examine in due course. It is directed at a higher spiritual being for the purposes of adoration, propitiation, aversion, or attainment. Which is to say, prayer may be used to praise a deity, to gain favor with it by means of gifts or sacrifices, to turn away its wrath and punishment, or to achieve a goal either tangible or intangible.

All these components of incantation are without effect unless the right inner state of mind is achieved when the incantation is uttered:

> The efficacy of all words used as charms and spells lies in what the Aryans call the Vâch, a certain latent power resident in Âkâsha. Physically, we may describe it as the power to set up certain measured vibrations, not in the grosser atmospheric particles whose undulations beget light, sound, heat and electricity, but in the latent spiritual principle or Force—about the nature of which modern science knows scarcely anything. No words whatever have the slightest efficacy unless uttered by one who is perfectly free from all weakening doubt or hesitancy, is for the moment wholly absorbed in the thought of uttering them, and has a cultivated power of will which makes him send out from himself a conquering impulse. Spoken prayer is, in fact, an incantation, and when spoken by the "heart," as well as

by the lips, has a power to attract good and repel bad influences. But to patter off prayers so many times a day while your thoughts are roving over your landed estates, fumbling your money-bags, or straying away among any other worldly things, is but mere waste of breath.[4]

From the most ancient times, it has been recognized that the life-force resides in the breath and in the blood. The breath is the life-force of the mind, the blood the life-force of the body. Early man observed that when the breath stops, or when the blood flows out, the result is death, even though no other injury has occurred. The blood is contained in the body. When sacrifice was made of human beings or beasts, the blood of the sacrifice was reserved for the god to whom the sacrifice was given. The breath is not held captive in the body but passes in and out. The intellect can shape the life-force of the breath by causing the breath to vibrate and carry forth sounds and words. In this way the creative life-force may be projected beyond the body onto things in the greater world.

The raw vital force of the breath and the focused creative energy of the voice have been recognized in all cultures from the most ancient times, but in modern magic we often use them in an offhanded manner without understanding that they are the primary taproot of magic by which its transformative power is released and shaped. To use this power intelligently, it is necessary to become familiar with all its aspects. I have set them forth in the following pages in what I hope is a clear and rational arrangement that will make you a better informed student of magic if you are a scholar, or a more effective worker of magic if you are a magician.

---

4. Nasarvanji F. Bilimoria, *Zoroastrianism in the Light of Theosophy* (Bombay: Blavatsky Lodge, Theosophical Society, 1898), 20. The term "Aryan" is here used in its original sense, to designate the Indo-Iranian peoples of ancient times.

One
Living Breath

Everything begins with the breath, which contains the vital life-force by which all things may be created. The first act of God in the first chapter of the first book of the Torah, called *Bereshit* ("in the beginning") from its first three words, was to breathe upon the waters of chaos: "In the beginning God created the heaven and the earth. And the earth was without form, and void; and darkness was upon the face of the deep. And the Spirit of God moved upon the face of the waters. And God said, Let there be light: and there was light." [5]

The "spirit of God" in the text was the breath of God. The Hebrew word for spirit, *ruach*, also means breath. The Spirit of God and God's breath are one and the same thing. This was a common understanding in the ancient world. The Latin word for "breath" is *spiritus*. The Romans understood the breath to contain the life-force. The ancient Greeks had a similar understanding. Greeks called the spirit *pneuma*, which means "breath." *Agia Pneuma* means "Holy Breath" as well as "Holy Spirit." The Sanskrit word *prana*, the vital force in yoga, means "breath of life."

The waters of chaos, called in the Bible the "deep," were a still and perfect mirror into which God looked and saw his own face reflected.

---

5. Genesis 1:1–3 (King James Version).

Understand this in a symbolic sense—of course God does not have a face in the physical sense that we have a face. As he hovered above the waters, the breath from his nostrils, the "spirit of God," stirred the surface into ripples, thereby breaking his reflected image into fragments. This caused an imbalance, prompting God to speak. When God spoke, the breath from his lips was articulated in the form of the words, "Let there be light" (*Yehi ohr*: "light will be") and this primal incantation from the mouth of God created the first thing that was not void—light.

The creation of humanity is described in two separate places in the text. The first place, Genesis 1:26–27, describes the creation of the body of Adam in the image of God. His body was shaped from the dust of the ground, but this human form lying on the ground was lifeless. In the second passage, Genesis 2:7, God "breathed into his nostrils the breath of life; and man became a living soul." The *spiritus* or *pneuma* of God became the soul of Adam. Note that the breath of God was breathed into the nostrils of Adam, not into his mouth. This is symbolically significant. We receive into ourselves the vitality in the atmosphere that sustains us during life through the nostrils. We use the mouth to project this power in the form of sounds and articulate speech. As yet, Adam had not spoken. His first use of language occurs in Genesis 2:19–20: "And out of the ground the Lord God formed every beast of the field, and every fowl of the air; and brought them unto Adam, to see what he would call them: and whatsoever Adam called every living creature, that was the name thereof. And Adam gave names to all the cattle, and to the fowl of the air, and to every beast of the field."[6]

The birds and beasts received their essential identities with the names spoken by Adam. The power of his breath was projected outward from his mouth in an articulated form, each name being different and unique. These words were words of power in a magical sense, and their speaking was the first incantation spoken by a human being, just as the creation of light by God was the first incantation in our universe spoken by God.

After making the beasts and birds from the dust of the ground, in the same way he had formed the body of Adam, and allowing Adam to name them, God used the life-force that was already present inside Adam, symbol-

---

6. Genesis 2:19–20 (KJV).

ized by his rib (euphemism for the bone in his penis), to make the woman, Eve. Many animals have a penis bone to stiffen the penis, but humans do not. This biblical myth may have served as an explanation to why this is so.[7] Creative force was understood in ancient times to reside in the erect penis, but ancient texts often refer to the penis with various euphemisms, not from reasons of delicacy but because the vital creative force was sacred and not to be profaned. For example, when Pythagoras met the Hyperborean magician Abaris, he is said by his biographer Iamblichus to have shown Abaris "his golden thigh," which was said to be the wonder of the world.[8] This is a polite way of saying that he had sex with Abaris.

In the Genesis account of the creation of Eve, the penis of Adam becomes through mythic euphemism his rib. The implication is that Eve was generated from Adam by an act of ejaculation, probably in the same way the Egyptian god Atum was supposed in myth to have created the other Egyptian gods. In Egyptian mythology Atum was variously said to have created the other gods by spitting saliva from his mouth, by his mouth (a veiled reference to articulate speech), by his hand, and by masturbation. The passage from an Egyptian funeral text given by E. A. Wallis Budge in his *Gods of the Egyptians*, which is in that text attributed to another Egyptian creation god, Khepera, is illuminating on several counts. This description also applies to the god Atum: "In the story of the creation Khepera is made to say, 'I had union with my hand, and I embraced my shadow in a love embrace; I poured seed into my own mouth, and I sent forth from myself issue in the form of the gods Shu and Tefnut.'"[9]

We see from this passage that Atum (Khepera) created the gods by ejaculating into his own mouth and then spitting forth his semen. Creative fire is in the semen, but the articulate act of creation, by which the other gods were shaped, was a spoken act from the lips of Atum, who gave names to the gods

---

7. Genesis 2:21–2. Refer to Scott F. Gilbert and Ziony Zevit, "Congenital Human Baculum Deficiency: The Generative Bone of Genesis 2:21–23," *American Journal of Medical Genetics* 101, no. 3 (May 2001): 284–85, doi:https://doi.org/10.1002/ajmg.1387.

8. Iamblichus, *Iamblichus' Life of Pythagoras, or Pythagoric Life*, trans. Thomas Taylor (London: A. J. Valpy, 1818), 67.

9. E. A. Wallis Budge, *The Gods of the Egyptians*, vol. 1 (London: Methuen & Co., 1904), 297.

and thereby defined them on his living breath, just as Adam had defined the animals in the Garden of Eden by naming them.

Obviously, much is left unsaid in the brief Genesis account of this magical act of creating Eve. The esoteric mystery concealed in the passage is that the life-force in Adam, concentrated in his semen, was extended in the same way the flame of a candle can be extended to light a second candle. And it is by this principle of extension of the original breath of God down through the human generations that we all possess our souls. All human breath is the breath of God.

The creation story that appears in the Hebrew Pentateuch is very ancient indeed. It may have been derived by the Hebrews from the mythology of the Babylonians during the period in the sixth century BCE when the Hebrews were held as captives in Mesopotamia. After their release from captivity, the Hebrews carried this creation myth back to Jerusalem with them and made it part of their own mythology. The story of the Garden of Eden, of Noah and the Great Flood, of the Tower of Babel—all come from Babylon. On this matter Ernest Wright observed in his work *Biblical Archaeology*:

> Consequently, an increasing number of scholars have been coming to the conclusion that many of these ancient traditions regarding origins must go back to an earlier period. In fact, it seems most probable that some of the traditions about the Creation, the Garden of Eden, the Flood, the stories of Nimrod (Gen. 10:8ff.) and of the Tower of Babel (Gen. 11) were brought from Mesopotamia by the Patriarchs themselves. How else explain why Israel had them but Canaan did not? [10]

From this biblical fable we learn several important magical truths. The breath holds within itself the power of creation. Our breath is the same breath that was in God, the very breath that was used to create the universe. There is no essential difference between the breath of God and the breath of a man or a woman. That power of creation that lies within us can be transmitted from us outwardly upon the breath through the mouth to affect other

---

10. G. Ernest Wright, *Biblical Archaeology* (Philadelphia, PA: Westminster Press, 1962), 45.

external things, without in any degree diminishing its vitality within us, in the same way a candle flame is not diminished in any way when it is used to light another candle.

What was it about the breath that made it figure so significantly in the story of creation? For one thing, it was observed by the ancients that when the breath stopped, life stopped. When a child was born from the womb, it drew its first breath, and when in old age it drew its last breath, it died. The life of a human being was rounded by the breath. This is not true of the heart, which circulates that other great seat of the life-force in the human body, the blood. The heart beats before birth, while the child is still in the womb. It is only the breath that begins at birth and ends at death.

Another significant aspect of the breath is that it passes into the body from outside it, and then passes back out again. The breath transcends the barrier of the skin, uniting microcosm with macrocosm, the lesser world with the greater world. It thus forms a bridge between inside and outside and is a perfect vehicle to project the creative power of the life-force beyond the limits of the body of the individual. It was observed that it could be used to transfer or convey information in the form of words, linking the mind of one human being with the mind of another after the manner of a bridge.

From a magical point of view, we can say that the breath embodies the raw power of creation, which by extension is also the powers of transformation and destruction, since whenever a thing is created, something that went before it is destroyed, and by the same token, whenever something is destroyed, something new is created by the act of transformation. This is an important concept in magic, so I will give some examples. If you break a glass, you destroy the glass by shattering and transforming its pattern into shards, but the pile of shards that results from this destruction is itself a new thing, newly created. Conversely, if you create a pot on a potter's wheel from a heap of wet clay, you are simultaneously destroying the heap of clay, which was a thing in its own right, no less real or complete than the pot.

We can distinguish deliberate, willed creation from creation that occurs by happenstance, as a result of destruction. Usually, willed creation involves the building up of organized complexity of detail in the created thing. This may be accompanied by a greater concentration of potential energy in the product of creation. When God breathed into the nostrils of Adam, he concentrated his life-force in the body of clay and animated it, giving it warmth. Life is accompanied by warmth, and cold is a characteristic of death. The breath is always warm. A living human body holds more energy than a dead body, as indicated by these differences in temperature. Even the breath of a cold-blooded creature contains some internally generated warmth, since its life processes by their very nature must produce heat.

The Breath of the World

When the air around us is drawn into our bodies, it becomes our breath. The exhalation of our living planet becomes our inhalation. It gives us life and sustains us for the interval between one breath and the next. The free oxygen in the air is drawn into our blood through our lungs, and when we exhale, the waste product carbon dioxide that passes from our blood into our lungs is expelled. Note that carbon dioxide is not solely a waste product. The amount of carbon dioxide in our blood regulates our rate of breathing.

More than anything else, our breath unites us with the greater world around us. Our skin is a barrier that has been designed to exclude parasites, bacteria, viruses, and other noxious forms of life that would prey on our bodies. We take in food from the outside. We excrete wastes to the outside. Only our breath is in constant flux, flowing in and out rhythmically several times per minute. With our breath we both take in and give out from our bodies in a ceaseless rhythm throughout our lives.

The Greeks called the living planet Gaia. According to the poet Hesiod, this goddess was the first to come forth after Chaos: "Verily at the first Chaos came to be, but next wide-bosomed Earth, the ever-sure foundations of all the deathless ones who hold the peaks of snowy Olympus."[11] From herself without sexual union, Gaia brought forth the sky, the mountains, and the seas. "And Earth first bare starry Heaven, equal to herself, to cover her on every side, and to be an ever-sure abiding-place for the blessed gods. And she brought forth long Hills, graceful haunts of the goddess-Nymphs who dwell amongst the glens of the hills. She bare also the fruitless deep with his raging swell, Pontus, without sweet union of love."[12]

---

11. Hesiod, *Theogony*, in *Hesiod, the Homeric Hymns and Homerica*, trans. Hugh G. Evelyn-White (London: William Heinemann, 1920), 87.

12. Hesiod, *Theogony*, 87, 89.

In 1979 James Lovelock gave to the world his Gaia hypothesis with the publication of his book, *Gaia: A New Look At Life On Earth*. The book sets forth the idea that it was living organisms that had shaped the biosphere of planet Earth in such a way that it is fit to support life. This is one of those great ideas which, once it is grasped, seems impossible to deny because it is so obviously true. Lovelock wrote concerning his early researches into the Gaia hypothesis: "Our results convinced us that the only feasible explanation of the Earth's highly improbable atmosphere was that it was being manipulated on a day-to-day basis from the surface, and that the manipulator was life itself." [13]

The living, vital breath of Earth is our breath. By it we are connected to all life on this planet. As the goddess breathes, so do we. Just as the individual cells in our bodies help sustain the body and are at the same time sustained by it, so are we sustained by the breath of Gaia, and at the same time we contribute to her sustaining. We are the living cells of her body but also her children, the most recent in a long line of evolving generations.

The Gaia hypothesis echoes a much older concept in Greek philosophy known as the *psychè kósmou*. The Romans called it the *anima mundi*, and we know it today as the Soul of the World. In his dialogue *Timaeus*, Plato called it "a Living Creature endowed with soul and reason," and stated concerning it, "For since God desired to make it resemble most closely that intelligible Creature which is fairest of all and in all ways most perfect, He constructed it as a Living Creature, one and visible, containing within itself all the living creatures which are by nature akin to itself." [14]

The intelligible creature fairest of all and most perfect is, of course, humanity. The macrocosm was made to resemble the microcosm. The Stoics held this world soul to be the only vital force in the universe and believed it to be a combination of the elements Air (by virtue of its rapid motion) and Fire (by virtue of its heat). It is *pneuma* that enables *logos* (the articulation of divine will) to penetrate and shape matter. *Pneuma* is an emanation, or one might better say, an exhalation, of the Soul of the World. There is no separateness to

---

13. James Lovelock, *Gaia: A New Look at Life on Earth* (Oxford: Oxford University Press, 2000), 6.

14. Plato, *Timaeus*, in *Plato in Twelve Volumes*, vol. 9, *Timaeus, Critias, Cleitophon, Menexenus, Epistles*, trans. R. G. Bury (London: William Heinemann, 1929), 55, 57.

life, no such thing as solitude. Each time we breathe in, we unite with the Soul of the World, and each time we speak, we define an act of creation.

The Power in the Air

Occultists have called the esoteric energy to create that exists on the breath by various names in different times and cultures. Fans of the Star Wars movies know it as the Force. In the nineteenth century it was sometimes called Odic force, a name given to it in reference to the god Odin by the German occultist Baron Carl von Reichenbach (1788–1869). It will come as no surprise that Reichenbach was influenced by the teachings of the German physician Franz Mesmer (1734–1815), who believed that a universal vital force existing all around us could be controlled by the human will and directed with passes of the hands to various parts of the body for purposes of healing. The English writer Edward Bulwer-Lytton (1803–1873) called it *vril* in his 1871 novel, *The Coming Race*.[15]

The Chinese Taoists call it *chi* and the Japanese practitioners of the martial arts by a similar word, *ki*. The yogis of India know it by the Sanskrit word *prana*. All these terms share something in common—they refer to a subtle energy or power that resides in or on the air. This energy may be drawn into the body on the breath and can be controlled, circulated, concentrated, and directed by the human will.

William Walker Atkinson (1862–1932), writing under the penname Yogi Ramacharaka, commented on this matter:

> Occultists, in all ages and lands, have always taught, usually secretly to a few followers, that there was to be found in the air a substance or principle from which all activity, vitality and life was derived. They differed in their terms and names for this force, as well as in the details of the theory, but the main principle is to be found in all occult teachings and philosophies, and has for centuries formed a portion of the teachings of the Oriental Yogis....Many occult authorities teach that the

---

15. Edward Bulwer-Lytton, *The Coming Race* (Edinburgh, Scotland: William Blackwood and Sons, 1871), 46–48.

principle which the Hindus term "Prana" is the universal principle of energy or force, and that all energy or force is derived from that principle, or, rather, is a particular form of manifestation of that principle.[16]

This energy is present latently in the air around us at all times and may be drawn into the body and concentrated there by inhalation. When drawn into the body, it becomes ignited or energized by the divine spark that is within us and can then be used for willed magical purposes of a personal nature, such as incantations. The air around us is the exhalation of the Soul of the World, energized in a general way by her spirit. When we inspire, it becomes our breath, and our individual human spirit further energizes it in more specific ways. This is, of course, a metaphor, but the occult principles and forces that underlie it are quite real and very potent in works of incantation and enchantment.

---

16. Yogi Ramacharaka, *The Hindu-Yogi Science of Breath* (Chicago: Yogi Publication Society, 1904), 16.

Two
Vowels

The vitality of the breath expresses itself in the form of vibration. Many of these vibrations are too high in pitch or too low to be heard, but those we can hear reach our consciousness as sounds, carried from the breath itself through the air to our ears. The larynx is an incredibly versatile organ of the body, capable of producing a wide range of forceful sounds, as well as the spoken languages by which humans communicate. What concerns us most, from the point of view of practical magic, is the vibrations of the vowels.

Each language has its own set of vowels, and these vowels differ from those used in other languages, although of course there is overlap. In theory, there is an infinite number of possible vowel sounds, because sound forms a continuous spectrum, just as the number of possible tones in music is infinite or the number of possible colors is infinite. However, certain vowel sounds tend to stand apart and distinguish themselves in any given language, just as music tends to divide itself into scales and modalities and colors into a limited number of recognizable types.

Vowels are a kind of word singing. Richard Paget wrote in his book *Human Speech*, "Considered as a musical instrument, the human voice is really a little orchestra of wind instruments." [17] Elsewhere, in his book *Babel*, he observed, "Shortly put, the human voice is a multiple musical instrument, in which an adjustable reed (the 'trumpeter's lips' within the larynx) blows its varying melody through a series of cavities, each of them not unlike the cavity of an ocarina, while the number and size of these cavities is constantly modified by the action of the human tongue, lips, soft palate, epiglottis, and false vocal cords." [18]

The cavities in which the sounds of the vowels resonate are the throat, mouth, and nasal passages. Paget wrote, "The throat and mouth cavity is variously subdivided into two, three, or probably sometimes even more, connected cavities—like an hour-glass with more than one waist, and consequently more than two bulbs—each of which produces a definite musical effect on the soughing or humming air which passes through it." [19]

All musical instruments require two parts: one part to make the sound and another part to amplify the sound and give it depth or color. In the case of an acoustical guitar, the sound of the vibrating strings is amplified in the large box that forms the instrument's body and emitted through the open hole in its top; in a piano, the sound of the vibrating strings is magnified by a sounding board, which fulfils much the same function as the body of a guitar. A trombone magnifies the sound produced by the vibrating lips of the player in the hollow body and bell-shaped horn of the instrument. For the human voice, it is the vocal cords within the larynx that produce the sound, and the cavities in the chest, throat, mouth, and sinuses that magnify and color it.

The Seven Greek Vowels

The seven vowels of the classical Greek language are different from those used in modern English and also slightly different from those in modern Greek, where only five vowels are used. Joscelyn Godwin wrote of the seven,

---

17. Richard Paget, *Human Speech* (London: Kegan Paul, Trench, Trubner & Co., 1930), 97.
18. Paget, *Babel* (London: Kegan Paul, Trench, Trubner & Co., 1930), 26.
19. Paget, *Babel*, 24.

"These are the letters that the gods taught to men, or, in other words, that the cabalistic priests attributed to the gods." [20]

A α	Alpha (a)
E ε	Epsilon (short e)
H η	Eta (long e)
I ι	Iota (i)
O o	Omicron (short o)
Υ υ	Upsilon (u)
Ω ω	Omega (long o)

As you can see in this list above, Eta and Omega were long vowels; Epsilon and Omicron were short vowels; but Alpha, Iota, and Upsilon could be either long or short.

The seven Greek vowels were regarded as the sounds made by the seven planets as they revolved in their crystalline spheres around the earth. The first-century Pythagorean philosopher Nicomachus of Gerasa, in his lost work *Theologoumena arithmeticae* (*The Theology of Arithmetic*), called them "the primary sounds emitted by the seven heavenly bodies." [21] In his *Harmonicum enchiridion* (*Manual of Harmony*) he wrote: "These are described as unpronounceable in themselves and in all their combinations by wise men since the tone in this context performs a role analogous to that of the monad in number, the point in geometry, and the letter in grammar." [22] By "unpronounceable," Nicomachus meant impossible to articulate, not silent. It is the consonants of speech that turn the vowel sounds into words, by imposing stops and patterns upon them. The consonants are the body that gives shape to the vowels, which are the living spirit.

The vowels were usually assigned to the planets in the Ptolemaic order of the planets, an ordering that was also used by the Egyptians and Pythagoreans.[23] The Abbot Jean Jacques Barthélemy (1716–1795) wrote, "The Egyptians

---

20. Joscelyn Godwin, *The Mystery of the Seven Vowels* (Grand Rapids, MI: Phanes Press, 1991), 64.

21. Godwin, *Mystery of the Seven Vowels*, 24.

22. Stephen Gersh, *From Iamblichus to Eriugena* (Leiden: E. J. Brill, 1978), 295.

23. Godwin, *Mystery of the Seven Vowels*, 21.

and Pythagoreans also arranged the planets: Moon, Mercury, Venus, Sun, Mars, Jupiter and Saturn, and in consequence, the vowel *Alpha* characterized the Moon, *Epsilon* Mercury, *Eta* Venus, *Iota* the Sun, *Omicron* Mars, *Upsilon* Jupiter, *Omega* Saturn." [24]

The bishop of Lyon, Irenaeus (c. 130–c. 202 CE), in his work *Against Heresies*, quoted the Gnostic Marcus, who asserted, "And the first heaven indeed pronounces *Alpha*, the next to this *Epsilon*, the third *Eta*, the fourth, which is also in the midst of the seven, utters the sound of *Iota*, the fifth *Omicron*, the sixth *Upsilon*, the seventh…utters the elegant *Omega*." [25] Other assignments that did not follow the Ptolemaic order were also sometimes recorded, but the rational assignment would seem to be to place the vowels on the planets of traditional astrology in ascending order, with *Alpha* on the Moon, the nearest "planet" to us, and *Omega* on Saturn, the most distant planet from us known to the ancients.

A α	Moon
E ε	Mercury
H η	Venus
I ι	Sun
O o	Mars
Υ υ	Jupiter
Ω ω	Saturn

Each planetary sphere of the heavens was evoked by singing all seven of the vowels in an order that was specific to that heaven. The first-century Greek writer Demetrius of Tarsus, author of *De Elocutione* (*On Style*), wrote in that work, "In Egypt the priests, when singing hymns in praise of the gods, employ the seven vowels, which they utter in due succession; and the sound

---

24. Jean Jacques Barthélemy, "Remarques sur les médailles d'Antonin frappées en Egypte," in *Oeuvres de J. J. Barthélemy*, vol. 4 (Paris: A. Berlin, Bossange Père et Fils, Bossange Frères, 1821), 185. My translation.

25. Irenaeus, *Against Heresies*, in vol. 1, *The Ante-Nicene Fathers* (New York: Charles Scribner's Sons, 1903), 338.

of these letters is so euphonious that men listen to it in place of aulos and cithara." [26]

The French writer Barthélemy may have discovered the actual esoteric vowel names the Greeks used for the spheres of the planets. In the ruin of a Greek theater at Miletus, in Turkey, that was unearthed in the seventeenth century, there are seven columns, each column inscribed by sets of the seven vowels, below which is the prayer "Holy one, preserve the city of Miletus and all its inhabitants." The line of vowels immediately above the prayer, which is the same on each column, shows the vowels in their natural order, except that with each successive column the letters have been rotated one space forward, so that on the first column appears the vowel set AEHIOYΩ, on the second EHIOYΩA, on the third HIOYΩAE, and so on for the remaining four.

If we assume, as Barthélemy did, that the spheres of the planets are signified by the initial vowels, each column is dedicated to a different planet—the first to the Moon, the second to Mercury, the third to Venus, and so on. The esoteric name of the planet would be the vocalization of the seven vowels in the order that occurs when the vowel of the planet is moved to the front. This esoteric name, when combined with the prayer common to all the pillars, would yield this meaning for the first pillar: "Moon, O holy one, placed at the head of the planets Mercury, Venus, Sol, Mars, Jupiter, Saturn, preserve the city of Miletus and all its inhabitants"; but this meaning for the second pillar: "Mercury, O holy one, placed at the head of the planets Venus, Sol, Mars, Jupiter, Saturn, Moon, preserve the city of Miletus and all its inhabitants"; and so for the rest, with the vowel of a different planet heading each vowel string.

Barthélemy did not go so far as to suggest that these vowel strings represented the universally accepted names for the planets, but he believed that the vowels were used in different ways for this purpose in different places in ancient Greece. He wrote, "I am not saying that in all times and all places, the same combinations of vowels have designated the same planets, I have

---

26. Demetrius of Tarsus, *De Elocutione*, in *Demetrius On Style*, trans. William Rhys Roberts (Cambridge: Cambridge University Press, 1902), 105. Some authorities ascribe this work to Greek writer Demetrius of Phalerum (fourth century BCE), but Roberts disagreed.

seen different ones on other monuments; but in such a matter one should not expect an exact uniformity of usage."[27]

Barthélemy believed the initial line of vowels on each pillar, which is not in its Ptolemaic order, indicated the melody with which the vowels of the planet name were to be chanted or sung. Here the vowels were taken to indicate notes on a musical scale. This is pure speculation on Barthélemy's part, however. What we can be reasonably confident about is that the seven pillars represented the seven planets and that each permutated Ptolemaic sequence of vowels was esoterically associated with its corresponding planet, signified by the initial vowel in the vowel set.

Magic Square of the Seven Greek Vowels

I will take these vowel sets a step further here, as a tool of practical magic, and propose a magic square made up of the seven esoteric vowel names for the seven planets. Its construction is simple enough. Each successive row in the square shifts the first letter in the vowel set to the back of the line.

A	E	H	I	O	Υ	Ω
E	H	I	O	Υ	Ω	A
H	I	O	Υ	Ω	A	E
I	O	Υ	Ω	A	E	H
O	Υ	Ω	A	E	H	I
Υ	Ω	A	E	H	I	O
Ω	A	E	H	I	O	Υ

I suggest that you make this magic square of Greek letters on cardboard so that it is seven inches by seven inches in size. In each cell draw the corresponding Greek vowel in black. Color the background of the cells with colored pencils using the traditional planetary colors. The traditional colors for the planets are as follows:

---

27. Barthélemy, *Oeuvres de J. J. Barthélemy*, vol. 4, 186. My translation. For a different arrangement of the Greek vowels to designate the planets, see Hans Dieter Betz, ed., *The Greek Magical Papyri in Translation*, 2nd ed. (Chicago: University of Chicago Press, 1992), 150.

Moon: Silver or light gray

Mercury: Orange

Venus: Green

Sun: Gold or yellow

Mars: Red

Jupiter: Blue

Saturn: Black or dark gray

When you color the backgrounds of the Saturn cells, make sure the vowel is still easy to see. I suggest dark gray for Saturn.

To make the Greek letters really stand out and come alive, employ the contrasting "flashing colors" that were used by the Hermetic Order of the Golden Dawn, an English Rosicrucian society that flourished at the close of the nineteenth century. Flashing colors are opposites on the color wheel. When they are brought together side by side, they appear to dance and flash due to their contrast. This gives them a kind of animation or living energy. Make the letters themselves the planetary colors and their backgrounds the opposite colors on the color wheel.

Vocalizing the Greek Vowels

With the magic square of the Greek vowels in front of you where you can easily see it, sit comfortably or stand with your back straight. Regard the first row of the square, the name of the Moon, and draw in a complete breath. Retain it for a single beat, then vocalize the Greek vowels in their natural Ptolemaic order one after another beginning with Alpha, drawing them out on your breath each for a single beat. Time the beats so that when you finish the seventh vowel, your lungs are nearly empty. Draw a second complete breath, and vocalize the second row of vowels, the row of Mercury, beginning with Epsilon. Continue in this way through the seven sets of vowels, so that all the planetary vowel names are vibrated in order. Do not strain your voice or your lungs during this exercise. When you complete one set of seven breaths, relax and breathe normally for half a dozen breaths, then repeat the square. Do seven repetitions of the square.

The sounding of the Greek vowels may be made as follows:

A, Alpha: "ah" as in f*a*ther

E, Epsilon: "eh" as in g*e*t

H, Eta: "ay" as in *ei*ght

I, Iota: "ee" as in tr*ee*

O, Omicron: "aw" as in *o*tter

Υ, Upsilon: "ou" as in fl*u*te

Ω, Omega: "oh" as in v*o*te

Strive for clear, round vowel sounds, each distinct from all the others. You can use a kind of light bouncing rhythm as you sound the vowels successively. This exercise will familiarize you with the sounds of the Greek vowels and also get you comfortable vocalizing them. There are other ways to sound these vowels, of course. Modern Greek differs from ancient Greek, and even different dialects within a language sound the vowels in different ways. But this will provide a general sense of what the Greek vowels sound like on your voice.

Use of the Vowels in Magic

The vowels played a central role in the magic of Egypt during that period when Egypt was ruled by the Ptolemaic Dynasty (305 BCE–30 BCE). During this time Greek became the dominant language in Egypt, at least among the educated class. It remained the dominant language of Egypt even after the Romans took control of Egypt in 30 BCE. The Greek magical papyri of this time are filled with incantations that contain, in addition to written instructions, long chains of extended vowel sounds that were to be vibrated on the breath by the magician.[28]

Although the majority of the surviving incantations are in Greek, it is likely that the practice of extending the vowels on the breath in magical incantations originated with the Egyptians, whose skill at magic was legendary throughout the ancient world. Janet H. Johnson observed in her introduction to the *Demotic Magical Papyri*, "Even in the spells written in Greek, the religious or

---

28. See Hans Dieter Betz, ed., *The Greek Magical Papyri in Translation, Including the Demotic Spells*, 2nd ed. (Chicago: University of Chicago Press, 1992). An example of a series of extended Greek vowels appears on page 16, line 98.

mythological background and the methodology to be followed to ensure success may be purely Egyptian in origin."[29] The Greeks who came to Egypt to rule that land picked up the practice from the Egyptian magicians and priests and made it their own. Even after the Romans conquered Egypt and took control of that nation, the use of extended vowel sounds for magic purposes continued.

The way the vowels of the planets were expressed by the Egyptian priests is in sharp contrast to the ways Greek witches used vocal sounds to call up infernal spirits. The intonations of the Egyptian priests were beautiful on the ear; those of the witches were ugly and unpleasant. This distinction reflects the difference between theurgic and goetic magic, the magic of heaven and the magic of the underworld.

We find a veiled reference during the reign of the Roman emperor Nero to the use of vowel sounds by witches in the epic poem *Pharsalia* by Marcus Annaeus Lucanus (39–65 CE), better known as Lucan, who wrote concerning the witch Erictho:

> Last came her voice
> More potent than all herbs to charm the gods
> Who rule in Lethe. Dissonant murmurs first
> And sounds discordant from the tongues of men
> She utters, scarce articulate: the bay
> Of wolves, and barking as of dogs, were mixed
> With that fell chant; the screech of nightly owl
> Raising her hoarse complaint; the howl of beast
> And sibilant hiss of snake—all these were there;
> And more—the wail of waters on the rock,
> The sound of forests and the thunder peal.
> Such was her voice.[30]

Who can doubt that these howling, barking, screeching sounds made by the witch are any other than the Greek vowels extended on the breath? Here, the vowels are not sounded by themselves with beautiful, bell-like tones, as

---

29. Janet H. Johnson, introduction to Betz, ed., *The Greek Magical Papyri in Translation*, lv.

30. Lucan, *The Pharsalia of Lucan*, trans. Edward Ridley (London: Longmans, Green, and Co., 1896), bk. 6, lines 810–21. Lucan began writing his epic around 61 AD.

they were by the Egyptian priests, but roared, barked, and growled out, as
befits the practice of goetic or chthonic magic, and intermingled with harsh
consonants and guttural stops. Erictho was supposed by the author Lucan to
be a witch who dwelt in Thessaly, in northern Greece, in the middle of the
first century BCE, but Lucan probably had direct personal knowledge of the
use of vowel sounds by actual witches in his own day at Rome.

The use of vowels in magic was still alive a century later when the Hermetic books were written, as the *Discourse on the Eighth and Ninth* shows:

> A
> OOEE
> OOO EEE
> OOOO EE
> OOOOOO OOOOO
> OOOOOO UUUUUU
> ooooooooooooooo
> ZOZAZOTH
> Lord, grant us wisdom from your power that reaches us,
> that we may relate to ourselves the vision of the eighth
> and the ninth.[31]

The eighth and ninth referred to in this Hermetic text are, of course, the
eighth and ninth spheres, respectively the sphere of the fixed stars, and the
crystalline sphere of the waters above the firmament; or by some authorities
the *primum mobile*. According to the Hermetic doctrine, the aspiration of the
soul was to ascend through the heavens up to the sphere where God resided.

The editor of the passage I have quoted, William Barnstone, remarked in
a footnote: "This is glossolalia, speaking in tongues, speaking in ecstasy."[32]
He was quite wrong. The use of extended vowel sounds was not accidental or
inspirational, but was deliberate and based upon an established method, most
of the explanation of which, unfortunately, has not come down to us. Magic is
never random. It adheres to fixed principles that are unchanging. Sometimes

---

31. Willis Barnstone and Marvin Meyer, eds., *The Gnostic Bible* (Boston: Shambhala, 2003),
516. The *Discourse on the Eighth and Ninth* was written in Egypt in the Greek language
in the second century BE.

32. Barnstone, *The Gnostic Bible*, 516n7.

these principles can be inferred, if enough accurate information exists. Very likely many of the texts such as the one quoted above contain copying errors and omissions in the vowels, which makes interpretation even more difficult.

It may be observed of the quotation that the vowels begin with Alpha, the first letter of the Greek alphabet, and end with Omega, the final letter. Used in this way, the vowels were designed to draw down the power of the god who is named Zozazoth, which may be broken down into the two names "Zoz" and "Azoth." The name "Zoz" will be familiar to those who know the magic of Austin Osman Spare.[33] "Azoth" is a word of power that combines the first and last letters of the Latin (A–Z), Greek (A–O), and Hebrew (A–Th) alphabets. It was used in European magic and alchemy of the Renaissance period.

The use of pure vowel sounds in charms and chants was not confined to ancient times but appears throughout human history. It survived in the form of folk songs in England down to modern times, although those singing the songs had no idea that by using the vowel sounds, they were liberating magic power. At the beginning of the twentieth century, it was the custom for English farm laborers on Plough Monday (the first Monday after January 6) to blacken their faces or wear masks and to go around from house to house singing and dancing at the front door in the hope of receiving gifts of money or beer. If they were rejected, they would threaten to plough up the doorstep. This is what they sang:

> O, O, E, I, O,
> Up with the shovel and the hoe,
> Down with the fiddle and the drum.
> No more work for poor old neddy,
> Now that the ploughing's done.[34]

This seemingly harmless bit of doggerel is actually a compulsion charm, intended to force the householder to give gifts to these revellers with the hope of sending them away. The power in this charm lies in the vowel sounds. It is

---

33. Spare spelled the name "Zos," but the final letter in the name stood for a reflected Z. Symbolically, it suggests twin serpents rising on either side of the solar disk. I am not suggesting a direct relationship between the "Zoz" of the *Discourse on the Eighth and Ninth* and the "Zos" of Spare, but the similarity is intriguing.

34. Arthur Robinson Wright, *English Folklore* (London: Ernest Benn, 1928), 40.

very unlikely that any of the laborers singing the charm realized that it was an act of magic.

How to Sound the Vowels

There is one passage among the Greek magical papyri that offers some insight into how the extended vowels were to be sounded. We can be grateful to the unknown scribe who copied the spell that he decided to provide some hints for those who would come after him and read his work, because by understanding how the Greek vowels were used, we can better understand how to use the English vowels. I will quote the passage here:

> AOIAŌ EOĒY (nine letters):
> The "A" with an open mouth, undulating like a wave;
> The "O" succinctly, as a breathed threat,
> The "IAŌ" to earth, to air, and to heaven;
> The "Ē" like a baboon;
> The "O" in the same way as above;
> The "E" with enjoyment, aspirating it,
> The "Y" like a shepherd, drawing out the pronunciation.[35]

I have given the ordering of the vowels as it appears in Betz's *Greek Magical Papyri*. However, it seems to me that an error was made by someone in the ordering of the vowels, since the first letter in the word "EOĒY" is the short vowel Epsilon, and the third letter, the long vowel Eta, but in the descriptive lines Eta is described first, then Epsilon.

These instructions are somewhat obscure, but we are fortunate even to have them. At least they offer some guide. Note that nine vowels appear in the first line, two of which, the Alpha and the Omicron, are repeated, so that there are seven unique Greek vowels in this line (AOIAΩ EOHY). The guide to pronunciation is also divided into seven distinct lines. It is evident that the two names of power, AOIAŌ EOĒY, which are entirely of vowels, were to be pronounced one vowel at a time, with the exception of the name of God IAŌ that occurs in the first name. This seems to have its own unique manner of pronuncia-

---

35. Betz, ed., *Greek Magical Papyri*, 101–2.

tion. It may be that the IAŌ was sounded while tilting up the head, so that the first vowel was voiced looking at the ground, the second while looking at the horizon, and the third while looking up to the heavens. If so, the up tilting of the head would have been one continuous movement while the vowels were vibrated one after the other and run together.

The sounding of the A (Alpha) is clear enough—undulating like a wave. This suggests a regular change in pitch to create a rolling or trilling sound, which is called ululation. It is produced by moving the tongue rapidly from side to side, or up and down against and away from the teeth, while sounding the vowel. The O (Omicron) is sounded more briefly with an extended huff of air. The Ē (Eta) "like a baboon" may refer to the vocalizations of the cynocephalus ape so prominent in Egyptian mythology, which appears perched atop the Great Balance in the Papyrus of Ani.[36] The second O (Omicron) is sounded in the same way as the first O (Omicron). The second E (Epsilon) is said to be pronounced "with enjoyment, aspirating it." This is a different sound from the first Ē (Eta), since it is a different vowel. Finally, the Y (Upsilon) is sounded in a drawn-out fashion, "like a shepherd" calling to his flocks across the hills.

It should be noted that there were two ways in which the vowels were sounded to release their power in the Greek magical papyri. They were either extended on the breath in a sustained howling sound, or they were sounded individually in sacred names made up wholly of vowels, such as the names AOIAŌ EOĒY in the quotation above. The vowels also appear in incantations as part of ordinary words, but these seem to have been vocalized in the usual way, as words, although they were probably uttered forcefully in a ritual manner. It is a safe assumption that the names composed wholly of vowels were more significant and more potent than the sacred names composed of combined vowels and consonants.

There was method to the sounding of vowels, which were the most important part of the incantation. All the power was in the vowels, which were called

---

36. Papyrus no. 10,470, sheets 3 and 4, British Museum, https://www.britishmuseum.org /collection/object/Y_EA10470-3. See E. A. Wallis Budge, *The Gods of the Egyptians*, vol. 1 (London: Methuen & Co., 1904), color foldout plate following page 144. This plate appears in the 1969 Dover Publications edition at the end of volume 2 as a tipped-in color plate.

in one Greco-Egyptian papyri "the shudderful names: A EE ĒĒĒ IIII OOOOO YYYYYY ŌŌŌŌŌŌŌ."[37] The increase by one number in the repetition of each successive vowel suggests both an extension of its sounding on the breath and that these vowels were to be written down in a triangular pattern in seven rows, the A (Alpha) at the top, the EE (Epsilon) in the second row, the ĒĒĒ (Eta) in the third row, and so on.

Use of the Vowels in Magic

Exactly how the magicians of the Egyptians, Greeks, and Romans understood the use of the vowels is difficult to determine, since it was never written forth in an explicit way, or at least, not in any preserved text. All we have are examples of spells in which these vowels were used. My own belief is that each vowel represented a divine hierarchy of power, and that by sounding the vowel, the magician was able to summon and command the individual beings in that hierarchy, or the esoteric energies represented by that hierarchy, for works of magic. A key association in these seven vowel hierarchies would have been the seven astrological planets of ancient times; another would be the gods or goddesses associated with the planets; yet another element would be the seven archangels linked with the seven heavenly spheres of the planets by Jews, Christians, and Muslims.

When the Elizabethan scholar Dr. John Dee and his crystal scryer, Edward Kelley, received the system of Enochian magic during a series of séances conducted toward the close of the sixteenth century, the angels informed Dee through Kelley that each Enochian letter was a unique spirit. When the Enochian letters were gathered into words, their potency was magnified. In pronouncing Enochian words, each individual letter is vocalized in succession, as a way of giving these spirits of the letters life on the living breath of the magician. The priests of Egypt must have understood the Greek vowels in a similar way, as unique living vessels of power, each with its own set of associations.

Numerical groups or clusters of extended vowels may have had particular meanings and uses that are unknown to us. Even as in ancient rune magic, repetitions of specific runes appear in rune spells engraved on such things

---

37. Betz, ed., *Greek Magical Papyri*, 102. Elsewhere in the Greek papyri, a magician says, "Lord, I imitate you by saying the seven vowels; enter and hear me, A EE ĒĒĒ IIII OOOOO YYYYYY ŌŌŌŌŌŌŌ." *Greek Magical Papyri*, 178.

as swords and shields, but the meanings of the number of their repetitions have been lost. It may be that the runes were sounded in an extended way on the voice by rune masters, even as the Greek vowels were sounded by the Egyptians, Greeks, and Romans. However, there is a difference—the groups of repeated runes in ancient rune spells are not all vowels. It is with the special power of the vowels that we are concerned.

IAO

One specific use of Greek vowels in the ancient world stands out. It is the three vowels I, A, and O (Iota-Alpha-Omega), which were joined together to form the sacred name of God, IAΩ. How old this name is would be difficult to judge, but it was used by the Chaldeans for the supreme name of God among the Hebrews. This name in Hebrew (יהוה) has four letters and may be transliterated as IHVH or YHWH (Hebrew: Yod-Heh-Vav-Heh—note that Hebrew letters are written from right to left). In the most ancient surviving copies of biblical books from the Old Testament in the Greek language, these two forms of the name appear. In some manuscripts, the Greek letters Iota-Alpha-Omega form the name of God, and in other manuscripts the Hebrew letters Yod-Heh-Vav-Heh are inserted for this name.

For example, in the first century BCE manuscript Papyrus Fouad 266, the name of God is given in the four Hebrew letters that were called by the Greeks the Tetragrammaton.[38] But in manuscript 4Q120, a Greek fragment of Leviticus 26:2–16 that is also of the first century BCE, the Greek form of the holy name, IAO, is used.[39] It seems that the Greeks and Romans regarded these two names as equivalent. The Roman writer Varro, writing toward the

---

38. Bruce M. Metzger, *Manuscripts of the Greek Bible: An Introduction to Greek Paleography*, corrected ed. (Oxford: Oxford University Press, 1991), Rahlfs 848 on page 60 and photograph 3 on page 61. Fouad 266 consists of three fragments listed as Rahlfs 847, 848, and 942. The Hebrew letters are almost impossible to see in this low contrast black-and-white photograph but are clearer in color photographs because the Hebrew letters are written in red ink.

39. Patrick W. Skehan, "The Divine Name at Qumran, in the Masada Scroll, and in the Septuagint," *Bulletin of the International Organization for Septuagint and Cognate Studies* 13 (Fall 1980): 14–44. See page 29 of this essay, where the manuscript is referred to by its alternative title, "4QLXXLev^b."

close of the second century BCE, said of IAO that it was the Jewish God, and that the form of the name IAO was used in the Chaldean mysteries.[40]

This leads me to speculate that the way IAO was sounded esoterically must have been similar to the way IHVH was sounded by the Hebrew priests. It may provide a clue to the accurate vocalization of IHVH, which has been lost since the fall of the Second Temple in 70 CE.

The significance of IAO for our study is that the name is composed of vowels. And not just any arrangement of vowels. These three vowels I-A-O are the three vowels in the specific, invariable order of what the great German folklorist Jacob Grimm (1785–1863) called *ablaut reduplication*.[41] A little explanation is needed here. Reduplication is the term for a manner of speaking in which words are repeated to form a phrase, such as "bye-bye" or "humdrum." Ablaut reduplication is a special form of reduplication discovered by Jacob Grimm in which the vowels of the parts of the expression are ordered in a very specific way.

These phrases always have the vowels in the order I-A-O. For example, in "singsong" the I comes before the O. In "chit-chat" the I comes before the A. In "ding-dang-dong" the vowels are ordered I-A-O. Grimm found this rule of ordering the vowels to be invariable. You never say "dong-dang-ding," for example. It is always "ding-dang-dong." "Chatchit" never happens—it is always "chitchat." Something in the cadence of the vowels compels the mind to order them this way when they are used to construct reduplicate expressions. This is true not only in English but also in many languages that descend from the Indo-Aryan root language.

Knowing this, we may strongly suspect that the three vowels that make up the divine name of God, IAO, are not happenstantial in their selection or sequence, but they have a concealed underlying power that arises from their specific pattern. Because the name is composed only of pure vowels, it

---

40. This is according to the historian John the Lydian (sixth century), writing in *De Mensibus* IV 53: "But the Roman Varro, when discussing him, says that among the Chaldaeans, in their mystical [writings], he is called 'Iaô,' meaning 'mentally perceived light' in the language of the Phoenicians, as Herennius [Philo] says." John Lydus, *On the Months*, trans. Mischa Hooker, 2nd ed. (2017), 104.

41. Jacob Grimm, *Deutsche Grammatik*, vol. 1 (Göttingen, Germany: Dieterichschen Buchhandlung, 1819), 543.

is possible to sustain all three vowels on the same breath and to pass seamlessly from one vowel to the next: "IIIIIAAAAAAOOOOO." It seems to me very likely that this is how the Greeks sounded this name when using it in their magical incantations. As mentioned above, it is possible that on some occasions IAO was vibrated while raising the face from the ground to the heavens.

The Hebrew alphabet is said to contain no vowels. Spoken Hebrew has vowel sounds, of course, or it could not be articulated, but these vowel sounds are not represented among the twenty-two Hebrew letters. This is of profound importance from the magical point of view. It shows that the ancient Hebrews, and other cultures who used a similar division of the vowels from the consonants of the alphabet, held the vowels in great reverence and understood that they are distinct in a fundamental way from the letters of the alphabet. In modern English we think of the vowels as just letters, not much different from all the other letters, but the Hebrews viewed the vowels as too sacred to record in written form.

Ancient Hebrew used no vowel markings at all in written texts—older versions of the Pentateuch contain no vowel indications. Those who wrote and read them had to know the correct vowels for each word in order to speak it accurately. In more modern centuries a system of diacritical vowel markings known as "vowel pointing" was used to visually indicate the correct vowels in written Hebrew. They continue to be used today. Modern Hebrew still has no vowel letters in its alphabet.

English Vowel Spectrum

By sounding all five English vowels one after another in order on a single breath, what I call the "vowel spectrum" may be produced. The vowels may be sounded as indicated by the example words in the list below. That is, the "a" sounded long as in the word "name," the "e" long as in the word "feet," and so on. The sounding of the vowel corresponds with the name of the vowel, except for "u" which is sounded "oo" rather than "you."

A: "name"
E: "feet"
I: "hire"

O: "bone"

U: "loot"

All vowels should be sustained with the same volume and force for the same duration. This requires practice in order to control the exhalation so that all vowel sounds are of the same strength.

The vowel spectrum is useful for drawing down power from the greater universe and concentrating it in your own body or in your magic circle. This can be done just prior to conducting specific works of magic within the circle. It is also useful for channeling power into an object you wish to charge with occult potency. For this purpose, the object should be placed in the center of the altar top, if you are using an altar in your magic. If you are not using an altar, you can hold the object in your hands close to your face, and allow your breath to play over it as you sound the vowels.

If the sequence of the vowels is reversed and they are sounded in the order U-O-I-E-A, the effect is to draw power up from below or to attract spirits from below to the place of working. This can be useful when working chthonic or demonic magic or when doing necromancy in which you seek to raise up the spirits of the dead. It is a general rule in magic that infernal or demonic magic reverses the usual order of things. For example, in European Satanism of past centuries, the pentagram was inverted; when the Black Mass was conducted, the Lord's Prayer was recited backward; witches performing malefic magic danced "widdershins," which is to say, against the direction of the sun's movement across the sky; and so on. Reversing the vowel sounds does not make them evil, but it causes them to attract the opposite kinds of energies and spirits. Instead of drawing down, they draw up. Instead of drawing light, they draw shadows.

When doing the vowel spectrum, the vowels should be sounded on a single breath, and this vowel chant repeated while you allow your mind to lose focus and follow the sounds of the vowels. The effect is to alter the state of your consciousness and to induce a trance state. When sounding the vowels in their natural order, allow the pitch of your voice to rise. When sounding them in their opposite order, allow the pitch of your voice to drop. Do not count the number of repetitions. Stop the exercise at the moment that feels right to you. Trying to do a specific number of repetitions is likely to break the trance state and destroy the effect of the vowel chant.

In sounding the five English vowels of the vowel spectrum in their natural order, it can be useful to visualize the sun or have an image of the sun before you. When sounding the vowel spectrum in reverse order, have the image of the moon in your mind or set it before your sight.

English Vowel Associations

We know that the ancient Egyptians, Greeks, and Romans associated the vowels with the seven planets of astrology and the gods and goddesses of those planets, but this is of limited use to us when working with the English vowels since they are five, not seven. If we really wish to use the English vowels in the same manner as the Greek vowels, we could extend their number to seven by adding the occasional English vowels Y and W and by sounding them in slightly different ways from the other five. However, if we wish to use the five English vowels in their own right, not as substitutes for the Greek vowels, we can make a rational correspondence between the five pure vowels of English and the five elements of Western magic and alchemy.

The use of the five elements has a long history in Western magic, and in a practical sense the occult energies of the elements are more useful than the occult energies of the planets. The elements consist of the four lower elements, Fire, Air, Water and Earth, and the fifth element, or quintessence, Spirit, which is also sometimes called Light. Spirit is somewhat different from the lower four elements. It pervades each of them and vitalizes them, giving them their unique natures. By itself it is pure spiritual energy, formless and colorless, invisible and insensible.

The English vowels may be linked with the five elements in the following set of associations:

A ("name"): Spirit
E ("feet"): Fire
I ("hire"): Air
O ("bone"): Water
U ("loot"): Earth

By linking a vowel sound to an element, it becomes possible to invoke that element by sounding the vowel on the breath. These vowels are particularly useful when raising the energy of specific elements. By chanting a vowel repeatedly, the corresponding elemental energy may be intensified, and elemental spirits associated with the element may be drawn close and manifested. The vowel sound becomes a kind of mantra of the element. Remember, the final vowel is not sounded as "you" but rather as "oo."

You can be creative in coupling vowels to be sounded on the breath. For example, explosive energy can be released by joining E (Fire) with I (Air). The elements Fire and Air form an explosive mixture. They may be sounded by drawing out the E sound, then finishing with the I sound using a kind of yipping shout of exultation (EEEEIII). A heavy, sleepy effect may be achieved by joining the vowels O (Water) and U (Earth). Drop the pitch as you transition from the O to the U vowel and extend the U downward (OOOUUUU). Conflict may be created by sounding two vowels whose elements conflict—E (Fire) with O (Water), for example (EEEEOOO). Water is the enemy of Fire. Make the two vowels sound as different as possible by abruptly dropping the pitch when you transition from the E to the O. A particular element may be elevated or spiritualized by joining its sound with that of A (Spirit), the quintessence (fifth essence) of the elements that pervades and underlies them all (for example, AAAOOOO).

The same triangular method of writing the vowels down in a charm that we saw for the Greek vowels can be used for the five English vowels and will yield this potent vowel pattern:

A

E E

I I I

O O O O

U U U U U

This can be sounded by vibrating on the breath each line in succession, extending the duration of each line by one beat, so that the first line is sounded for one beat, the second for two, the third for three, and so on.

The other way of writing down the vowels to make a vowel charm that was used by the Egyptians and Greeks is to write out the vowels in a line, then below it write them out again, but move the first vowel to the end of the line; below that in the third row write the vowels, but move the first two to the back of the line; and so on until you have made a magic square of vowels.[42] We have already encountered this method in Barthélemy's description of the seven pillars at Miletus.

When we employ this method for the English vowels, we get the following vowel pattern, which can be placed on magic charms, talismans, and amulets—a magic square of twenty-five vowels.

A	E	I	O	U
E	I	O	U	A
I	O	U	A	E
O	U	A	E	I
U	A	E	I	O

The same exercise suggested above on page 22 for the magic square of the seven Greek vowels can be used for the magic square of the five English vowels.

Cry of the Bacchantes

Very little is known about the original Greek cult of the bacchantes, women also known as maenads who met at night in sacred groves to worship the god of wine and ecstasy, who was called Dionysus by the Greeks and Bacchus by the Romans. This god represented the immanence of the divine in matter. Consequently, his rites were sensual in the extreme, so much so that in 184 BCE the Roman Senate found it necessary to issue a decree for the suppression of the festivals of Bacchus throughout Italy.

> The naked women ran about, exciting and inviting the men by obscene words and gestures, and the latter never thought of what had become in that crowd of their wives, their sisters, or their daughters. They little heeded the shame, which was reciprocal. In a word, there was no kind of licentiousness which was not improved upon

---

42. Betz, ed., *Greek Magical Papyri*, 150.

on this occasion. At last the night that had spread its veil over this scene of abomination fled before the car of Phoebus, and the god was restored to the *arca ineffabilis* [box that held the image of Bacchus]. The men staggering, filled with wine, and enervated by their lusts, returned to their deserted homes, where they were gradually joined by their wives and children, dishonoured and defiled.[43]

In earliest times no men were admitted to these rites, during which the maenads were said to have dishevelled their long hair and torn at their garments in their frenzied excitement, which was no doubt heightened by the drinking of wine. In later times the priestesses who presided over the festival of Dionysus, or Bacchus, were fourteen in number and chosen for this honor from among older women.

> The priestesses of Bacchus were fourteen in number; they were called *Gerarai*, from *Gerasko* (*to grow old*), because they were chosen when advanced in years. They had fourteen altars, and presided at the offering of fourteen sacrifices; they were the real Bacchantes, but subsequently the name was extended to all the females that took part in these outrageous scenes. Some authors have maintained that the Bacchantes were virgins, and continued to be so, defending themselves against all attacks amidst the most extravagant sensualities and Bacchantic libations.[44]

The bacchantes or maenads were famous for their use of a particular call or cry which they directed at their god. This cry was composed completely of Greek vowels. It is commonly transliterated into English and other languages

---

43. Stanislas Marie César Famin, *The Royal Museum at Naples* (London: Privately Printed, 1871), 18. This is an English translation of Famin's *Musée Royal de Naples, Peintures, Bronzes et Statues Érotiques de Cabinet Secret, avec leur explication par M. C. F.*, first published in Paris in 1816. The square brackets in the quote are mine.

44. Famin, *Royal Museum at Naples*, 16–17.

based on the Latin alphabet as "Evohe!" although it has been given other forms (Euoi, Evhoe, Evoe). Note that the V in the transliteration is intended for the Greek vowel Upsilon. The original Greek for this word is εὐαῖ or εὐοῖ.

This was not the only word the maenads cried out during their worship. They were said to shriek "Evoe Bacche! Io! Io! Evoe! Iacche! Io Bacche! Evohe!" but it is the cry "Evohe!" that is most remembered in ancient histories and poetry.[45]

In Greek myth, it was these female worshippers of Dionysus who tore Orpheus to pieces in their fury when he tried to calm their ecstasy with the music of his lyre. This scene is presented with great dramatic effect by the Abbot Marc Antoine Bayle in his work, *The Pearl of Antioch*:

> The song of Orpheus does not mitigate the fury of the Bacchantes. An unusual frenzy possesses them.
>
> "Let the lyre be hushed and the drum resound! Death to the wretch who blasphemes Bacchus and his mysteries. Evohe! Evohe! Brandish the thyrsus ornamented with ivy. Honor the god who has given the intoxicating grape to man to drive away care. Rush together and strike the madman who dares invoke modesty and amiable graces. Nothing shall check the transports of the Bacchantes nor prevent them from following Bacchus. Evohe! Evohe!"
>
> The Menades precipitate themselves upon Orpheus. The one, who had urged on her companions, brandished her thyrsus and with a heavy blow wounded the head of the divine songster. Blood stains the laurel encircling his brow. The sight inebriates the Bacchantes. One seizes the left arm of Orpheus and without effort tears it from its socket. Another does the same to the arm which had drawn such harmonious sounds from the lyre. All together they tear to pieces his palpitating flesh. Confused cries are heard on all sides. The dying

---

45. E. H. Barker, *Lempriere's Classical Dictionary, Abridged for Public and Private Schools of Both Sexes*, ed. Joseph Cauvin (London: Longman, Brown, Green, and Longmans, 1843), 213.

groans of Orpheus are overpowered by the howlings of
the Menades.[46]

This Greek cry was carried over to the Roman Bacchanalia and used by
those celebrating the rites of Bacchus in Italy, which came to be hugely popular owing to the free dispensation of food and wine and the ready availability
of willing or unwilling sexual partners. From the continued use of the Greek
word by the Romans, we may presume that it was held to have esoteric significance by those who used it. It was, and is, most certainly a word of power.
Modern witches regard it as a cry of joy.

My own interpretation is based on the myth of the death of Orpheus, who
was dismembered and killed by the maenads. If Dionysus does represent
the embodiment of spirit in matter, which seems reasonable given his link
to wine, which is by its nature spirit in matter—alcohol is even called "spirits"—then the cry "Evohe!" expresses the liberation of spirit from matter. By
his dismemberment, the spiritual presence and energy of Orpheus was liberated from his body. His body was literally opened up by the maenads to
permit the release of his spirit. The cry of "Evohe!" is thus the ecstatic release
of spirit on the living breath.

Correct pronunciation of this Greek word of power is unknown. Certainly, pronouncing the Upsilon as "v" is wrong, yet this is usually done in
modern Wicca, where the word is sounded "ee-voh-hay!" We know it was
sounded with great force, because it was said to make the hills ring when it
was shouted. It is my strong sense that each of the four vowels was sounded
separately, although they were run together, and that the final letter was
emphasized with an ecstatic uplift of the voice. A pronunciation of "Eh-ooo-
aaah-eeee!" or perhaps "Eh-ooo-awww-eeee!" with the first vowel somewhat brief, the others progressively lengthened, and the final vowel rising
into a shriek and terminating in a kind of yipping noise may be something
near to the original way the word was sounded.

The word was connected intimately to the god Dionysus and should probably be used in rituals when invoking excited or ecstatic states of consciousness, to arouse passion and to let loose psychic energy. It is the quintessential
shout of emotional liberation, the primal scream of the ancient world.

---

46. Marc Antoine Bayle, *The Pearl of Antioch* (Baltimore, MD: Kelly, Piet and Company,
1871), 147–48.

Three
Composing Incantations

In this chapter we will look at the features in common that contribute to make incantations more focused and powerful. We will examine them from the point of view of both their structure and their content.

Brevity

One of the first things you notice about spoken spells and chants is that they tend to be quite brief. This is not invariably true of all forms of magic—the elaborate ceremonial magic of the European grimoires often includes prolonged incantations of several printed pages directed at various classes of spiritual beings, along with prayers derived from the Bible. But in most surviving examples of folk magic, which is the magic actually worked by the common people, the incantations are brief. This naturally tends to make them more concentrated. With fewer words, each word becomes correspondingly more important. Words must be chosen with greater care to convey the maximum amount of meaning.

As an example, I will quote from the *Long Lost Friend* a short incantation intended to cause fire to pass over a place without doing it harm. The incantation is lent greater force by the use of rhyme, which I will discuss a little further along in this chapter.

Wild-fire and the dragon, flew over a wagon,
The wild-fire abated, and the dragon skeated.[47]

This would have been spoken by farmers in the nineteenth century, particularly those living on the prairie, upon sighting the smoke of a grass fire approaching their crops and barns. Such fires, driven by high winds, fly through the air on sheets of flame. The winged dragon is the spirit of the fire, which is directed to pass over using the imagery of fire flying upon the air over a wagon without burning it. Today, this incantation might be used to good effect by residents of California during brush-fire season, when their homes are threatened with destruction.

Repetition

In effective spells, patterns tend to be repeated. The same wording may be used in successive lines or verses. The same names occur multiple times. References may be repeated, or similar references may be made. All this serves to intensify the charm in the mind of the magician using it, while also making it easier to remember.

The repetition is usually not random but guided by numerical considerations. Threefold repetitions are very common. The number three has always held an extra measure of magic, resulting in threefold repetition being often used in spells, even when it is not numerically expedient.

In 1932, John Abbott had this to say concerning the number three:

> The Hindu and the Muhammadan both associate finality with the number three. When finality is desirable three is deliberately chosen as a limit, but when finality means disaster three becomes a number to be avoided....Anything said or done by a Muhammadan three times acquires a legal sanction, *tre dafah shari*. He pronounces his *tilak* or declaration of divorce three times; the bride acknowledges three times her acceptance of the bridegroom, *ijāb kabul*. To invoke the blessing of God the hands are raised three times after prayer;

---

47. John George Hohman, *The Long Lost Friend* (Harrisburg, PA, 1850), 14.

three recitations of the Koranic verse, *Kul Huvallah*, are
equal to one recitation of the whole Koran.[48]

The author of *Alice's Adventures in Wonderland*, Charles Lutwidge Dodgson (1832–1898), who wrote under the penname Lewis Carroll, used the magic of three in his nonsense poem *The Hunting of the Snark*:

> "Just the place for a Snark!" the Bellman cried,
> As he landed his crew with care;
> Supporting each man on the top of the tide
> By a finger entwined in his hair.
>
> "Just the place for a Snark! I have said it twice:
> That alone should encourage the crew.
> Just the place for a Snark! I have said it thrice:
> What I tell you three times is true."[49]

There are two places where repetition is constantly used, and both involve magic, although the magic in these aspects of human life is usually not recognized or understood. One place is in nursery rhymes and fairy stories. Children love repetition. By repeating a thing, it acquires importance and becomes impressed on the memory. Nursery rhymes and fairy stories introduce young children to basic problems of life, while at the same time reassuring them that these problems can be solved.

The other aspect of common life where repetition is constantly used is in popular songs. Many of our most beloved popular songs consist of little except repetition. The same phrase will be repeated over and over, and by this repetition it acquires a strange kind of power, even though the exact meaning of the phrase may remain elusive to the listener, who will replay the song many times in an effort to makes sense of this perceived but obscure potency and meaning. The effect of repetition persuades the listener into believing that a secret message must be hidden inside the song, since the words have so much power yet seem to convey no explicit sense. This is the power of repetition.

---

48. John Abbott, *The Keys of Power* (London: Methuen & Co., 1932), 285.

49. Lewis Carroll, *The Hunting of the Snark* (London: Macmillan and Co., 1876), 3.

An example of the use of repetition occurs in the following incantation from Chaldea, an ancient kingdom in southern Mesopotamia that flourished from the ninth to the sixth centuries BCE. It is directed at the god of the sun, and its purpose is to remove a "ban" or curse from the household of the speaker and from the land in which he dwells. The curse probably took the form of disease, which the sun has the power to burn away. I will reproduce the portion that best illustrates the use of repetition.

> O Sun-god, stand still and hear me!
> Overpower the name of the evil ban that has been
>   created,
> whether the ban of my father, or the ban of my
>   begetter,
> or the ban of the seven branches of the house of my
>   father,
> or the ban of my family and my slaves,
> or the ban of my free-born women and concubines,
> or the ban of the dead and living, or the ban of the
>   adult and the suckling,
> or the ban of my father and of him who is not my father.
> For father and mother I pronounce the spell; and for
>   brother and child I pronounce the spell.
> For friend and neighbour I pronounce the spell, and
>   for labourer and workman I pronounce the spell.
> For the field thou hast made and thy pasturage I
>   pronounce the spell.
> May the name of my god be a father where there is no
>   justice.
> To mankind, the flock of the god Ner, whatever be
>   their names, who are in field and city,
> speak, O Sun-god, mighty lord, and let the evil ban be
>   at rest.[50]

---

50. Archibald Henry Sayce, "The Sacred Books of Chaldaea," in *Lectures on the Origin and Growth of Religion as Illustrated by the Religion of the Ancient Babylonians* (London: Williams and Norgate, 1887), 321.

Alliteration

Anything that makes an incantation stick in the mind aids in giving its words power. A very ancient poetic technique for lending weight to words is alliteration. It is defined as the repetition of initial consonant sounds in successive or closely related syllables in groups of words. You will find this used extensively in old Anglo-Saxon poetry, as well as in the sagas of Iceland and Norway. In general, alliteration was popular with poets across northern Europe. Alliteration is not much used in modern poetry, but it is still an effective technique for charm making.

Alliteration also occurs in what are known as tongue-twisters—phrases difficult to speak quickly. An example is the tongue-twister "Around the rocks the ragged rascal ran." Here, the "r" consonant sound is repeated with stress five times. Another familiar example begins, "Peter Piper picked a peck of pickled peppers."

We also find alliteration in one of the best-known sayings of modern witches and pagans, which lists the four necessities of life: "Flags, flax, fodder, and frig." This saying had its origins in the 1960s, although it is often claimed to be an old Saxon blessing.[51] "Flags" stands for flagstones that form the floors of houses, or in a more general sense for the dwelling place; "flax" represents clothing, which was often woven out of linen thread in Europe in olden times, and thus for all clothing; fodder represents the food that is necessary for our sustenance; and frig is for Frig (Old English) or Frigg (Old Norse), the northern European goddess of motherhood. Frigg (from the proto-German *frijjo*, which means "beloved") was the wife of Odin. She is the goddess of Friday and was associated by the Romans with Venus. She is in this sense love, both spiritual and carnal, and by extension the goddess of marriage and children. The four essentials are thus shelter, clothing, food, and love. By casting them into an alliterative form, they become both more memorable and more forceful.

One of the more prominent examples of alliteration used in poetic composition occurs in the Anglo-Saxon epic poem *Beowulf*. Since this is written

---

51. The expression seems to have been first used in the private letters of the English witch Robert Cochrane, written in the 1960s to Joseph "Bearwalker" Wilson, founder of the 1734 tradition of American witchcraft.

in Old English, which very few people read, I will give an extract translated into modern English that preserves the original meter and overall structure:

> So their lord, the well-beloved,   all at length they laid
> In the bosom of the bark,   him the bracelet-giver,—
> By the mast the mighty king.   Many gifts were there
> Fretted things of fairness   brought from far-off ways![52]

In reading this kind of alliterative verse, there is a sense of jogging along on a horse as the voice moves from one stress to another—because this kind of verse was always intended to be recited aloud, never to be read silently from a scroll or book. Its power comes from the living breath of the bard. Personally, I find alliterative verse more powerful than rhyming verse, but modern poets disagreed with my judgment, and for the past five centuries or so have favored rhyme over alliteration.

If you can hear the singing of alliteration in your mind, it is quite easy to compose potent incantations using this literary device. I will compose a charm now, extempore, as I write these words, to show you how alliteration may be used in modern magic.

> Earthen-bedded at birth of babe
> Whose name is writ on root-clasped rock;
> Set in soil when wailing welp
> Drawn from womb, his cord was cut;
> Grow and gain in girth and might,
> Tall and true, straight and strong:
> While standing fast in secret fold,
> No blade or shaft shall work his weird.

This charm, which I've written in an antique style that suits alliteration, is designed to safeguard a male child from the edged weapons of his future foes. By changing "his" to "her" it can be applied to a female child. It is to be recited at the planting of a tree. The best choice for a male child is an ash tree,

---

52. This quote is from a partial translation of *Beowulf* by Stopford A. Brooke, *The History of Early English Literature* (New York & London: Macmillan and Co., 1892), 27. Concerning his translation, Brooke wrote: "I used alliteration whenever I could, and stressed as much as possible the alliterated words." Ibid., ix.

because in Germanic lore the first man was formed from an ash tree, but other trees such as the oak may be used. For a female child, a pine or willow will be appropriate. As the tree, planted in secret along with a stone at its roots that has carved upon it the birth name of the baby, grows and increases in strength, so the babe will grow in might, and no edged weapon wielded by his enemy will ever cut him down. The child's "weird" is, of course, his fate, or death. The tree must be planted in a safe place where it will not be felled during the course of a lifespan.

Assonance

Somewhat similar to alliteration, assonance is the poetic device of using the same vowel sounds repeatedly in stressed syllables to achieve an effect of harmony. It is subtle but can be effective when used rightly. It differs from alliteration in that alliteration is the repetition of the same letters or sounds at the beginning of words, whereas assonance is the repetition of vowel sounds. This term may also be applied to the repeated use of consonant sounds in the same manner, although it is more common to call this practice consonance rather than assonance.

Assonance can occur in rhyming words, but words don't need to rhyme for it to be present. An example of assonance from Shakespeare is the familiar line from the play *Romeo and Juliet*: "**O** Rom**eo**, Rom**eo**, wherefore art th**ou** Rom**eo**?" The significant assonant vowel sounds are in bold type. Note that there is no rhyme here, but the sentence has a melodic lilt due to assonance and repetition.

The best way to use assonance when composing charms is to listen for the music of the words. If the words dance and trip along, the sound of one word helping and emphasizing the next, you are probably using assonance. I will compose a brief assonant charm of fertility for couples trying to conceive a child.

> My Lord the Sun, my Lady the Moon,
> Strengthen his seed, open her womb,
> A babe will come and bless them soon.

This should be recited twice a day out of doors, at noon and at midnight, with the eyes raised and the hands uplifted, for a full lunar cycle.

Rhyme

Rhyme has a use that is similar to that of alliteration, in that it enhances the force of the charm as it is uttered, but the effect of rhyme is different from the effect of alliteration. Rhyme is a softer, gentler emphasis. Whereas alliteration may be said to be masculine in its nature, rhyme is feminine. An advantage to the use of rhyme is that it acts as an aid to the memory. In English poetry, alliteration gave way to rhyme as the principle poetic device around the same time modern English emerged from Middle English.

Nursery rhymes are short, simple poems that use rhyme. The rhyme acts as a memory aid for children, the audience to whom nursery rhymes are directed. Here is a familiar verse from the nursery tale of "Jack and the Giants," which was old when William Shakespeare quoted two lines of it in his 1605 tragedy, *King Lear*.

> Fi, fee, fo, fum!
> I smell the blood of an English man!
> Be he alive or be he dead,
> I'll grind his bones to make my bread! [53]

We know the character Jack from the fairy tale of "Jack and the Beanstalk," but the lore of Jack the Giant-Killer is more extensive than this, and according to the English poet and novelist Sir Walter Scott, was brought to England by the first Saxon invaders. In an 1819 essay on the antiquities of nursery literature, Scott wrote, "Jack, commonly called the Giant Killer, and Thomas Thumb landed in England from the very same keels and warships which conveyed Hengist and Horsa, and Ebba the Saxon." [54] In modern times the first line of this ancient verse usually reads "fee, fi, fo, fum" which, perhaps because of the ordering of the vowels, sounds more satisfying.

As simplistic as this verse is, it shows the structure of many rhyming charms that have been used in European folk magic for centuries. Short lines,

---

53. There are countless different wordings to this little verse. The version I have quoted is from James Orchard Halliwell's *Popular Rhymes and Nursery Tales* (London: John Russell Smith, 1849), 74.

54. Walter Scott, "Fairy Tales, or the Lilliputian Cabinet, Containing Twenty-Four Choice Pieces of Fancy and Fiction, Collected by Benjamin Tabart," *The Quarterly Review* 21 (January & April 1819), 97.

simple words, and rhyming couplets. But note that the first line is seemingly made up of nonsense sounds derived from four vowels, which, when combined with the letter F, become alliterative, and thus gain great, thumping power. It is quite possible that this first line was not meaningless in the early Saxon versions of this tale (if Scott was correct, and it did indeed descend from the Saxons), any more than the vowel sounds used by the Egyptians in their magic were meaningless.

Rhyming verse has a persistence that is quite remarkable. The tales of the hero Jack are in prose, but scattered amid the prose are poetic verses such as the one above.[55] The prose changes considerably from version to version of the tales, but the poetry is always there, preserved, although it too undergoes minor modifications. Children may forget the wording of the tales, but they remember the wording of the verses.

Rhymes can either be perfect rhymes or near-rhymes. Owing to the inherent limitations of language, it is sometimes necessary to resort to near-rhymes when composing incantations, but perfect rhymes are more satisfying and contain greater force. For example, a perfect rhyme is "man-can" but a near-rhyme is "man-land." The sounds of the words are similar but not quite the same. The use of near-rhymes gives you a greater number of words to choose from when composing your charms.

Most often, rhyming couplets will be used—two lines that are together and end in rhyming words. Additional force can be achieved by using a rhyming triplet—three lines together that end in rhyming words. This is not always possible because good triple rhymes are rare in English. It is better to use couplets that are clear and exact in their meaning than to try to make a triplet by straining the sound or its sense. A good rhyming charm should feel effortless and give the impression that it has always existed somewhere, even if never before revealed to mankind. Strong incantations have a rightness about them that is satisfying both in sound and in meaning.

---

55. See the anonymous chapbook *Jack the Giant-Killer* (Glasgow: J. Lumsden & Son, [c. 1815]), 24. This version of the verse reads:
Fa, fe, fi, fo, fum,
I smell the blood of an Englishman;
Let him be alive, or let him be dead,
I'll grind his bones to make me bread.

I'll compose a rhyming charm to banish fatigue when walking long distances to show you what can be done with short lines and simple words:

> Tired legs, lagabout,
> Wake 'em up, stretch 'em out;
> Hi there! ho there!
> Ride all day on shanks' mare.

As you speak the words, "Hi there! Ho there!" give each leg in turn a little thrust and shake as you are walking, so that your legs know you are addressing them directly. Recite this charm to the rhythm of your walk. It will restore strength to your legs.

A rhyming word does not always need to follow at the end of the next line, nor, for that matter, do rhyming words need to occur at the ends of lines of verse—they can be embedded in the body of the lines. The freer your structural requirements, the easier it is to allow the charm to come forth naturally from within your subconscious mind, like a kind of mental birth.

Purpose

When you deliberately compose an incantation, you do so for a specific purpose, which you have in mind at the time of its composition. It is essential that the charm express that purpose if it is to be magically potent. It is best to keep your purpose simple and singular. If you try to express something that is complex or multiple, the magic will lack effectiveness because of its lack of focus.

Before you attempt to compose an incantation, take some time to reflect on what you want it to do so that its purpose is absolutely clear in your own mind. When you are quite sure of the one thing you want the charm to do, go to a quiet place and compose it. Do not force the lines of the charm. If you are trying to use certain words to express your purpose and they refuse to fall into an apt order, try a different set of words, a different approach to the same end.

Suppose you wished to compose a simple charm to recite whenever you are seeking to find lost items that you yourself have misplaced. The purpose is singular—finding what you have lost—even though the lost items will vary. By not specifying a single lost item, you can use the same charm again and again for locating your keys, your wallet, your eyeglasses, your pen, or whatever you have a tendency to put down in different places and forget about. The words "lost" and "found" can play a useful part in the charm since together in this sequence they express your purpose. I will now compose the kind of charm I am talking about so that you can see how it is put together.

> Seek high and low, seek what you know,
> Seek all around, it shall be found;
> Where you put it, where you set it,
> There you'll find it, there you'll get it;
> This charm I speak to show the way,
> That lost be found upon this day.

The final line of the charm indicates that the lost item will be found on the same day you begin to search for it. If the thing you look for has been moved by someone else, the charm is broken. It is designed to find things where you yourself have put them, then forgotten.

Analogy

Analogy is the comparison of one thing with another thing. You use analogy in an incantation when you compare what you wish to achieve with something that is well known to happen. For example, if we were dealing with a love charm, we might incant, "As the horse gallops across the meadow, so my love hastens to my bed." We saw analogy used in the first charm I composed in this chapter, in which the growth of a man is linked with the growth of a tall, straight tree that has the man's name written on a stone at its roots.

What lies at the root of the use of analogy in charms is a principle of magic that is sometimes called the "principality of similarity." The magician links one thing to another, and then what is done to that thing also occurs to the thing with which it is occultly joined. Samuel Liddall "MacGregor" Mathers, Aleister Crowley's teacher in the Hermetic Order of the Golden Dawn, once took a packet of dried peas and baptized each pea in the magical name of one of his enemies. He then put the peas into a sieve and shook them so that they rattled around inside. Evoking the demons Beelzebub and Typhon-Set, he instructed them to torment his enemies so that they would constantly bicker. In this way he made his enemies fight amongst themselves, by analogy.[56]

As an example of analogy in a charm, suppose you wished to cause a person to come with haste to your present location. You might write the name of the person in full upon one side of a slip of paper and hold the paper above a candle so that the heat of the candle warms the paper. Then you might recite these words I have composed below, in such a way that your breath touches the slip of paper and moves it slightly:

> As the lodestone draws the steel,
> As the flower draws the bee,
> As the candle draws the moth,
> So is this one drawn to me.

Touch the slip of paper to the candle flame and allow it to be burned to ashes while concentrating on the face of the person named. All of the writing of the name must be fully consumed by flame.

Always remember, magic helps those who help themselves. It is better if the person you seek to draw knows you and best if that person is somewhere not too far away. If you try to attract a complete stranger from the other side of the world, it may take some time before this charm fulfills itself. Use common sense in magic, as in all walks of life.

Authority

Another way of lending power to an incantation is to call upon the authority of a potent spirit, angel, or god to enforce its fulfillment. This is one of the most ancient and yet most common devices of magic. There are several ways of doing this. You can call upon the power of a higher being by speaking their name and describing the spirit's well-known abilities and attributes as a way of attracting the attention of that being; you can implore the aid of the spirit with prayer or demand it through threats; or you can take on the power of the spirit by assuming its name and attributes upon yourself, through invocation, so that the spirit's power becomes your power.

---

56. Francis King, *Modern Ritual Magic* (London: Neville Spearman Limited, 1970; repr., Bridport, Dorset, England: Prism Press, 1989), 71–72.

In Christian Europe, by far the most common authority to invoke for the empowering of an invocation has been Jesus Christ. Calling upon Mary, Mother of God, is common in Roman Catholic countries, as is calling upon the authority of the saints. In pagan times, it was the old gods and goddesses who were invoked to empower the magic. Sometimes the pagan names of gods were replaced in by the names of Christian saints on ancient healing charms, as a way of making the magic Christian: "To replace the names of idols, the Church generally enforced the use of some one of the designations of God or of Christ, such as Deus, Emanuel, or Adonai….The names of saints, of apostles, and especially of the evangelists, were also permissible substitutes for Heathen appellations." [57]

For example, an Anglo-Saxon charm to heal the leg of a horse that has lamed itself invokes the powers of various Nordic gods and goddesses:

> Then Sindgund charmed it, and Sunna, her sister;
> Then Volla charmed it, and Frija, her sister;
> Then Woden charmed it, who could charm it well:
> Leg luxation, and blood luxation, and limb luxation,
> Bone to bone, blood to blood,
> Limb to limb as they were glued together. [58]

After Europe was Christianized, the same charm to heal the leg of a horse continued to be used for the same purpose, but the authority of the pagan gods of the north was replaced by the authority of the Trinity:

> Our Lord rade, his foal's foot slade;
> Down he lighted, his foal's foot righted.
> Bone to bone, sinew to sinew,
> Blood to blood, flesh to flesh:
> Heal in the name of the Father, Son, and Holy Ghost. [59]

Let's suppose we want to protect a small child from sickness. We might compose a charm calling upon the protection of the Queen of Heaven, who

---

57. Felix Grendon, "The Anglo-Saxon Charms," in *The Journal of American Folk-Lore* 22 (April–June 1909), 114.

58. Grendon, "The Anglo-Saxon Charms," 149.

59. Grendon, "The Anglo-Saxon Charms," 149.

may be regarded as pagan or Christian, depending on your point of view. Many Catholics identify the Queen of Heaven, who is described in Revelation 12:1–3, with the Virgin Mary, mother of Jesus, although the name "Queen of Heaven" (*Regina Coeli*) is not actually used in this place in the Bible. If you do an internet search for "prayers to the Queen of Heaven," you will find many Christian prayers. Others believe her to be a pagan goddess, and in this persona she is mentioned in various ancient texts that refer to goddesses such as Ishtar and Isis.[60]

If we were to request the protection of this goddess for the child, we would do so with a sincere prayer that mentions the mercy and kindness of the goddess, particularly toward infants and children, and we would ask her to protect the wearer of the charm. This incantation would be inscribed and enchanted on an amulet to hang around the child's neck. I will compose here a possible wording of the charm, which should go something like this:

> Airy goddess, Queen of All,
> Twelve stars crown your head;
> The sun your mantle of gold,
> The moon your silver slipper.
> As you love the littlest ones,
> Guard the wearer of these words;
> Shield this child from every hurt,
> Protect this babe from all harm.

If, instead of appealing to the kindliness of this goddess through prayer, you choose to invoke her into yourself, so that you can assume her power and authority directly for the purpose of protecting an infant from disease, you might use wording something like this:

> Sky goddess am I,
> Cloaked in the sun,
> Twelve stars my crown;
> The moon is my boat
> On the ocean of night.

---

60. See Jeremiah 44:15–8 (King James Version).

The small and the weak
Best do I love;
The sleeping child
Who lies in its crib,
Wrapped up in dreams.

By these circles three,
Water, air, earth,
No pestilence of day,
No sickness of night,
Shall touch this child.

This would be uttered over an infant or young child sleeping in their crib or bed to turn aside sickness. Before the speaking of each verse, a circle would be inscribed in a sunwise direction around the child with your right index finger or with an instrument of power such as a wand. Three verses, three circles. Why only three elements? Because fire does not transmit disease; it cleanses it. You are barring from the child the approach of disease by the three lower elements, water, air, and earth, for each of which you draw a circle as a barrier of protection.

If you wish, you can inscribe the circles upon the air using physical representations of the three elements—a bowl or cup of water to draw the circle of water, a feather or smoking stick of incense to draw the air circle, and a dish of salt to draw the earth circle. At the end of this invocation, kiss the sleeping child upon the forehead in your persona as the Queen of Heaven.

Forms of Prayer

When incantation is used within the framework of organized religions, it is called prayer. Early Christianity developed various forms of prayer for different purposes. These forms can be used to good effect by both Christians and non-Christians. They are esoteric tools and owe no allegiance to any particular belief system. The grimoires are filled with prayers for various functions. Some forms of prayer have little application in works of magic—prayers of confession, for example. I will list the more important types of prayer that may be used with advantage in occult work.

1. Adoration

If you are working in the Christian tradition, you will be dealing with God the Father, as well as with Jesus and Mary, the angels of God, and perhaps also the saints if you are Roman Catholic. If you are working in the tradition of the Kabbalah, you will deal with God the Creator and the angels of God. If you are Wiccan, you will interact with the Goddess. To form a more personal and intimate relationship with a deity or higher spirit whose qualities you admire, prayers of adoration or love should be used.

Express your love in a personal way, as though speaking to someone you greatly adore, by praising the god for his or her virtues. This should not be done with an attitude of subservience, but rather with respect and affection. Do not use this type of prayer with any ulterior motive or expectation that you will get anything back from it. Use it strictly to become more familiar and intimate with a deity you genuinely love.

2. Supplication

This is perhaps the most common form of prayer. A deity or spirit is supplicated to grant your request for assistance or guidance in your life. It does not concern the life of any other person. This is you, asking for help. You would use it if you wished to change your life for the better, to find your way when lost either physically or spiritually, or to give up some self-destructive habit such as alcohol or drugs. It is best directed at a spiritual being you have reason to believe is interested in your life and your happiness.

3. Intercession

When you ask a god or spirit to help someone else, you are making a prayer of intercession, which is also known as a prayer of petition, because in it you petition a spirit to aid another person. This prayer must be made with no thought or expectation of personal gain. It must be motivated only by concern for the suffering or deprivation of someone else.

4. Blessing

Speak this type of prayer when you wish to call down the blessing of God upon another person or upon a spirit. Ask the deity to help and comfort the person or spirit you wish to have blessed. You might include in this prayer the reasons you believe the person or spirit merits the deity's blessing, which will enable the one blessed to enjoy happiness and peace.

5. Protection

When you pray for protection for yourself or for someone else, you use this type of prayer. The protection can be from any kind of danger that you perceive as an imminent threat, which you would specify in the wording of the prayer, or it can be protection in a general sense against all dangers that may threaten, known or unknown.

6. Consecration

In ceremonial magic it may be necessary to consecrate ritual tools, materials, or objects. To consecrate is to make holy, to give something in service to a deity. The occult power of the deity then adheres in that material or object. In Christianity, water is consecrated to make it into holy water. Magic rituals may involve the consecration of ritual instruments such as the wand, the sword, pentacles, candles, and so on.

7. Invocation

A prayer of invocation calls down a god or spirit to be present in a perceptible way with the magician. It is a way of establishing a close and clear communication with the spirit, and a way to assume the power and authority of the spirit to whom it is addressed. When you invoke a deity, it becomes present within your mind and body, and to some degree you merge with it. This prayer can be used to take on the authority of a deity or higher spirit so that you can command lower spirits who obey that authority.

Four
Names and Words of Power

In diverse cultures around the world and throughout human history, names have always possessed a great magic. A sorcerer who knows the true name of a person has power over that person, because magic that is worked on the name affects the holder of the name. The essence of an individual is crystallized in the name given at birth. This is the entire basis of the system of divination called numerology, which relies on the manipulation of number values of the letters in the birth name to reveal hidden or unknown matters connected with the individual.

The Cambridge philosopher F. M. Cornford wrote concerning the power of names, "To form a representation of the structure of Nature is to have control over it. To classify things is to name them, and the name of a thing, or of a group of things, is its soul; to know their names is to have power over their souls. Language, that stupendous product of the collective mind, is a duplicate, a shadow-soul, of the whole structure of reality; it is the most effective and comprehensive tool of human power, for nothing, whether human or superhuman, is beyond its reach." [61]

---

61. Francis Macdonald Cornford, *From Religion to Philosophy* (London: Edward Arnold, 1912), 141.

In many primitive cultures, it is considered bad luck to reveal your name, especially to a stranger. One way to avoid this was to have a true name given to a child at birth and a nickname for common use. The true name was seldom revealed, and the person was known by the nickname. The fear was that if the true name were revealed, it laid the possessor of the name open to malicious magic. This reluctance to reveal one's name was current even into the late nineteenth century among the Irish and Welsh according to Oxford professor John Rhys, who in his influential essay "Welsh Fairies" wrote on this matter: "The student of man tells us that the reason for the reluctance to disclose one's name was…that an enemy should not get possession of anything identified with one's person, such as a lock of one's hair, a drop of one's blood, or anything closely connected with one's person, lest it should give the enemy power over one's person as a whole, especially if such enemy is suspected of possessing any skill in handling the terrors of magic." [62]

Rhys made the bold and often quoted assertion, based on the similarity between the Irish words *ainm*, "name," and *amm*, "soul," along with other word correspondences in various languages, that to the ancient Celts, the name was the soul: "Lastly, the lesson which the words in question contain for the student of man is, that the Celts and certain other widely separated Aryans, unless we should rather say the whole Aryan family, believed at one time not only that his name was a part of the man, but that it was that part of him which is termed the soul, the breath of life, or whatever you may choose to define it as being." [63]

It is significant that Rhys not only connected the birth name with the soul and with the breath, but he also stated that the name *is* the soul and the breath that gives life (the *anima*, which signifies not only the soul but the breath). The ancient Celts did not make a clear distinction between them. It was perhaps this insight by Rhys that the name is the soul that formed the seed of Cornford's assertion that language, by which things are named, is a duplicate shadow-soul of reality. He wrote, "Speech is the *Logos*, which stands to the uni-

---

62. John Rhys, "Welsh Fairies," in *The Nineteenth Century: A Monthly Review* 30 (October 1891): 566.

63. Rhys, "Welsh Fairies," 567.

verse in the same relation as the myth to the ritual action: it is a descriptive chart of the whole surface of the real." [64]

The ancient Egyptians were given two names, one of which was regarded as their true name and known only to themselves and their parents, and the other was the name by which they were known to others. This practice was believed by them to descend from the gods. In a myth of Ra, the god of the sun, Ra states, "I am he who has many names and many forms…my father and my mother told me my name, it is hidden in my body since my birth so that no magic power may be accorded to anyone who might wish to cast a spell over me." [65] Isis, the sorceress, injects poison into Ra to force him to reveal to her his true name. When he does so, she immediately removes the poison from his body.

This practice of giving two names to a child, one secret and closely guarded and another that was used openly, was surprisingly widespread. It was used in ancient China, and also in India, where on the tenth or twelfth day after a child's birth, the child was given two names, one of which was known only to the parents but was later revealed to the child when he or she became old enough to understand its significance.[66] The common name, used casually in day-to-day life, was believed to lack power because it was only a nickname. No magician could turn it against its owner as a weapon. With this understanding, it is easy to see how important the given name is in magic.

Modern magicians will often take upon themselves a magical name to signify their transformation through occult study into a higher order of being. They regard this new name as the true expression of their nature and their birth name as something they have moved beyond. They often will keep this magical name private, lest it become known by their enemies and used against them.

We see the same general practice in the Roman Catholic Church, when monks and nuns put off their given names and adopt religious names when they take holy orders, to signify their ascension to a higher level of spiritual understanding. However, their new names are not kept secret. We also

---

64. Cornford, *From Religion to Philosophy*, 141.

65. Maurice Bouisson, *Magic: Its Rites and History*, trans. G. Almayrac (London: Rider & Company, 1960), 102.

66. Bouisson, *Magic*, 103.

see the adoption of a new name in the popular entertainment world among musicians and actors, who often cast off their birth names and adopt names that to them seem better suited to express their transformed consciousness. Robert Zimmerman in this way became the folk musician Bob Dylan. Marion Robert Morrison became the famous Western film actor John Wayne.

When composing an incantation for a person who has changed their name, you must consider which name is more appropriate to use—the birth name or the adopted name the person currently goes by. The birth name will always possess power, because it was imposed on the person at or near the time of coming into the world, the moment for which the astrological birth chart is cast. However, some individuals may have so greatly transformed themselves in their lives that the name they have chosen to represent them has become a better express of their true being. For example, the magician Harry Houdini was born Erik Weisz, but who would assume that "Weisz" is a more powerful or more accurate expression of his soul than "Houdini?"

Barbarous Names in the Grimoires

Western magic has a body of texts written over the span of more than two thousand years that contain instructions on various magical techniques, including the use of charms and incantations. These books were known in France collectively as the grimoires (from the Old French *grammaire*, a grammar or book of instruction). The word came into common English usage only in the second half of the nineteenth century. The books vary widely in subject matter and quality of both their writing and their contents, but they are the legacy of European magic to us in the modern age and as such are a precious resource.

Many of the grimoires contain names and words that seem to have no meaning. Some are obviously the names of demons or pagan gods that have been corrupted by careless copying. The early grimoires came into existence before printing and were copied and recopied by hand by those who used them. During this copying, it was easy to misspell names that were totally unfamiliar to the copyist. Other words in the incantations of the grimoires do not appear to be derived from names and are wholly incomprehensible. These were called by the Greeks the barbarous names of power or, more generally, the barbarous words of power. Another term for them is *voces mysti-*

cae (literally "mystical voices"), "those 'words' or 'terms' in a spell that do not represent ordinary language." [67] For the ancient Greeks, anyone who was not Greek was a barbarian. They were called names and words of power because they were believed to have great efficacy in the working of magic.

Writing on this subject, Edward Clodd observed, "There is no essential difference between Names of Power and Words of Power, and the justification of any division lies wholly in its convenience. For although the implication may be that the one is associated with persons, and the other with things, we have sufficing evidence of the hopeless entanglement of the two in the barbaric mind. Both are regarded as effective for weal or woe through the magic power assumed to inhere in the names, and through the control obtained over them through knowledge of those names." [68]

The names of power can be so corrupted, and the words of power so incomprehensible, that it is sometimes difficult to separate them. A word of power may once have been the name of some ancient deity, or it may simply be a corruption of a word in a foreign language, which over time was copied and recopied until the errors were compounded to such a degree that it lost all connection with its origin. This is particularly true of Hebrew words, because almost none of the magicians in Europe who used Hebrew words and names of power could actually read Hebrew, and also because of the nature of the Hebrew alphabet, which has letters that are very similar in shape and easy to confuse with one another (Heh with Cheth, Vav with Yod, Beth with Kaph, and so on).

Sometimes, by puzzling over these names, it is possible to make an educated guess about which deity was intended. For example, in the fifth chapter of one of the most ancient grimoires, the *Key of Solomon*, the following string of barbarous names appears in a conjuration of spirits to visible appearance from the four quarters of the world:

> I conjure ye anew by these other names of God, Most
> Holy and unknown, by the virtue of which Names ye

---

67. John G. Gager, ed., *Curse Tablets and Binding Spells from the Ancient World* (Oxford: Oxford University Press, 1992), vi.

68. Edward Clodd, *Magic in Names and in Other Things* (New York: E. P. Dutton & Company, 1921), 157.

tremble every day;—BARUC, BACURABON, PATACEL, ALCHEEGHEL, AQUACHAI, HOMORION, EHEIEH, ABBATON, CHEVON, CEBON, OYZROYMAS, CHAI, EHEIEH, ALBAMACHI, ORTAGU, NALE, ABELECH (or HELECH), YEZE (or SECHEZZE); that ye come quickly and without any delay into our presence from every quarter and every climate of the world wherein ye may be, to execute all that we shall command ye in the Great Name of God.[69]

The name Eheieh (I Am) jumps out from the list as an uncorrupted name of God, and Chai is short for El Chai (Mighty Living One), but the others are less obvious. After this list of barbarous names, the editor of this edition of the *Key of Solomon*, the noted English magician Samuel Liddell "MacGregor" Mathers, added this footnote: "I give these Names as they stand, they do not all appear to be Hebrew; some of them suggest the style of the barbarous names in the Graeco-Egyptian Magical Papyri."[70]

Another example of barbarous names that I will give here appears in a Latin manuscript of necromantic magic from the fifteenth century kept in the Bavarian State Library, *Codex Latinus Monacensis 849*. At the end of a magical operation "For Obtaining Information About a Theft by Gazing into a Fingernail" (in folios 44v 45v of the manuscript), the following barbarous names appear: "Egippia, Benoham, Beanke (vel Beanre), Reranressym, Alredessym, Ebemidyri, Fecolinie, Dysi, Medirini, Alhea, Heresim, Egippia, Benoham, Haham, Ezirohias, Bohodi, Hohada, Anna, Hohanna, Ohereo, Metaliteps, Aregereo, Agertho, Aliberri, Halba."[71]

Those who have not experienced firsthand the efficacy of these barbarous incantations, when they are correctly vibrated on the breath, are inclined to dismiss them as no more than a random collection of pagan names that have, through ignorance, devolved into mere uncouth noises. Concerning these

---

69. Samuel Liddell MacGregor Mathers, trans., *The Key of Solomon the King (Clavicula Salomonis)* (London: George Redway, 1889), 25.

70. Mathers, trans., *The Key of Solomon the King*, 25.

71. Richard Kieckhefer, *Forbidden Rites* (University Park: Pennsylvania State University Press, 1998), 246.

barbarous names, Pazig wrote disparagingly, "Last of all, we further infer the futility of Incantations from the fact that they are very often so fabricated that they have evidently no meaning at all, and the Magicians are ignorant of their signification; and although it is acknowledged that a foreign tongue is the parent whence they have been derived, still they are so mutilated and corrupted that you can scarcely, if even at all, guess what import they bear."[72] Elsewhere he called them "a monstrously uncouth jargon of outlandish words."[73]

The veneration with which this class of names was regarded by the magicians of the ancient world is indicated by the reference to them in the *Chaldean Oracles*, a set of wisdom sayings which were fabled to have been the sayings of Zoroaster: "Change not the barbarous Names of Evocation for there are sacred Names in every language which are given by God, having in the Sacred Rites a power Ineffable."[74] The Christian writer Origen (b. 185 CE) gave much the same advice concerning the various names for God that were used by the Hebrews. "We must pronounce the holy names in their original language, for it is the sound itself which is operative while the translation is inoperative and useless."[75] Writing at greater length on this subject, Origen noted that incantations lose their force when translated to other languages.

> And while still upon the subject of names, we have to mention that those who are skilled in the use of incantations, relate that the utterance of the same incantation in its proper language can accomplish what the spell professes to do; but when translated into any other tongue, it is observed to become inefficacious and feeble. And thus it is not the things signified, but the qualities and peculiarities of words, which possess a certain power for this or that purpose. And so

---

72. Pazig, *Treatyse of Magic Incantations*, 46.

73. Pazig, *Treatyse of Magic Incantations*, 42.

74. W. Wynn Westcott, ed., *The Chaldean Oracles of Zoroaster* (Wellingborough, Northamptonshire, UK: The Aquarian Press, 1983), 57. The true origin of these sayings is a matter for conjecture, but they seem to have come into general knowledge in the second century as part of the works of Julian the Theurgist, who lived during the reign of the Roman Emperor Marcus Aurelius (r. 161–180).

75. Bouisson, *Magic*, 105.

on such grounds as these we defend the conduct of the Christians, when they struggle even to death to avoid calling God by the name of Zeus, or to give Him a name from any other language.[76]

Concerning the importance and use of barbarous names of power, the magician Cornelius Agrippa had this to say:

> Therefore we may not for any reason whatsoever change them; therefore *Origen* commandeth that they be kept without corruption in their own characters; and *Zoroastes* also forbiddeth the changing of barbarous and old words; for as *Plato* saith in Cratylus, all divine words or names have proceeded either from the gods first, or from antiquity, whose beginning is hardly known, or from the barbarians: *Jamblicus* in like manner adviseth, that they may not be translated out of their own language into another; for, saith he, they keep not the same force being translated into another tongue.
>
> Therefore these names of God are the most fit and powerful means of reconciling and uniting man with God, as we read in Exodus, in every place in which mention is made of my name, I will be with thee, and bless thee; and in the book of Numbers, the Lord saith, I will put my name upon the sons of Israel and I will bless them.
>
> Therefore divine *Plato* in Cratylus, and in Philebus commandeth to reverence the names of God more than the images or statues of the gods: for there is a more express image and power of God, reserved in the faculty of the mind, especially if it be inspired from above, than in the works of men's hands.
>
> Therefore sacred words have not their power in magical operations, from themselves, as they are words,

---

76. Origen, *Origen Against Celsus*, in vol 4., *The Ante-Nicene Fathers* (New York: Charles Scribner's Sons, 1907), 406–7.

but from the occult divine powers working by them in the minds of those who by faith adhere to them; by which words the secret power of God as it were through conduit pipes, is transmitted into them, who have ears purged by faith, and by most pure conversation and invocation of the divine names are made the habitation of God, and capable of these divine influences.[77]

It should not be assumed that the occult power inherent in names is an academic topic of past centuries. Today there is great debate about the use of the name "Jesus" in prayer and for such magical works as healing and exorcism. Some religious sects associated with the Sacred Name and Hebrew Roots movements believe that the name only has occult force in its original Hebrew form, "Yeshua." When the apostle Paul wrote, "For whosoever shall call upon the name of the Lord shall be saved," did he mean the Hebrew form "Yeshua" or the Greek form "Iesous" or the Latin form "Iesus"?[78] For devout followers of Christ this is a matter of no small significance, when it is believed that the exact form of a name carries its power in its very shape and sound. Modern Christians should not concern themselves greatly with this matter. The form of the name "Jesus" has been used long enough and widely enough by passionate believers that it has acquired its own inherent occult power for salvation, healing, and exorcism.

Barbarous Words

The strings of seemingly meaningless words contained in some of the ritual procedures of the grimoires are puzzling. They do not appear to be the corrupted names of pagan gods. The folklorist Felix Grendon called them "an incoherent jumbling of words, miscellaneously derived from Latin, Greek, Hebrew, Gaelic, and other tongues," and added, "This gibberish was often arranged in rhythmical lines, with frequent assonant rhymes. Such jingles were in great favor even among later Greek physicians of a superstitious

---

77. Henry Cornelius Agrippa, *Three Books of Occult Philosophy*, ed. Donald Tyson (St. Paul, MN: Llewellyn Publications, 1993), 475–76.

78. Romans 10:13 (KJV).

bent."[79] He gave an example from the writings of the physician Alexander of Tralles (c. 525–c. 605), which is a charm to cure gout.

> Meu, treu, mor, phor,
>
> Teux, za, zor,
>
> Phe, lou, chri,
>
> Ge, ze, on.[80]

This list of single syllables creates a kind of singsong effect when chanted aloud. The influence of the Greek language is obvious in this list, but it has no apparent meaning. Grendon called it "gibberish." However, merely because it is without meaning does not mean it is without method. It is possible that these strings of seemingly meaningless barbarous words in the grimoires were the result of divine inspiration on the part of the theurgists who originated the rituals in which they appear. We see a similar phenomenon today in Protestant churches in the form of what is known as "speaking in tongues," or glossolalia.

During their meetings, the American Christian religious order known as the Shakers received visitations of various spirits they believed to be spirits of the dead, who took part in their rituals. Sometimes these spirits would bring with them songs, which the entire congregation would sing and dance to. The song of the channeled spirit that identified itself as Shawnee war chief, Tecumseh, well illustrates the use of repetition, alliteration, and nonsense words in incantations:

> A way wig a wig a war,
>
> Way wig a war war,
>
> Way wic e wic a war
>
> Way wick e war war.
>
> A way walla wampum,
>
> Willa walla wano,
>
> Tecumseh am e noon,
>
> Villa volia vin de vo.[81]

---

79. Grendon, "The Anglo-Saxon Charms," 114.

80. Grendon, "The Anglo-Saxon Charms," 114.

81. Anonymous, *Extract from an Unpublished Manuscript on Shaker History* (Boston: E. K. Allen, 1850), 22.

The way barbarous words work is to provide a focus for the mind of the magician, who understands implicitly that the words have occult power that can be released by chanting them aloud on the breath. Their very lack of specific meaning helps amplify their power, because they become channels for the unconscious will of the magician who chants them, or as Agrippa put it in the quote on page 67, "by which words the secret power of God as it were through conduit pipes, is transmitted." The same phenomenon may be observed in devout Catholics who, ignorant of the Latin language, recite prayers in Latin for various blessings and helps. The lack of specific meaning in the barbarous words opens them to whatever meaning the magician seeks to derive from them.

The magician Israel Regardie (1907–1985) believed that those invocations that contained barbarous words whose sense had been forgotten or degenerated or that were never more than meaningless jargon were the most potent invocations of all. He noted in his 1932 work *The Tree of Life* that such meaningless words in ancient invocations were always vibrant and sonorous, writing, "That is their sole virtue, for they are particularly effective when recited with magical intonation, each syllable being carefully vibrated. For some reason or other it has been found that the recitation of these names is conducive to the exaltation of the consciousness, exerting a subtle fascination on the mind of the Magician." [82]

It is no coincidence that strings of barbarous words in the grimoires resemble the nonsense rhymes chanted by children. Compare the charm against gout with this bit of children's doggerel, a rhyme for counting out:

> One-ery, two-ery,
> Tick-ery, tee-vy;
> Hollow-bone, crack-a-bone,
> Pen and eevy. [83]

The imaginations of the children supply whatever meaning is necessary to give the words power in their games, whatever purpose their chanting is designed to achieve. The use of barbarous words in magic functions in much

---

82. Israel Regardie, *The Tree of Life* (New York: Samuel Weiser, 1969), 143–44.

83. Halliwell, *Popular Rhymes and Nursery Tales*, 134.

the same way. The sounds of the words guide the deep mind in directing power at the magical purpose for its fulfillment.

In order to release the power of barbarous words, it is necessary to chant them for their sounds, without regard to their possible meaning. The vowels in these words should be extended slightly, but not enough to distort the sound of the words beyond recognition. As you vibrate the words, allow your mind to step from one vowel sound to the next as though walking up a flight of stairs effortlessly. Or imagine that you are crossing a stream and dancing from one stepping stone to the next to avoid falling into the water. Your mind must be balanced and poised as it rides the vowels from word to word. The sounds are everything, the meanings nothing, when chanting barbarous names or words.

Abracadabra

There are a handful of words of power that have transcended their time and place and in some mysterious manner have managed to become familiar words in our own time, although very few people who hear and use these words have any idea that they owe their origin to ancient magic. The term "hocus pocus" today signifies something deceptive or illusionary, but how many know that it was used by English conjurors in the sixteenth century as words of power? The term is believed to be based on the Latin words *hoc est corpus*, from the Latin Catholic Mass: *Hoc est corpus meum* (This is my body).

Thomas Ady, in his 1661 book *A Perfect Discovery of Witches*, described how a street conjuror would make use of these potent words of transubstantiation of the body of Christ:

> Then begin the silly people to wonder, and whisper, then he sheweth many slights of activity as if he did them by the help of his Familiar, which the silliest sort of beholders do verily beleeve; amongst which he espyeth one or other young Boy or Wench, and layeth a tester or shilling in his hand wetted, and biddeth him hold it fast, but whilst the said Boy, or silly Wench thinketh to enclose the peece of silver fast in the hand,

he nimbly taketh it away with his finger, and hasteneth the holder of it to close his hand, saying, Hold fast or it will be gone, and then mumbleth certain words, and crieth by the vertue of *Hocus, Pocus, hay passe prestor, be gone;* now open your hand, and the silly Boy or Wench, and the beholders stand amazed to see that there is nothing left in the hand.[84]

We see in this quotation how at one time stage magic and real magic were confused together and how entertainers may have borrowed actual words of power used in incantations to impress their audiences in the marketplace.

The most famous of these words of power is "Abracadabra." Most people recognize it as a word used by stage magicians when they pull a rabbit out of a top hat, but it didn't start that way. Its earliest appearance in surviving written form is in the medical text *De medicina praecepta* by the late second-century Roman writer and physician Quintus Serenus Sammonicus (d. 212 CE), where it is presented as a cure for fever:

Thou must on paper write the spell divine,
Abracadabra called, in many a line.
Each under each in even order place;
But the last letter in each line efface:
As by degrees its elements grow few,
Still take away, but fix the residue,
Till at last one letter stands alone,
And the whole dwindles to a tapering cone.
Tie this about the neck with flaxen string,
Mighty the good 't will to the patient bring:
Its wondrous potency shall guard his head,
And drive disease and death far from his bed.[85]

---

84. Thomas Ady, *A Perfect Discovery of Witches* (London: R. I., 1661), 37.

85. W. Sparrow Simpson, "On a Seventeenth Century Roll Containing Prayers and Magical Signs, Preserved in the British Museum," *Journal of the British Archaeological Association* 40 (1884): 308.

The word is written as a charm in the form of an inverted triangle of eleven lines, each successive line with the final letter removed until on the last line there remains only the first letter. This way of writing a charm was by no means unique to this word but was used extensively in Greco-Egyptian and Jewish magic. As an incantation, the lines of the charm are to be vocalized one after another, and as the lines diminish, so does the fever.

ABRACADABRA

ABRACADABR

ABRACADAB

ABRACADA

ABRACAD

ABRACA

ABRAC

ABRA

ABR

AB

A

Each line of this charm can be pronounced if you give a vowel to the letter R when it appears at the end of the word and pronounce it "er." The lines are pronounced thus: "Ab-ra-ca-dab-ra, Ab-ra-ca-dab-er, Ab-ra-ca-dab, Ab-ra-ca-da, Ab-ra-cad, Ab-ra-ca, Ab-rac, Ab-ra, Ab-er, Ab, Ah."

There was a difference of opinion about whether this charm should be written centered, as I have given it above, or with the first letter of each line in a vertical column, so that successive lines diminished on the right side.[86] Sometimes examples of this charm have not only the last letter of the word, but the first and last letters removed from each successive line.[87] This results in an inverted triangle of letters that has only six lines. In the margin of a British Library manuscript of Serenus's work that was copied by a scribe at

---

86. Quintus Serenus Sammonicus, *De medicina praecepta saluberrima* (Leipzig: I. G. Mülleriano, 1786), 150, note to line 944.

87. Erich Bischoff, *Die Kabbalah* (Leipzig: Th. Grieben's Verlag [L. Fernau], 1903), 93. See also Louis Baudet, *Préceptes Médicaux de Serenus Sammonicus* (Paris: C. L. F. Panckoucke, 1845), 102n100. Also W. Sparrow Simpson, "On a Seventeenth Century Roll Containing Prayers and Magical Signs, Preserved in the British Museum," 309.

the Abbey of St. Augustine at Canterbury, England, in the thirteen century, the Abracadabra charm appears with the first letter removed from each successive line, rather than the last letter.[88] There was clearly uncertainty about the exact way the charm should be used, although general agreement about its potency and efficacy.

E. A. Wallis Budge believed the charm to be much older than the second century CE. He accepted the interpretation of Bischoff that Abracadabra is derived from the Chaldean words *Abbada ke dabra* and that it signifies "perish like the word."[89] Others speculate that the word is derived from the Hebrew *Ha Brachah-dabarah* and means "name of the Blessed."[90] However, some scholars believe it to be a corruption of the Hebrew *ebrah k'dabri*, meaning "I will create as I speak." Budge asserted that the patient was to vocalize each line of the charm. He did not state it explicitly, but it seems to me that Budge intended that each day one of the lines should be spoken until none remained. He wrote, "As the formula diminished the fever became less."[91] It could scarcely be expected that the fever would vanish instantly—therefore, to speak a line per day until no lines remain seems like a reasonable way of proceeding.

Budge gave the charm in a triangle that is formed from Hebrew letters after the example of Bischoff. In Hebrew, the word has only nine letters because there are no vowels in the Hebrew alphabet. It may be transliterated into Latin letters as Aa-B-R-A-K-D-B-R-A (עברא כדברא). Remember that Hebrew letters are written from right to left. Note that although the letter A in the Latin alphabet is a vowel, the corresponding Hebrew letter Aleph (א) is not. Nine seems like a more significant number, in a magical sense, than eleven. In Greek the word was also written in eleven letters: ἀβρακαδάβρα.

Concerning the use of the charm, the 1910 edition of *Encyclopaedia Britannica* stated that it is to be written on a paper that is then folded into the form of a cross. I take this to mean that it is to be folded twice so that the folds make a cross on the paper when it is opened. In its folded state, it is hung around

---

88. Royal MS 12 E XXIII, British Library, London.

89. See Bischoff, *Die Kabbalah*, 95.

90. Don C. Skemer, *Binding Words: Textual Amulets in the Middle Ages* (University Park: Pennsylvania State University Press, 2006), 25.

91. E. A. Wallis Budge, *Amulets and Superstitions* (London: Humphrey Milford, 1930), 221.

the neck of the sufferer on a strip of linen so that it rests against the pit of the stomach, and it is worn in this way for nine days. On the night of the ninth day, before sunrise, the wearer is to cast it over their shoulder into a stream, the waters of which are flowing toward the east.[92] From the number of days cited, it seems likely that this instruction was meant to be applied to the charm when written in Hebrew letters, although Serenus gave only the Latin version of it. The Latin version of the charm would need to be worn for eleven days.

This charm could also be written in reverse, as a malevolent spell to cause another person to become ill and eventually die. In this use, the magician would link the charm to the person to be ill-wished, then recite a line of it each day, gradually intensifying the illness. If the Hebrew etymology *ebrah k'dabri*, meaning "I will create as I speak," is accepted, it suggests that the charm was used to intensify the working of magic, fair or foul. In either its diminishing or increasing form, it illustrates the power inherent in repetition. Similar charms using other words of power were constructed in the same way for various purposes, to diminish or intensify effects.[93]

The word has had an interesting history. It was used by the Basilidean Gnostic sect of the second century as a charm against disease and misfortune and was inscribed in one form or another on Gnostic gems.[94] Serenus himself was a Gnostic. Daniel Defoe wrote in his book *A Journal of the Plague Year* that the Abracadabra charm was used in 1665 by Londoners to ward off the plague: "This was in wearing Charms, Philters, Exorcisms, Amulets, and I know not what Preparations, to fortify the Body with them against the Plague; as if the Plague was not the Hand of God, but a kind of Possession of an evil Spirit; and that it was to be kept off with Crossings, Signs of the Zodiac, Papers tried up with so many Knots; and certain Words, or Figures

---

92. *Encyclopaedia Britannica*, 11th ed., vol. 1 (1910), 69. The reference to the pit of the stomach appears to be derived from the essay cited above by W. Sparrow Simpson, page 310, who quoted from John Jones, *Medical, Philosophical and Vulgar Errors, of Various Kinds, Considered and Refuted* (London: T. Cadell Jun. and W. Davies, 1797), 31.

93. See the "Charm to Restrain Anger" in Betz, ed., *The Greek Magical Papyri*, 143.

94. R. Walsh, *An Essay on Ancient Coins, Medals, and Gems* (London: Howell and Stewart, 1828), 51 and plate 2.

written on them, as particularly the Word *Abracadabra*, form'd in a Triangle, or Pyramid."[95]

The enchanted talisman was nailed to the doors of houses, in imitation of the practice of the Israelites in Egypt, who splashed their doorframes with the blood of sacrificial lambs to turn aside the plague of God that killed the firstborn of the Egyptians.

The preacher Samuel Mather (1626–1671), elder brother to Increase Mather of New England fame, encountered a healer in Ireland in 1664 who possessed the Abracadabra charm, which he had derived from the *Three Books of Occult Philosophy* of the German magician Cornelius Agrippa.[96] Mather was not impressed by this wonder worker and, according to his biographer Erasmus Middleton, penned an essay to expose this fraud: "About this time he had an interview with one Valentine Greatarick, who pretended to cure diseases by stroking; a man of a strong imagination, whom he found to have read Cornelius Agrippa, and had got his Abracadabra. Dr. Stubbes having printed some letters in his favour, the people of Dublin crowded after him. Mr. Mather therefore wrote a piece to expose his pretences. But though it was read with approbation by some persons of figure, he was not allowed to publish it."[97]

Increase Mather mentioned the same man and the same Abracadabra charm. Drawing on information he probably received from his brother Samuel, he wrote: "That insignificant word, *Abrodacara*, is by Sammonicus mentioned as a magical spell; which hobgoblin word the late miracle-monger or Mirabilarian stroaker in Ireland, Valentin Greatrix, attempted to cure an ague by."[98] Although the spellings of the healer's name and of the charm itself differ, both brothers are clearly talking about the same individual, who was celebrated in Ireland for a brief time as a wonder worker.

It may be noted in passing that Greatrix appears to have used much the same therapeutic method that would later be developed by the more celebrated

---

95. Daniel Defoe, *A Journal of the Plague Year* (London: E. Nutt, J. Roberts, A. Dodd, J. Graves, 1722), 39–40.

96. Agrippa, *Three Books of Occult Philosophy*, 476.

97. Erasmus Middleton, *Evangelical Biography*, vol. 3 (London: J. Stratford, 1807), 322.

98. Increase Mather, *Remarkable Providences Illustrative of the Earlier Days of American Colonisation* (London: John Russell Smith, 1856), 183.

German occultist Franz Anton Mesmer (1734–1815), who employed hand passes above the body and stroking of the body to cure illness.

The magician Aleister Crowley (1875–1947) believed that the word Abracadabra held great power, but that it had been misspelled. Crowley changed the spelling to Abrahadabra for numerical reasons, so that the numerical sum of its letters would total 418, which he considered a more significant number. To achieve this sum, Crowley converted the Latin letters into their Hebrew letter equivalents and added their values:

A—Aleph—1

B—Beth—2

R—Resh—200

A—Aleph—1

H—Heh—5

A—Aleph—1

D—Daleth—4

A—Aleph—1

B—Beth—2

R—Resh—200

A—Aleph—1

In this form, Abrahadabra, the word appears in Crowley's prophetical *Liber AL vel Legis*, otherwise known as the *Book of the Law*, which was received psychically by Crowley through his guardian angel, Aiwass, in Cairo in 1904.[99] The sum of the letters in the Greek version of the name "Aiwass" is also given by Crowley as 418, which he called the number of the magical formula of the Aeon of Horus.

Divine Names

The words with the greatest power in Western magic have always been the names of the gods or, in the case of monotheistic cultures, the names of God. In pagan times, each deity had numerous names or titles that expressed var-

---

99. Aleister Crowley, *Liber AL vel Legis* (South Stukely, Quebec: 93 Publishing, 1975), 57.
   "Abrahadabra" is the first word of the third chapter of this work.

ious aspects of the god. The Germanic and Norse god Woden (Odin) in particular was noted for the large number of titles by which he was known. He was called *Forni* (Ancient One) due to his white hair and long white beard, *Bolverker* (Evil Doer) because his appearance was sometimes accompanied by ill-fortune, *Gangleri* (Wanderer) due to his habit of wandering the earth in the disguise of a lowly traveler, *Geirvaldr* (Spear Master) because his weapon of choice was the short spear, *Grimr* (Masked One) due to his forbidding aspect, *Ygg* (Terrible One) due to his remorseless nature, *Hangi* (Hanged One) in reference to his hanging of himself from the world ash to learn the secret of the runes, and numerous other titles, each conveying some aspect of his divine nature.[100]

The advantage to all these titles is that a magician could tailor the god by selecting for his incantation only those qualities of his nature that had a bearing on the magician's purpose. If one wished to empower runes, the magician would call upon Odin in his role of Hangi (Hanged One); if one wished to prevail in battle, summoning Odin by his title Geirvaldr (Spear Master) would better serve the purpose; if one worked magic against an enemy, Odin might be called by his title Bolverker (Evil Doer); if one sought revenge, the god might be called by his name Ygg (Terrible One).

The use of divine names was carried to its highest level of sophistication in the magic of the Jewish rabbis of the Middle Ages. A Jewish magician was known as a *Baal Shem* (Master of the Name). They used the various names of God that occur in the Torah (first five books of the Old Testament) for different, specific purposes in their magic. Just as Odin had over a hundred titles by which his various functions and qualities were described, so the God of Moses was called by many names in the Old Testament books. Among these Hebrew names of God are *Adonai* (Lord), *Eheieh* (I Am), *Elohim Gibor* (God of Battles), *Eloh* (Almighty), *Elohim Sabaoth* (God of Hosts), *El Chai* (Mighty Living One), *Adonai Malekh* (Lord and King), *El* (Mighty One), and *Shaddai* (Almighty).

Many of these names lack a specific function. Some are clear enough—Elohim Gibor means the God of Battles, and its use in magic would be obvious. Others, such as Eloh and Eheieh, are less clear in their practical application.

---

100. For an extensive listing of the various names of Odin, see Jean I. Young, trans., *The Prose Edda of Snorri Sturluson* (Cambridge, UK: Bowes & Bowes, 1954), 31 and 48–50.

However, the Jewish magician had a method for combining divine names with specific functions. It was simply this—whenever a name of God appears in a sacred verse of the Torah, study its context and that will give you the function of the name; but whenever an action or function of God is described in the holy writings, by using methods of the Kabbalah, a name of God presiding over that function can be extracted.

This method may be extended beyond the five books of Moses to the entirety of the Old Testament and indeed to the New Testament as well:

> The general rule of these is, that wheresoever anything of divine essence is expressed in the Scripture, from that place the name of God may rightly be gathered; but in what place soever in the Scripture the name of God is found expressed, there mark what office lies under that name. Wheresoever therefore the Scripture speaks of the office or work of any spirit, good, or bad, from thence the name of that spirit, whether good, or bad, may be gathered; this unalterable rule being observed, that of good spirits we receive the names of good spirits, of evil the names of evil.[101]

This is not the place to delve into the complexities of the Kabbalah, but I will provide a simple method by which the name of God, or the name of an angel, may be derived from holy scripture for a specific function. It will work as well for the New Testament as the Old Testament.

Find the passage in the Bible that expresses the achievement of your magical purpose as clearly and as concisely as possible. If you are seeking a name of God, let the passage describe an action of God; if you are seeking the name of an angel, let it express the action of an angel. Then take the initial letters of the significant words in that passage. Ignore little words such as "a" and "the" and "of" since they have no occult virtue. This will result in a set of letters. In order to turn these letters into the name of God, or the name of an angel, it may be necessary for you to add vowels. Try to add in as few vowels as possible in order to make the name easy to pronounce aloud.

---

101. Agrippa, *Three Books of Occult Philosophy*, 538.

Names Live on the Breath

It is important that you grasp one point when using names of power. A name has power in magic only when it is spoken. A name is something expressed on the breath by the lips, tongue, and other speaking organs of the body. Writing down a name is merely a way of recording it so that at a later time the one who wrote it, or another person, can read the name and thus speak it, either aloud or in the mind. A name that is only spoken in the mind, silently, has less power in magic than a name spoken aloud on the breath. The more clearly you can hear a name in your mind when you read it or think of it, the more power it will possess, but it will never have as much power as a name uttered aloud with the lips.

Coupled with the utterance of the name, there must be a clear certainty in the mind of the magician that the name is a conduit of occult power, that by speaking the name, you open a valve that allows the specific type of magical force that you associate with the name to flow through to the physical universe. By knowing the meaning of the name, you focus its power on a specific purpose when you give it life by uttering it on the breath. However, as mentioned earlier, if you are using barbarous names, whose meanings are unknown, yet you have a firm belief and expectation in their magical potency, their power will still manifest itself. Your own meaning will fill the words the way water fills empty vessels and will determine their shapes for the purpose you have in mind.

Tetragrammaton

It remains only that we speak of the supreme name of power in Western magic, the name of God that the Greeks called *Tetragrammaton* (four letters) because this name has four letters in its original Hebrew form. Of all the many names of God used by the Jews, it stands above and apart. It is said to be the only name of God that is not a descriptive title but is the actual personal name of Deity. For this reason, it rules over all other divine names and all names of spirits both good and evil. It is said by the rabbis that the pronouncing of this name created the world, and that if it were spoken aloud again in an accurate way, the world would be unmade—or rather, remade in another form, for every destruction is a kind of creation of something else.

The correct pronunciation of the name was a great secret kept by the Jews for many centuries. When the Romans pulled down the Temple at Jerusalem, killed the Jewish priests, and scattered the Jews across the world in 70 CE, the pronunciation of the name was gradually forgotten. Today, no one can say with assurance that they know its correct way of voicing on the breath— although there are many magicians who have claimed to know it.

I don't want to delve too deeply into the Kabbalah, which is the subject for another book. It is enough that you remember that the Hebrew alphabet has no vowels. The Tetragrammaton, as the Greeks called it, is made up of four Hebrew consonants, which are Yod, Heh, Vav, and a second Heh. They are often transliterated into English as IHVH or YHWH. In order to pronounce this name, vowels must be added. Before the fall of the Temple at Jerusalem, the Jewish priests knew the vowels and their pronunciation, so they could on holy days whisper the name during rituals in a very low voice so that those gathered to worship could not hear it above the sound of drums and the piping of flutes. With the loss of the priesthood, the correct voicing of the name was lost.

In Western magic the name is usually written as its four Hebrew letters (יהוה), is transliterated into Latin capital letters (IHVH), or is transliterated into three Greek letters (IAΩ), or the Greek name for it (τετραγράμματον) is written out in Latin as "Tetragrammaton." All these forms were considered to possess occult potency in past centuries, and you will find them all represented in old woodcuts and book engravings. The purest form is the original unpointed Hebrew, with four Hebrew letters. Bear in mind that Hebrew is read from right to left, not left to right like English or Latin. The י in the name is equivalent to the I, the ה in the name is the H, and the ו in the name is the V.

The general practice when vocalizing the Tetragrammaton during rituals or other works of magic is to sound each of the Hebrew letters individually, one after another. There are various ways to pronounce the Hebrew letters in English, because their pronunciation has varied from century to century, and from country to country. A good working pronunciation is to sound them in this way: "*Yooode—Haaaay—Vaaaav—Haaaay.*" The "o" in Yod is long, the "a" in Heh is also long (an "a" doesn't appear in the extended transliteration of the letter, "Heh," but the sound is the long "a" sound), and the "a" in Vav is a short "a" sound. If you wish to make your pronunciation conform exactly with modern spoken Hebrew, you can find the Hebrew letters vocalized aloud as sound files on the internet.

In the history of Western magic, the Tetragrammaton has more authority and more power than any other name. Magicians used it in a variety of ways. One way is to assume the authority of IHVH to command lesser gods and angels. The magician speaks aloud to the spirit, commanding it to perform its appointed task by the authority of IHVH. For example, if you wished to command the archangel Michael, who is considered second in power only to God in Christian folklore, to make a river flow backward, you would say, "I command you, Michael, warrior angel of heaven, to reverse the waters of this river, by the authority and power of Yod-Heh-Vav-Heh, supreme God of Creation."

When you command spirits by a name of power, you assume the authority to do so by virtue of your strength of will and clarity of purpose. You must believe yourself worthy to use the power of the name, or your inner uncertainty will take away the power, and the spirit you command by it will not obey you. By using the Tetragrammaton, you become an agent of God, appointed by God to use his name in your works. Unless those works are spiritual in nature and for the greater good, they are not appropriate as works of God, so you cannot expect the Tetragrammaton to command lesser spirits to perform them. Only those who are enlightened and pure in purpose can make practical use of the highest name of power, and only for works of greater good.

Five

Vibrating Words

In previous chapters we examined the occult potency inherent in the breath itself, as well as the liberation and focus of that power through the use of vowels, numbers, words, and names in various forms of composition, such as rhyme, alliteration, and so on. Here, we will look at different ways the words of incantations can be vibrated on the breath in order to use its inherent latent power to accomplish different purposes.

The manner of vibration should always suit the purpose of the magic. You will remember the quotation from Demetrius of Tarsus, who wrote that the voices of the Egyptian priests were so beautiful when they sang the seven Greek vowels in succession that men would stop and listen to them in preference to the music "of aulos and cithara."[102] By contrast, according to the Roman poet Lucan, when the witch Erictho incanted, her voice resembled the baying of wolves, barking of dogs, screeching of owls, howling of beasts, and hissing of snakes.[103]

The Egyptian priests had a beautiful purpose in mind, to please the gods with the sound of their chants, whereas the witch had an ugly purpose, to work malicious magic through the aid of the spirits of the

---

102. Demetrius of Tarsus, *Demetrius on Style*, 105.
103. Lucan, *The Pharsalia of Lucan*, trans. Ridley, 182.

underworld. Each expressed the power of the breath, focused and articulated in the form of vowels, in a way that reflected the purpose of the incantation. In magic, as in modern architecture, form follows function.

If you were to evoke a demon using a beautiful song and pleasing harmonies, the scent of rose incense, sweet offerings of food and drink, and bright, cheerful flowers, the demon would experience pain when standing in the triangle, because these things are inimical to its world and its very nature. Conversely, if you were to invoke an angel with ugly symbols, foul incense, dark colors, bitter food offerings, and harsh, clashing sounds, it would experience discomfort and probably would not appear.

To evoke the spirit of the dead, you would use things associated with death. Your invocation would have a dead sound. The colors around you during the ritual would be black and gray; or you would do the evocation in a place appropriate to the dead, such as a graveyard or battlefield where people had died.

To make incantations to the gods and goddesses of the seven planets of the ancients, you would use word imagery and a manner of vibration appropriate to the deity addressed—for example, soft and loving sounds for Venus, but hard and warlike shouts for Mars. To each his own.

The following are various modes or styles of incantation. Each of them is flexible and may be used for many different purposes, but each will be more appropriate to some circumstances than to others.

Golden Dawn Method

The Hermetic Order of the Golden Dawn was a Rosicrucian order of English occultists that flourished more than a century ago. Its members developed a particular style for vibrating words and names of power. The Golden Dawn method of vibration is a bit theatrical, but that should not be surprising since one of the great actresses on the London stage at the time, Florence Farr, was a leading member of the order and used this method many times in her group ritual workings.

Victorian actresses and actors did not have electronic voice amplification. They had to rely on the innate power of their voices to reach the back of large theaters and to move the emotions of audiences. The method of vibrating words taught by the Golden Dawn descends in part from this reality of the stage and in part from the training methods applied to the professional opera singers of the time, who also worked without voice amplification. The function of the Golden Dawn method of vibration is to project the full power of the voice upon the breath.

When correctly done, the effect of this method can be quite startling. The voice takes on an otherworldly quality, a greatness of resonance and depth that seems almost beyond the capacity of the human body to achieve. It echoes not only in this world, but in the worlds above and the worlds below. Spirits are able to hear it clearly, just as they can see images that are strongly and persistently held in the mind. When you visualize a symbol strongly, it comes into existence on the astral planes, and when you vibrate words using this method, they echo and resound like thunder across the astral realms.

Here is the actual method, which is called in the Golden Dawn teaching texts the Vibratory Mode of Pronouncing the Divine Names:

> The ordinary mode of vibrating is as follows: Take a deep and full inspiration and concentrate your consciousness in your heart....
>
> Then formulate the letters of the Name required in your heart, in white, and feel them written there. Be sure to formulate the letters in brilliant white light, not merely in dull whiteness as the colour of the Apas Tattwa. Then, emitting the breath, slowly pronounce the Letters so that the sound vibrates within you, and imagine that the breath, while quitting the body, swells [...] so as to fill up space. Pronounce the Name as if you were vibrating it through the whole Universe, and as if it did not stop until it reached the further limits.[104]

---

104. Israel Regardie, *The Golden Dawn*, 6th ed. (St. Paul, MN: Llewellyn Publications, 1989), 487. Note that I've made a slight correction to the text in the quotation. The original reads "swells you so as to fill up space." But it is the breath that fills space, not the self-image of the magician. Breath could scarcely swell the body of the magician as it is leaving the body. The word "you" has been cut, as indicated by the square brackets in the quotation. The Apas Tattwa is the tattwa of elemental water.

The letters of the vibrated name are visualized in white in the heart center because the energy to form them is to be drawn down from the highest source of divine power, called Kether (the Crown) in the Kabbalah, and the color of this source is brilliant white. Another name for Kether is the "White Head." The heart center itself may be visualized as a sphere around the size of a baseball in the center of your chest. The Golden Dawn gave the color orange to this power center of the body in its Knight's Color Scale, so you should visualize the white letters floating within this semitransparent orange sphere.

Another short description on how to vibrate names occurs in the Golden Dawn ritual, the Enterer of the Threshold, which I will quote:

> Another formula of Vibration is here hidden. Let the Adept, standing upright, his arms stretched out in the form of a Calvary Cross, vibrate a Divine Name, bringing with the formulation thereof a deep inspiration into his lungs. Let him retain the breath, mentally pronouncing the Name in his Heart, so as to combine it with the forces he desires to awake thereby; thence sending it downwards through his body past Yesod [the groin], but not resting there, but taking his physical life for a material basis, send it on into his feet. There he shall again momentarily formulate the Name—then, bringing it rushing upwards into the lungs, thence shall he breathe it forth strongly, while vibrating that Divine Name. He will send his breath steadily forward into the Universe so as to awake the corresponding forces of the Name in the Outer World. Standing with arms out in the form of a Cross, when the breath has been imaginatively sent to the feet and back, bring the arms forward in "The Sign of the Enterer" while vibrating the Name out into the Universe. On completing this, make the "Sign of Silence" and remain still, contemplating the Force you have invoked.[105]

---

105. Regardie, *Golden Dawn*, 345–46. The brackets are mine. The ninth emanation of creation, Yesod, corresponds on the human body with the groin.

The Golden Dawn was founded by three Freemasons, and it used various body postures for occult purposes, similar to the postures and gestures used in Freemasonry. The Sign of the Enterer is made by taking a half step forward on the left foot and thrusting the arms straight forward with the hands flat, palms downward, while staring intently forward over the backs of the hands.[106] The Sign of Silence is made by bringing the feet together and touching the lips with the forefinger of the left hand.[107] This is similar to the familiar gesture for silence that most people know. The right arm hangs down at the side of the body.

Do not be concerned about these Golden Dawn postures. Understand that you should formulate clearly in your mind the name you intend to vibrate as you take a slow, deep inhalation. Hold your breath and silently speak the name in your mind as you visualize it written in your heart center. With the force of your will, thrust the name down through your sex organs, drawing sexual force into the name as you do so, and into your feet. Push down with the breath being held in your expanded lungs to add force to this driving of the name into your feet. Briefly visualize it in your feet, then let it rebound upward into your lungs and vibrate the name aloud powerfully on your breath as you release your breath from your lungs to fill the greater universe.

Yet another brief explanation of the method appears in the Golden Dawn Ritual of the Pentagram: "In the pronunciation of all these Names, thou shalt take a deep breath and vibrate them as much as possible inwardly with the outgoing breath, not necessarily loudly, but with vibration thus: A-a-a-el-ll. Or—Em-or-r. Di-a-ll Hec-te-e-g-ah. If thou wilt, thou mayest also trace the letters [or] Sigils of these Names in the Air."[108]

---

106. Regardie, *Golden Dawn*, illustration on page 133, where the Sign of Horus is the Sign of the Enterer. Note that the right foot is advanced in this illustration, which is contrary to the usual practice. For a description, see page 371, the Saluting Sign (another name for this posture, which is also known as the Attacking Sign). See also Israel Regardie, *Gems from the Equinox* (Tempe, AZ: New Falcon Publications, 1974), photo on page 282, where Aleister Crowley makes a somewhat more forceful version of the sign.

107. Regardie, *Golden Dawn*, 133.

108. Regardie, *Golden Dawn*, 284. I have made a correction here, indicated by the brackets. The original text reads "trace the letters of Sigils of these names in the Air." Generally speaking, sigils are not formed of letters, so I believe the correct text is "letters or Sigils."

Al is a Hebrew divine name of God. *Emor Dial Hectega* is from the Eno-chian language and in Golden Dawn magic was associated with elemental Earth. Again, disregard these details and pay attention to the method. By "vibrate them as much as possible inwardly with the outgoing breath," it is meant that you must feel the vibration of the name inside your chest as you sound it upon the air. Your chest will resonate if you are vibrating the name correctly. The name should be voiced slowly and extended so that it is sounded completely. In my opinion there is no need to sound silent letters or to extend the sound of consonants, but the vowels must be extended when the name is vibrated. A sigil is a graphic symbol that represents a name. Its use is optional—you can vibrate names without tracing their sigils on the air.

Israel Regardie, a member of a later incarnation of the Golden Dawn and at one time the secretary to Aleister Crowley, advocated a different approach to the vibration of names in his 1932 work *The Tree of Life*: "Experience has shown that a shrill humming of the names to be pronounced is the most satisfactory method, a voice which vibrates rather than clearly pronounces being that which is required." [109] By this description, I take Regardie to mean a kind of nasal droning, like the drones of a set of bagpipes. In my own prac-tice I have not found clarity to be an impediment when vibrating names. However, Regardie appears to be saying that it is the vibration of the words, rather than the explicit articulation of the words, that penetrates through the higher and lower planes of existence.

There may be some basis for Regardie's statement, when we consider that the barbarous words are words that have lost their specific meaning but exist only as sound vessels that, when vibrated, become filled up with the general occult potency of the breath. Their very lack of meaning allows them to be charged with magic power, which can then be focused by the mind of the magician on a particular purpose or function.

The Golden Dawn teaching texts advise, "As a general rule, pronounce the Name as many times as there are letters in it." [110] Despite this explicit instruc-tion to vibrate a name as many times as it has letters, I do not advise it. Dif-ferent numbers have widely different significations. For example, three is of

---

109. Regardie, *The Tree of Life*, 141.

110. Regardie, *Golden Dawn*, 487.

spirit, four is of matter, five is of man, six is of God incarnate. It may happen that the number of letters in the name you vibrate is not a number you wish to associate with your work of magic. If you were seeking a material effect, you would not wish to repeat a name three times; if you were seeking harmony, you would not repeat it twice, the number of division and discord. My advice is to know the esoteric meaning of numbers and to repeat the name the number of times that is in harmony with the result you seek to achieve, always bearing in mind that rules are made to be broken, and this rule may be ignored to achieve specific desired purposes. Numeration is of less importance than content.

There may be occasions during your magical work when you wish to sound your incantations with great force. You can achieve this resonance by visualizing your throat as an open tube all the way down to your lungs, and your entire chest as hollow down to your diaphragm. Allow the sound to vibrate within your chest as if your chest were the body of a musical instrument. Keep your mouth open as you vibrate the words. When this is done correctly, you will experience a tickling or buzzing sensation in the back of your nose, where it meets your throat. There is no need to shout the words—the technique itself will carry them far across both physical space and across the spirit realms.

Chanting

Chanting is a technique that has been used within religions for thousands of years. It is employed extensively in Christianity, Judaism, Buddhism, and Islam. Its origin, like most aspects of magic, lies in prehistoric shamanism. When you chant, you repeat words or vowel sounds over and over. This creates a kind of trance state that opens the mind to higher levels of consciousness, including those levels on which we can interact with spirits.

The magicians of the Jewish Kabbalah, known as *Baalei Shem* (Masters of the Name), employed chanting in both their mystical study and their practical magic. G. R. S. Mead, who wrote a review of Erich Bischoff's 1903 work *Die Kabbalah*, translated from the German text a vivid portrait of a Baal Shem chanting the name of God:

The round panes of the half-opened window reflect but dully in their opaqueness the flickering light, whose gleam is yet more brightly seen in the metallic forms of certain astrological instruments lying near. But, how radiantly in contrast beam the rays o'er the rare symbols of the Kabbalistic tome spread open on the great oaken board, which now the old man, with what solemn deportment in his step, draws near. How dull and hollow sounds, in the sacred speech of his people, the murmur of his voice, blended with the Chaldean idiom's deep tones. From time to time he bows his head and the upper part of his body, each time, it seems, more profoundly and more earnestly. Glowing with a supernatural fire, his dark eyes, before half closed, begin to open now, as he articulates the great, thrice-holy, mysterious Name; red flicker the flames of the *menorah*, gloomy vapours rise and spread, the narrow chamber seems to widen into infinitude, while space and time both vanish. And ever through all chant forth the magical words of power.[111]

The four Hebrew letters of the Tetragrammaton can be permuted, or rearranged, into twelve distinct forms, which divide into four groups based on the letter that begins the forms in each group. It was by chanting these permutations that the renowned Master of the Name, Rabbi Judah Loew (1520–1609), the Maharal of Prague, breathed life into the Golem. These forms are sometimes known as the Twelve Banners of Tetragrammaton. Transliterated into English letters, they are:

IHVH, IHHV, IVHH
HVHI, HVIH, HHIV
VHIH, VHHI, VIHH
HIHV, HIVH, HHVI

---

111. George Robert Stow Mead, "A Kabbalistic Catechism," *The Theosophical Review* 34 (April 15, 1904): 184.

The twelve forms may be chanted as words, by inserting the vowels that are required to make them pronounceable; or they may be chanted by sounding the individual letters in sequence (Yod-Heh-Vav-Heh, Yod-Heh-Heh-Vav, Yod-Vav-Heh-Heh, and so on). I recommend the second method as an excellent meditation on God, in whatever form you may conceive the Supreme Creator.

It is best when chanting a verse that its lines be kept short. Chanting should be done rhythmically, over and over. If your incantation rhymes, so much the better. Alliteration is also helpful for focusing the mind and increasing the power of chants. As you speak the words on the breath in a kind of singsong way, mentally project them through the vastness of your imagination, which encompasses the universe. By this, I mean that you should hold the universe in your mind and send your chant across space as though launching a ship across the ocean. Push your magical purpose outward from your consciousness across this vast inner space while listening to the chant with both your ears and your inner mind. You may find it helpful to close your eyes as you do this.

Rather than chanting a specific number of repetitions, I find it more effective to just keep chanting until my intuition tells me that it is time to stop. You will get a sense that your chanted words have reached their objective and achieved their purpose. Stop the chant, and listen to the silence within yourself. Do not think of your purpose for making magic, or anything else, but merely take a minute or two to listen intensely to your inner silence. If you have outer physical activities to do in order to complete your working, then do them as much as possible without thinking about them. Keep your mind open and silent.

One of the most important skills you can learn is how to turn your thoughts off. Concentration on the magical purpose is important as well, but it will accomplish nothing unless you are able to turn your mind away from that purpose when you have finished your ritual. Chanting, all by itself, is a kind of ritual, but in magic it will usually be combined with other actions, such as the making of charms to be enchanted, or various physical gestures and postures. The trick you must learn is to know when your purpose has been achieved—it feels something like a key turning in a lock—and then to know how to withdraw your mind and allow your magic to work.

Turning off the mind is actually more important in magic than turning on the mind. When the work is done, you do not think about it anymore. It is done, accomplished, and fulfilled, and you know this in the deepest part of your mind, but you never dwell on this or fret about it. You must let your magic work itself apart from you, having full confidence that it will be accomplished, yet without dwelling on this confidence.

If you are using chanting alone to achieve something, the purpose will usually be expressed by the words of the chant. As an example, let's say that you are working magic to make an apple tree bring forth large, sweet apples. You might word your chant something like this one, which I have just composed:

> Water, sun, and soil to grow in,
> Tree is standing tall and strong;
> Apples big and red and sweet
> Will droop its branches low e're long.

You would chant this incantation while standing or sitting near the tree, ideally while resting your hands upon its bark, allowing the air from your lungs to go forth and physically touch the tree. In your mind you would hold an image of the tree, healthy and strong, bearing abundant fruit, the weight of which pulls down its boughs. Keep repeating the words of the chant over and over in a low voice. It is not necessary to use the technique of Golden Dawn vibration while chanting. Chants are usually made in an undertone. Do not focus your mind on the words of the chant. The chant is your instrument or tool. It is like a hammer, and the purpose you intend to achieve is like the nail. You focus on the nail, not on the hammer, when you use the hammer.

Singing

In the three major religions of the world based on the Torah, which are Judaism, Christianity, and Islam, prayers are not only chanted but also sung. The man who sings in the synagogue is known as the cantor or *hazzan*. He leads the gathered Jewish worshippers in prayer. In Christianity, the cantor is the person who sings solo passages, to which the church choir responds in song. Gregorian chants have been sung by Christian monks since at least the ninth century. Pope Gregory the First (r. 590–604) is sometimes credited with the invention of this form of sacred song—he is the patron saint of musicians and singers. The psalms of David, inspired by God, are not only prayers but songs as well that are sung in churches. The hymns of Protestant churches, songs written by humans rather than dictated by God, are prayers that are designed to be sung. In Islamic mosques, verses of the Koran are recited in a beautiful, melodious manner, which in my opinion can only be called singing, although Muslims are forbidden to call it that.

For the ancients, songs were more than just secular entertainment. They were foremostly shamanic offerings to the gods, a way to make the words of prayer more potent and effective. The Greek chorus in the fifth century BCE dramas of Aeschylus, Sophocles, and Euripides probably sang their words. They were not singing for the audiences assembled in the amphitheater to watch these plays, but for the gods listening and watching in the heavens above. Songs were sacred instruments of great power.

The Greek hymns of Orpheus, the date of which is uncertain, were both prayers that were sung and magical incantations. Plato (c. 429–347 BCE) mentioned them, which would put their composition prior to the fourth century BCE. This was the view of the classicist Thomas Taylor (1758–1835), who believed the Orphic hymns we possess today are the same as those referred to by the Greek philosopher.[112] Taylor wrote concerning these hymns, "But that they were used in the Eleusinian Mysteries is evident from the testimony of Lycomedes, who says that they were sung in the sacred rites pertaining to Ceres, which honour was not paid to the Homeric hymns, though they were more elegant than those of Orpheus; and the Eleusinian were the mysteries of Ceres."[113]

The power of song in incantation stems from the ability of music to move our emotions. When we sing, our voice follows a melody that affects us below the level of words. Singing the words of an incantation can be potent if the incantation is composed in such a way that it lends itself to melody. Applying a melody to a chant turns it into a song.

You can make up an original melody to go with the wording of your chant. When you do so, it should always be simple and clear. You don't want the act

---

112. Thomas Taylor, *The Mystical Hymns of Orpheus*, 2nd ed. (Chiswick, UK: C. Whittingham, 1824), xxxiv, xlii–xliii.

113. Taylor, *The Mystical Hymns of Orpheus*, xxxiv.

of singing to steal psychic energy away from your magical purpose; you want it to reinforce the incantation and make the voicing of it more powerful.

It is also possible to use the words and melody of existing songs as your incantation or part of your incantation. Popular songs can have great resonant power in the mind. You can repeat a line from a song over and over to increase its force by virtue of the power of repetition. When the line of a song suits your magical purpose, you may wish to sing it while hearing the music that accompanies the song in your imagination. Any song lyrics you choose to incorporate into your incantations should always be in harmony with your purpose and with the natures of the spirits you seek to contact: slow, heavy songs for communication with the dead or with chthonic spirits; light, airy melodies and bright words for aerial spirits; and so on.

It may be helpful to beat a small drum as you sing. This is a practice that has been used for thousands of years. Your mind can ride along on the rhythm of the drum the way a ship glides along on the wind that fills its sails. Or, if you have musical skills, you may wish to play upon an instrument as you vibrate your invocation in song. The use of the voice precludes musical instruments that rely on the breath, such as a trumpet or saxophone, but a guitar, a violin, and even a piano may be used to good effect when singing your incantations.

If you play a musical instrument while singing an invocation, take care to choose an instrument that is in harmony with your purpose. Percussive instruments, such as the piano, which makes its tones by hammers striking against strings, are best used with more masculine spirits and purposes of a harsher or more physical nature. Stringed instruments, such as the harp and the violin, are better suited to more feminine spirits and for gentle, mystical evocations. These are only general suggestions—let your musical intuition be your guide in this matter.

Wizards That Peep and That Mutter

It will often be necessary when you vibrate names and words or chant your incantations to do so in a way that is inaudible to others who may be near. One way to do this is to form the words on the breath without allowing the breath to vibrate over the vocal cords. The result is a kind of breathy whisper that can be kept as quiet as needed to avoid having others overhear what you are saying. This is where the quaint expression in the King James version of the Bible concerning wizards originates: "Seek unto them that have familiar spirits, and unto wizards that peep, and that mutter."[114] The muttering referred to is the wizard voicing his incantation under his breath, so as not to be understood by others who are standing near to him.

By using this breathy whisper, you take advantage of the power of your living breath to carry forth your magical purpose, but at the same time you avoid having your purpose exposed to others, as it would be if you stood in the middle of the town square and vibrated it using the Golden Dawn method. When working magic, secrecy is essential. The more people who know what you are doing, the more likely your magic is to fail. Indeed, it is best if you work your magic without anyone at all knowing that you are working it, not even the person you work it for. This is not always possible, but you should keep as much as you can of what you are doing secret.

As for the "peep" in the biblical quotation, it refers to the widespread belief that there is malign power in the gaze of a witch or wizard, especially when that gaze is cast from the corner of the eye. The evil eye does have some truth in it—there is indeed power in the gaze of a person skilled in magic, but that power is not necessarily hurtful, and it is not cast forth every time the magician's glance falls on something. We will examine the evil eye in greater detail in chapter 9.

Mental Vibration

At times it will be necessary to express your incantation without making any outward sound at all or giving any sign that you are expressing it. You may be in a crowded place and not wish to draw attention to yourself. Or it may be late at night, and you may not wish to disturb others asleep in the silent house, when even a whisper seems loud. This can be done by mental vibration.

To perform this technique, you use your imagination to "hear" the words you are expressing as clearly as possible in your mind, just as though you were vibrating them aloud on the breath. It is somewhat similar to reading without moving your lips, except most people, when they read silently, skip over words without sounding them fully in their minds. When using mental

---

114. Isaiah 8:19 (KJV).

vibration, you must recite the words of your spell slowly and fully in your mind, at the same speed and in the same way you would do so if you were actually saying them out loud.

You will find your throat silently working as you do this, because it will try to form the words as you sound them in your imagination. As much as possible, relax your throat. You don't want it taking energy away from the incantation. All your awareness when using mental vibration must be inward, in the imagination, which is actually vaster than the outer universe, since it contains and encompasses the physical universe, but is filled with the innumerable spiritual realms as well. As you mentally vibrate the words, send them forth across this inner universe to the realization of your purpose. Hold complete confidence in your heart that your purpose will be fulfilled. Repeat the incantation as many times as you intuitively feel is necessary for the working of the magic; or if you wish, you can repeat it a set number of times that is in occult harmony with your purpose.

When you have a sense that your incantation has fulfilled itself, stop chanting the mental words and relax your mind. Turn your thoughts to some everyday activity and put the act of magic completely out of your consciousness. It will remain in the back of your awareness as something that is done and accomplished and therefore needs no further attention. This is the great trick of magic—to know with full assurance that your magic has fulfilled itself and to completely stop thinking about it or worrying about it. Unless you can switch off your mind in this way after you work your spells, they will not be effective.

Six
Spellbinding

In traditional Western magic, the breath was used to control the wind. This was done by imitation. Blowing air from between the lips produced a tiny breeze, and the magician or witch could use this to either summon up a great wind in the sky or to calm a wind that was already blowing. In folk magic this was done by making an audible whistling noise and was called either "whistling up the wind" to call it up or "whistling down the wind" to diminish it. The person performing this act of magic identifies the sound of the breath and its motion of air with the greater wind of the outer world. The magician, whose body and mind are the microcosm, or little world, becomes in imagination the macrocosm, or greater world, and a resonance is created between the whistle of breath between the lips and the movement of the wind through the air.

Another way to raise the wind is the use of a device known as a bull-roarer. This is a small, flat piece of bone or wood with a reed of some kind attached to its surface. When air passes over it, the reed vibrates and produces a buzzing or roaring noise. It is tied to a length of cord and spun around in a circle. The harder it is whirled, the louder the noise it makes. The occult reasoning is that the sound of the bullroarer imitates the sound of the wind and in this way can be used to summon it. It is a type of sympathetic magic. On the island of Muralug, off the northern tip of Australia, magicians would increase the power of their bullroarers to call the wind by climbing as high as possible into the tops of trees.[115]

Knot Binding

The ability to whistle up the wind was a gift much admired in past centuries, particularly by European seamen whose ships were wholly wind-powered. It was a terrible thing to be becalmed at sea and to remain drifting under the sun day after day while the stores of fresh water were used up. A man who could whistle up the wind was treated like a god by the rest of the ship's crew.

However, it often happened that no member of a ship's crew was gifted with this particular power, and then the seamen sometimes took the precaution of buying winds from those known to possess this gift. The winds were purchased in the form of knots tied in string or twine by a witch or wizard, who captured the wind by blowing breath through the knot when it was loose and open, and at the same time drawing the knot tight around the breath. In this way the wind was bound into the knot. In Finland, "the Laplanders are in the habit of using a cord tied with three magical knots for raising the wind. When they untie the first knot, there blows a favourable gale of wind; which increases at the second, and becomes a perfect hurricane at the third." [116]

A seaman might purchase a length of twine with knots in it and would then comfort himself with the belief that he had the same number of winds to loose, should the need arise. The way to loose the witch wind was to untie the knot. When this was done, a breeze would spring up and then strengthen into a steady wind that would propel the becalmed ship on its way. But all the knots must not be loosed at the same time, or a catastrophic storm would result.

Underlying all forms of knot magic is the belief that a knot can capture and hold mana, or magic potential, when drawn tight. This mana is like electricity, neither good nor evil in its nature, but capable of serving either beneficial or malicious ends, depending on the intention of the magician. This potency is borne on the breath, which is why magicians breathe through the

---

115. Alfred Cort Haddon, *Magic and Fetishism* (London: Archibald Constable & Co., 1906), 8.
116. George Oliver, *The Pythagorean Triangle* (London: John Hogg & Co., 1875), 94.

knots when working knot magic. Words uttered into the knots as they are tightened give this mana shape and purpose for good or ill.

Knot magic was popular in Europe during the Middle Ages and indeed has been used throughout the world in many different cultures. There is a passage in the Koran (Sura 113, *Al-Falaq*) that reads, "I have taken refuge with the Lord of the Dawn from the wickedness of those women who blow upon knots." [117] The magic of knots was forbidden by Islam, as it was by Christianity and Judaism. Even so, it was widely resorted to by the common people.

The Sufi mystic and writer Idries Shah related a traditional folktale of the prophet Mohammed, who was bewitched by a Jewish sorcerer: "Nine knots were tied in a string, each knot 'binding' a curse, and the thread was then hidden in a well." [118] The story had a happy ending for Mohammed. The archangel Gabriel came to him and warned him about the existence of the binding charm, which was intended to cause the death of the prophet. The thread was pulled from the well, and before the knots could be untied to break the spell, Mohammed caused them all to untie themselves with a verbal command.

Shah does not say, but we can be fairly sure that the Jewish sorcerer enchanted the string by speaking nine curses as he was pulling the knots closed, so that his breath passed through their loops and was symbolically caught by them when the loops were tightened.

One aspect of knot magic involves making numbers of knots that are magically significant—for example, one knot for a willed purpose, two knots to sow discord, three knots for spiritual fulfilment, four knots for material realization, five knots to bind the human will, six knots to fulfill prayers, seven knots for glory, eight knots for wealth, nine knots for the weird, and ten knots for a final consummation leading to transition or for a death.

Diseases were sometimes cured using knot binding. Shah related the practice of Central Asian tribes to blow upon knots that were made in a cord of three colored threads, one green, one blue, and one red. A single knot was blown upon as it was tied each day. After seven days, the tricolored cord of seven knots was buried where it would not be found, and the disease for

---

117. Bouisson, *Magic*, 10.

118. Idries Shah, *Oriental Magic* (New York: E. P. Dutton & Co., 1973), 82.

which it had been tied was cured.[119] Here, it is probably the spirit of the disease that is captured and bound in the knots in the cord. Shah did not say, but one way to do this would be to pronounce the name of the spirit of disease in a diminishing way through successive knots, similar to that of the Abracadabra charm.

Names exist as sounds borne on moving air. That is their life. If the breath is blown through a knot as it is drawn shut, the living name spoken upon it can be captured. In this way a person or a spirit may be bound to the fulfillment of a specific duty and released from this obligation when the knot is untied or cut. Remember, when you bind someone with a knot, that you are stopping change. You can bind a person to fulfill a particular function over and over again, but that person will not be able to progress. If you bind a business or enterprise, that business will function in the way it was bound, but cannot transform itself or grow. Cutting or untying the knot releases what was bound into it on the breath, allowing it to progress and go through changes.

To bind a name in a knot, make the knot loosely in a piece of string or twine and speak the name as you hold the open knot close to your face. As you are speaking it, and as the air from your lungs is passing through the opening in the knot, draw the string slowly tight, and in your mind visualize the named thing being captured and retained by the pressure of the knot, just as if you were binding with ropes the person or spirit named. You can also bind things such as cars, ships, and houses and even places such as a field or a grove of trees. The thing to be bound is spoken through the closing knot, and the purpose for binding it is held in the back of the mind at the same moment.

There is a difference between untying the knot and cutting it. When you untie the knot, the power it contains is released gradually, but when you cut through the knot, the release is explosive. Cut the knot when you are seeking a more dramatic effect or when you require a burst of initial force, which may manifest itself on the physical or the psychic level, depending on what has been bound into the knot and the purpose of the binding.

One example of knots used in folk magic, a spell to bring about a dream vision of a future husband, appears in a nineteenth-century chapbook on divination titled *The Universal Fortune Teller*. The young woman seeking

---

119. Shah, *Oriental Magic*, 82.

this dream visitation must do this magic when she is sleeping in a house far removed from her usual residence. Upon going to bed, she must "knit the left garter about the right leg stocking, letting the other garter and stocking alone," and as she does this, she must recite the following incantation, making a knot at each of the six commas in the verse:

> This knot I knit, to know the thing I know not yet,
> That I may see, the man that shall my husband be,
> How he goes, and what he wears,
> And what he does all days and years.[120]

The tying of the left garter around the right stocking is symbolically the union of male and female, the union of opposites. The text does not specify this, but a knot should also be made at the final period of the verse. The total will then be seven knots, and seven is a number of great potency in magic, as well as the number of Venus, goddess of love.[121] When the woman falls asleep, she will dream of her future spouse, whom she will see dressed in the clothing or wearing the insignia of his trade or profession.

Witches' Ladder

A witches' ladder is a form of knot magic that in the past seems to have been most often used for malicious purposes, although in modern magic it is used for helpful or protective purposes as well. It is a length of twine or string with a series of knots tied in it that hold various objects of significance in the magic it works. Each knot holds one thing. A traditional witches' ladder made to curse an individual might hold a series of black feathers from a black chicken, crow, or other black bird. Black is symbolically the color of evil due to its association with darkness and shadows, hence the term "black magic."

---

120. Anonymous, *The Universal Fortune Teller* (London: W. S. Fortey, [1860]), 3 (unpaginated).

121. The link between Venus and the number seven is based on the Ptolemaic ordering of the seven planets of traditional astrology, coupled with the first seven magic squares, which for many centuries have been assigned to these seven planets. The smallest magic square, order three, was assigned to the most distant planet from the Earth, Saturn, and the successive squares placed on the remaining planets moving inward in the Ptolemaic order toward the Earth. The Moon and Sun were regarded as planets in traditional astrology. This resulted in the planets having the following numbers in Western occultism: Saturn, three; Jupiter, four; Mars, five; Sun, six; Venus, seven; Mercury, eight; and Moon, nine.

The witch would tie the feathers into knots one after another down the length of the string, and as a knot was made loosely so that it formed a loop, the witch would chant a curse against the person targeted by the charm, using the person's name to link the charm to that individual. As the name was spoken, the knot was drawn tight around the black feather. The result was a string of knotted feathers that somewhat resembled a ladder.

Other small objects could be bound into the knots, such as black iron nails, shards of glass, or pieces of bones from an animal or a human being. This is a very dark magic, but in modern times witches' ladders are often used for more helpful purposes, such as protecting someone from harm, preserving their physical health, keeping them bound to a promise they have made, or joining two persons together in love. The specific purpose for the magic depends on the incantations recited as the knots are tied, the nature of the objects bound into the knots, and the intention of the witch or magician who makes the ladder. The number of knots is also important, since some numbers are better suited for some purposes than others. Seven is considered a lucky number, for example, whereas thirteen is unfortunate.

The oldest existing example of a witches' ladder is not very old. In 1878 a length of rope was discovered between the ceiling and floor of a two-story house that was being demolished in Wellington, a hamlet in Somerset, England. It was described in 1887 by Dr. Abraham Colles in an essay in the *The Folk-Lore Journal*.[122] The rope, which still exists, has a loop at one end, presumably for hanging it up, and is a little over four feet in length. Woven into the twist of the rope are dozens of white cock's feathers that stick out on either side. Since no other example of this device was known to exist, and no practical use could be imagined for it, the assumption was made that it was used for magic. This was quickly confirmed by local people of the area, although the basis on which they made this confirmation is not recorded.

The renowned anthropologist James George Frazer (1854–1941) disputed the assumption by Dr. Colles that the knotted cord was used to curse. He believed that the witches' ladder was a device for magically stealing milk at a distance. Citing Robert Chambers' *Popular Rhymes in Scotland*, Frazer wrote, "Sometimes in Scotland the rope had to be made of hairs taken from the tails

---

122. Abraham Colles, "A Witches' Ladder." *The Folk-Lore Journal* 5, no. 1 (January–March 1887): 1–5.

of the cows whose milk was to be stolen; a knot was tied in the rope for each cow, and by pulling at the knots as if she were milking, and at the same time uttering a spell, the witch brought the milk into her pail." [123] The passage from Chambers referred to by Frazer is interesting because it contains the actual incantation supposed to have been used by the witch. I will quote it here.

> Meers' milk and deer's milk,
> And every beast that bears milk
> Between St Johnston and Dundee,
> Come a' to me, come a' to me. [124]

Frazer gave other examples of a knotted cord used to steal milk at a distance. However, this does not explain the feathers bound into the rope. Frazer hypothesized that the feathers were there to symbolically carry the magic through the air. [125] This view that the witches' ladder was only a magical device for stealing milk is disputed by W. H. Ashby, who in a letter submitted to the *Daily News* newspaper published on January 26, 1887, described the making of what he called a "real Somersetshire witches' ladder."

> I learn that the "witches' ladder" may be made of wheat-straw, called "elm," "ellum," or probably "haulm-straws." Take four straws, tie two together, top and bottom, for one side of the ladder. Tie the other two in the same manner, and then insert short straws between for steps. Now take small feathers and lace them up each side of the ladder, and you have a real Somersetshire witches' ladder. It is used in this way. Anything that goes cross-grained, if the ladder is waved to and fro a few times, and the request muttered at the same time with the swinging, the thing that was wrong will be righted. For instance, the fire will not burn, or the flats will not heat

---

123. James George Frazer, "A Witches' Ladder," *The Folk-Lore Journal* 5, no. 2 (April–June 1887): 81.

124. Robert Chambers, *Popular Rhymes of Scotland*, new ed. (Edinburgh: W. & R. Chambers, 1870), 329.

125. Frazer, "A Witches' Ladder," 81–83.

for ironing, or the lover will not come, or the husband stays out too late; swing the ladder, saying, "Burn fire," "Irons heat," &c, and all will be well….I was told that if a witch suspects a person of crime, or of witchcraft, or any offense whatsoever, she hangs her ladder outside her house; if the person comes to the door but cannot be induced to enter, the thing is proved against him.[126]

There is no mention in Ashby's letter of knots, but the lacing of the feathers into the rungs of this straw ladder has an aspect of binding similar to the insertion of feathers through the twist in a rope.

It is a reasonable assumption that the devices described by Ashby and Colles were used for magic other than milk-stealing, since similar devices are known. The folklorist Charles Godfrey Leland wrote that in Italy witches made something called a "witches' garland" in which black hen feathers were inserted through knots in a twisted length of twine. As each feather was knotted into place, the witch uttered a curse against the person for whom the garland was made. It was then placed into the person's bed to give the person bad luck or ill health. The old Italian woman who told Leland about this charm related that one instance of its use was to cause the death of a child: "They opened the bed and found what is called a *guirlanda delle strege*, or witches' garland. It is made by taking a cord and tying knots in it. While doing this pluck feathers one by one from a living hen, and stick them into the knots, uttering a malediction with every one." [127]

Note that the breath carrying the curses must pass through the tightening loops of the knots, so as to be captured there. Alternatively, if the objects are inserted in the twisted strands of a rope, the breath must pass through the opened twist before it is allowed to close around the object. The feathers of the witches' garland were plucked from a living bird because each feather plucked caused pain to the bird, and the feather retained that pain in an occult manner, which made the curse spoken over the feather and through the knot more potent. Also, living things or substances taken from living

---

126. W. H. Ashby, letter reprinted in *The Folk-Lore Journal* 5, no. 2 (April–June 1887): 84.
127. Charles Godfrey Leland, *Etruscan Roman Remains in Popular Tradition* (London: T. Fisher Unwin, 1892), 353.

things were supposed to possess vital energy that could be used to empower charms. Given the Italian name for this evil charm, it may be assumed that its ends were tied together to make it into a loop or garland.

This form of knot magic can be made even more personal by associating the objects tied into the knots in the twine with the person at whom the magic is directed. Small objects are gathered that have a strong link with the person for whom the magic is to be worked. They might be such things as a lock of hair, or even a single strand of hair from a comb, belonging to the person; a shard of a shattered mirror in which the person regarded his own image; a scrap of cloth from clothing worn by the person; a slip of paper with the person's signature written on it; and so on. If the charm is made for malicious purposes, also bound into the twine might be items intended to cause pain, such as razor blades, iron nails, pins, and the like.

Twisting in the Wind

On the grounds of a small seaside retreat near Halifax, Nova Scotia, there used to be a tree very near the water whose branches were hung with all manner of suspended objects but mostly bottles. When I asked what this was for, the woman who ran the retreat told me that it was for good luck. Each object had a wish attached to it. Different people would wish for something and hang an object from the tree on a length of string so that it moved in the wind. Some of these bottles probably held wishes that had been written down and placed inside them. The effect was that of a modern but very pagan Christmas tree.

Hanging from a tree something that represents a person so that it can move and twist in the wind was in ancient times considered a form of malicious magic. We still have echoes of the practice in the terms "left him hanging" or "left him twisting in the wind." Both phrases evoke the image of a hanged man, suspended between earth and heaven, unable to help himself because his feet cannot touch the ground. Such an image appears in the tarot as one of its trumps, or picture cards. In England and many other places in Europe, men and women condemned to death might be hanged by the neck from a scaffold located at a crossroads or hung up alive in an iron cage called a gibbet cage to die more slowly and be eaten by carrion crows. Such corpses were left swinging in the wind for prolonged periods, sometimes until the rope that supported them rotted and broke, as a warning to all who passed not to commit the same crimes.

One of the primary incidents in the mythology of the divine magician of the north, the god Woden (Odin), involves his voluntary suspension from the world ash tree, Yggdrasil, for nine days and nights. This is obviously a shamanic ordeal undergone by the priests or shamanic worshippers of this god. In the myth, Woden takes neither food nor drink for the entire nine days and then has a vision of the magic symbols known as the runes at the root of the great tree. With a cry, the god snatches up the runes just before falling into unconsciousness. When he awakens, he retains them and makes a gift of their magic to his faithful worshippers.

There is an obvious parallel between the ordeal of Woden on the world tree and the ordeal of Jesus on the cross of crucifixion. Both took neither food nor drink. Both sought spiritual revelation. Both cried out at the climax of their ordeal. The ordeal was a transition to a higher state of consciousness for both. In the case of Jesus, it involved the transition of death and rebirth. Symbolically, the shamanic ordeal of suspension exposed to the elements is also a death and birth—death of the old and birth of the new.

There is an interesting scene in John Boorman's film *Excalibur* in which the good knight Sir Percival is hanged from a tree bearing all the other knights who before him have failed to achieve his quest. While suspended between death and life, he has a vision of the Holy Grail, but before it can be fulfilled, the sharp spur of a dead knight hanging above him severs his rope, and the vision is cut short as he falls to the ground. In this scene, the knight himself becomes the object of magic suspended from the tree to twist in the wind, and his life quest the charm the object carries.

The wind is a significant factor because it is the instrument of torture or blessing. A charm is not simply bound to the tree or hidden inside the tree but is suspended from the tree. If the magic is benevolent rather than malevolent, as it can be when the chants used during the suspension of the object are blessings, the wind then carries the words of the magician to God or to the spirits able to fulfill the purpose of the charm, which will last as long as the object remains suspended. In a sense, the wind becomes the breath of God, sustaining on itself the magic of the charm. Cutting the cord that holds the charm up, or the natural breaking of the cord, ends the charm's efficacy.

When the suspended object is a bottle, the wind blowing across the open mouth of the bottle will often produce a sustained sound, like the note from a pipe organ. The ordeal of suspension in the wind empowers the charm. The wind carries its purpose to its fulfillment. An incantation expressing the purpose of the magic should be spoken through the knot as the object is tied to the tree. A written charm expressing the same purpose that is placed upon or inside the object is optional, but it strengthens the effect of the spell.

Binding with Hair

Hair is a very personal part of the identity of an individual. It seems alive because it grows, and thus appears to be a part of a person's living being, but this is an illusion. Hair is a dead thing, which is why it can be periodically cut off without pain or other negative consequences. Even though it is dead, the fact that it came forth from the living person gives it power in magic that is worked for good or ill toward that person. In past centuries, noblemen with many enemies would have their hair and their fingernail clippings carefully gathered up and disposed of by someone they trusted, to prevent them from falling into the hands of those who wished them harm.

Hair can be braided into thread if there is enough of it available, and this thread can be used for works of spellbinding. For example, hair can be braided into the twine used for a witches' ladder. If the hair is long enough, a single strand can be used to bind. Let's say you want a particular person to keep your secret and not betray you to anyone else. You might write the secret down on a slip of paper and place it into a small box, then use a strand of hair from the person who holds your secret to tie around the box so that it cannot be opened. As you tie the box shut, you would speak through the closing loop of the hair strand your purpose. As long as the hair remains unbroken, your secret will be safe.

A way to use a variation of knot magic to help or protect a person with long hair is to get the person to allow you to braid their hair for them. As you sit braiding their hair, lean your head close and murmur your magic purpose so that your breath passes through the strands of the braid as you are binding it. In this way the magic will be caught up into the braid and will endure until the braid is undone.

If you wish to bar the entry of a particular individual into a room, a house, or other place that has a door, you can use a single hair from that person's head to seal the door shut. Make sure that the hair extends from a tack in the door itself to a tack in the door jamb so that opening the door would break the strand, and seal the loop of hair with a knot—do not merely tape or stick it to the door and frame. As you draw tight the knot that holds the door shut, speak a binding charm through the closing loop so that your breath passes through it. Make sure you speak the name of the person to be kept out—or in. The charm might be something like this:

> John Smith, I bind this door with the hair of your
>   head;
> John Smith, I bind this door with the flesh of your
>   body;
> John Smith, I bind this door with the blood of your
>   veins:
> Hair of your hair, flesh of your flesh, blood of your
>   blood,
> No man has victory who strives against himself.

Repetitions of three are good for bindings, since with the number three, there is no material resolution, as there is with the number four. In this incantation I have not used alliteration or rhyme but have employed repetition to strengthen its effect. There are five lines, the number of humanity. The name of the person to be bound would be inserted into the blank verse in place of the generic name "John Smith," and the pronouns should be changed to correspond with the target's gender.

Binding with Words Alone

The natural historian Pliny the Elder (23–79 CE), author of *Natural History*, wrote of an ancient tradition that the Vestal Virgins knew a certain secret prayer that would bind runaway slaves to the ground they stood upon, provided they had not yet left the boundaries of the city of Rome.[128] The occult

---

128. Pliny the Elder, *The Natural History of Pliny*, trans. John Bostock and H. T. Riley, vol. 5 (London: Henry G. Bohn, 1856), 280.

authority of the Vestals was inextricably bound up with the city they served. Their powers ceased if they ventured beyond it. Elsewhere Pliny wrote, "There is no one, too, who does not dread being spell-bound by means of evil imprecations; and hence the practice, after eating eggs or snails, of immediately breaking the shells, or piercing them with the spoon." [129]

The opening in the half eggshell or the shell of the snail, being continuous and enclosing like a magic circle, was presumed to have encapsulated some of the essence of the person who devoured its contents. To prevent an evil magician from obtaining the shell and then torturing or injuring by malign incantations the person whose essence was imprisoned within it, the shell was broken, and this was believed to deprive it of its binding power.

When using words alone to bind, whether they be spoken, chanted, or sung, it is useful to turn the words themselves into a thread or cord that binds. The following example that I have composed is designed to compel the person it is directed at to reveal the truth and put right whatever current wrong the person may have committed.

> A net, a noose, a snare made right,
> These three bind by drawing tight,
> These words bind thee to the light,
> Speak the truth and do what's right.

You could target this spell in various ways. For example, by uttering it in a low voice while looking intently at the person to whom it is directed, who may be some distance away. Or you might speak it while gazing at the photograph of that person or immediately after writing and speaking the name of the person. It can even be targeted by strongly imagining the face of the person in your mind while vocalizing the words.

---

129. Pliny the Elder, *The Natural History*, vol. 5, 282.

Seven

Healing Spells

In ancient times, one of the most common uses for incantation was the treatment of those injured or sick. More healing spells have come down to us through history than any other type, with the possible exceptions of love spells and binding spells, both of which were also very popular. We will treat of other types of incantations in later chapters, but here we will consider their use to cure and heal.

After the Roman armies withdrew from England in the fifth century, the land was invaded by tribes from the Netherlands, Denmark, and northern Germany. We generally group them under the name Anglo-Saxons, although they consisted of different but related peoples from these regions of northern Europe. They brought with them their magic, which used the runes and was devoted to Woden, Thor, and the other gods of the north. Over time they were converted to Christianity, but they continued to apply the old leechcraft they had carried across the English Channel. The charms remained the same, even if the names of the old gods were replaced by the names of Jesus, Mary, and the Christian saints.

If we examine the Anglo-Saxon healing charms that have survived and been collected together, we find that a number of characteristics stand out. These can instruct us in the composition and use of our own healing incantations. Magic is timeless. The way it was worked twenty thousand years ago by Stone Age practitioners is the same way it is worked today. Only superficial details change—the underlying principles of magic remain the same.

In his essay "The Anglo-Saxon Charms," Felix Grendon codified a number of features common to these ancient incantations, most of which involve healing magic.[130] He noted that there was often an appeal to the power of a god or goddess—or in the Christianized version of the charms, to God the Father, Jesus, the Holy Spirit, or the Virgin Mary. This appeal to authority did not necessarily take the form of a prayer but more often was phrased in a narrative retelling of some feat or triumph of the god that expressed an aspect of his power. Names and words of power were often used in the invocation, which would be recited or sung over the body of the afflicted.

He wrote, "A peculiar feature of the English incantations is the frequent injunction that they be sung or written on certain parts of the body. The left side appears to have been preferred to the right." [131] This was probably because, in a magical sense, the left side of the body is feminine and receptive, whereas the right side is masculine and projective. It was desired by the healer that the incantation penetrate into the body. For the same reason, sometimes the incantation was sung into the sufferer's ear or into his mouth—openings that allowed the words to penetrate. More often it was directed toward the wound itself or toward that part of the body that was in pain. We see in this practice the application of the healing power inherent in human breath and in words or letters carried on the breath, which were sometimes written directly onto the skin of the sufferer. In earliest times the letters would have been runes.

An analogous practice was to apply spittle to the afflicted part of the body. Because it comes from the mouth, the organ of speech through which passes the breath, spittle was understood to be magically potent: "Saliva has always had a thaumaturgic if not a therapeutic value in folk-medicine. Spitting on the painful spot will prove helpful, according to charm A20. In C1, the healer is commanded to expectorate three times while treating a case of leprosy; and spitting is part of the ceremonial in other charms, such as E1." [132] The

---

130. Grendon, "The Anglo-Saxon Charms," 110.

131. Grendon, "The Anglo-Saxon Charms," 118.

132. Grendon, "The Anglo-Saxon Charms," 122.

letters and numbers in the quotation refer to individual charms, which need not concern us here.

In ancient times there was no knowledge of bacteria or viruses, many of which reside in the human mouth. The modern practitioner should bear this in mind before considering the use of saliva in magic for healing purposes. In particular it should not be applied to any sore or open wound.

Grendon divided the Anglo-Saxon charms into five groups or classes. It will be useful to examine each class.

A. Exorcisms of diseases or disease-spirits

B. Herbal charms

C. Charms for transferring disease

D. Amulet charms

E. Charm remedies[133]

A. Exorcisms

Prior to the Age of Enlightenment, it was widely believed that diseases were caused by evil spirits or by malicious magic involving the use and direction of evil spirits. To cure the sick, it was necessary to drive out the spirit that had taken possession of the body. This understanding of disease is very ancient indeed and goes back to the Mesopotamian kingdom of Sumeria (c. 4500–c. 1900 BCE), where every ill was ascribed to some demon. The same beliefs were still current in the later Babylonian Empire. "So we find the Babylonian physicians regarding disease as the work of demons, which swarmed in the earth, air and water, and against which long litanies or incantations were recited," writes medical historian Fielding H. Garrison.[134] Note that these demons are said to have occupied the three lower elements earth, air, and water, but not fire, which was generally understood to cleanse and purify disease, although it might also be associated with fever.

The exorcism of a spirit was accomplished by appealing for aid from a more potent god or spirit, such as Woden or Jesus, who held power over the

---

133. Grendon, "The Anglo-Saxon Charms," 123.

134. Fielding H. Garrison, *An Introduction to the History of Medicine*, 2nd ed. (Philadelphia: W. B. Saunders Company, 1917), 53.

demon of sickness and could command it to depart from the body. Alternatively, exorcism was done by tormenting the possessing spirit until it left the body of the sufferer to escape the torment. This torture of the possessing spirit could be symbolic—the spirit might be threatened with being chained down in the bottom of a dark pit, for example. Or the torture could be inflicted on the body of the possessed, with the understanding that the spirit inside the body would feel whatever pains the body felt. One way of doing this was to give the possessed person a noxious drink of bitter herbs.

This second method of exorcism is, unfortunately, still used today. From time to time we read in the news about a poor possessed child who is killed by well-meaning parents or relatives during a rite of exorcism to drive out a possessing demon. This kind of exorcism is unnecessary and should be strictly avoided. Spirits are nonphysical beings and can be made to suffer in nonphysical ways, by the vibrating of the names of God or the angels, for example, or by ritual cleansing. When necessary, binding incantations can be composed to exclude the spirit from the body of its victim. No possessed person should ever be tortured.

B. Herbal Charms

Herbs were used for their natural properties to heal the sick, but it was also the practice to pronounce incantations over herbs and to cut letters or words into them to enhance their curative power. Sometimes the incantations were spoken when the herbs were gathered, but at other times they were uttered as the herbs were pounded into medicinal salves. One Anglo-Saxon charm has an incantation spoken over a loaf of barley bread to empower the bread before it is fed to a sick horse.[135] We see here an obvious echoing, with no mocking intention, of the Christian rite of transubstantiation during the Mass, when the priest transforms the Eucharist into the blood and body of Christ.

C. Transference

It was a common practice of ancient healers to cure the sick by transferring the disease from the body of the sufferer to some external location, where

---

135. Grendon, "The Anglo-Saxon Charms," 197.

it no longer had the power to afflict the person. The separation effected between the sufferer and the disease was enough to end its symptoms. The disease might be transferred into the body of an animal, such as a donkey or a dog, but it was a very common practice to send it into a tree or less often into a stone or other inanimate object.

One way to accomplish this transference was to crawl through a gap or hole in the tree, stone, or other object into which the disease was to be transferred. This created a kind of doorway through which the sufferer transitioned from the condition of sickness to the condition of health.[136] The touch of the sick child against the tree caused the sickness to remain behind in the tree. Another form of gateway was created by stepping over the grave of a dead person. In this way the disease was left with the corpse beneath the ground.

D. Amulet Charms

In the same way that herbs were empowered by incantations before being made into medicines, the Anglo-Saxon shamans sometimes empowered amulets with their spoken words and their breath. These words or symbols were drawn on parchment or some other surface to create the amulet. Natural stones used as amulets for their inherent occult properties were not enhanced with incantation, according to Grendon.[137] However, I see no reason why this cannot, or should not, have been done. A well-composed incantation could multiply the power of a natural stone or crystal, just as it enhanced the power of herbs that were subsequently made into medicines.

E. Charm Remedies

These are simply remedies against injury or disease that derive their effectiveness from the actual wording of the incantation and the ritual gestures or practices that accompany it. There is nothing external to consider, no greater authority to call upon. For example, one remedy given to cure a "fiend-sick man, when a devil possesses a man, or ravages him internally with disease," is to cause him to drink a potion from a Christian church bell, using the bell

---

136. Grendon, "The Anglo-Saxon Charms," 130.
137. Grendon, "The Anglo-Saxon Charms," 135.

as his cup.[138] The magical reasoning here is that church bells are Christian things and that the Christian religion overthrew the older pagan beliefs. Hence, the sound of bells was abhorrent to possessing or tormenting "fiends" who consisted of pagan spirits of various types.

Although the Anglo-Saxon charms became Christianized over the centuries, they were never looked upon with favor by the Church, which always held them to be devilish and forbidden. St. Eligius (588–659 CE) is recorded to have spoken the following admonition against them in a sermon: "Before all things, however, I declare and testify unto you, that you should observe none of the impious customs of the pagans; neither sorcerers, nor diviners, nor soothsayers, nor enchanters; nor must you presume for any cause, or any sickness, to consult or inquire of them; for he who commits this sin immediately loses the sacrament of baptism." [139]

Despite this hostility on the part of the Roman Catholic clergy, these charms continued to be used, and in fact they never really ceased to be employed by those who considered themselves good Christians who were serving the greater glory of God by healing the sick. The forms of the charms mutated over time, but the essential principles upon which they were based, some of which we have just examined, remained unchanged.

Cunning Men and Wise Women

The cunning men and wise women of Europe and their counterparts in certain regions of America were often resorted to by the common folk for healing purposes in centuries past, since trained physicians were not only few in number in rural regions but were also far too expensive for the laboring class to use. These healers in the forested hills of the northeastern United States, which were largely populated by Germans and Scots, did not call themselves witches, in past centuries a term of malediction, but looked upon themselves as "pow-wows," a reference to Indigenous Americans.

The first appearance in print of the term "pow-wow" cited by the *Oxford English Dictionary* occurred in 1624, in E. Winslow's *Good News from New England*, where the older form of the word "powah" was used: "The office

---

138. Grendon, "The Anglo-Saxon Charms," 136.

139. Samuel Roffey Maitland, *The Dark Ages* (London: J. G. F. & J. Rivington, 1844), 150.

and dutie of the Powah is to be exercised principally in calling upon the Devill; and curing diseases of the sicke or wounded."[140] *Powah* is an Algonquin word signifying a medicine man. The native powah was identified with the European cunning man by Sir Walter Scott, in his 1830 work *Letters on Demonology and Witchcraft*, where Scott wrote:

> Even in North America, the first settlers in New England, and other parts of that immense continent, uniformly agreed that they detected, among the inhabitants, traces of an intimate connexion with Satan. It is scarce necessary to remark, that this opinion was founded exclusively upon the tricks practised by the native Powahs, or cunning men, to raise themselves to influence among the chiefs, and to obtain esteem with the people, which, possessed as they were professionally of some skill in jugglery, and the knowledge of some medical herbs and secrets, the understanding of the colonists was unable to trace to their real source—legerdemain and imposture.[141]

Cotton Mather wrote about the Narragansett tribes of Martha's Vineyard: "They generally acknowledg'd and worship'd many Gods; therefore greatly esteem'd and reverenc'd their *Priests*, *Powaws*, or *Wizards*, who were esteem'd as having immediate Converse with the *Gods*."[142] Mather reported that one of these powahs had the unerring ability to locate stolen goods, which he did by asking a *"god subservient to him, that the English worshipped."*[143] These powahs were renowned for healing the sick, and when someone was beyond the help of English physicians, the whites of the region would often seek the aid of the Indigenous healers.

In this way, the term "powah" or "pow-wow" came to be applied to the German, Scottish, and English faith-healers of New England and eventually

---

140. *The Compact Edition of the Oxford English Dictionary*, ed. J. A. Simpson and E. S. C Weiner, vol. 2 (Oxford: Oxford University Press, 1971), 1216.

141. Walter Scott, *Letters on Demonology and Witchcraft* (London: John Murray, 1830), 80–81.

142. Cotton Mather, *Magnalia Christi Americana* (London: Printed for Thomas Parkhurst, 1702), bk. 6, 52. The italics are Mather's.

143. Mather, *Magnalia Christi Americana*, bk. 6, p. 52. The italics are Mather's.

to the spells they used. They believed their healing power came from God. Letitia Wrenshall, who researched the folk customs of healers in Maryland and Pennsylvania in 1901, asked one such healer if she surrendered her will to God when she did her cures: "She looked at me in surprise, and said very seriously, 'If I didn't do that, I couldn't cure. That's the way I do it.' She then complained, almost to tears, that 'some people thought she did it in other ways, and said she was a witch, and nothing hurt her as bad as that.'" [144]

The woman was what we would call today a faith-healer. She was convinced her power came directly from Jesus. However, when we look at her practices, we see that they are really no different from the healings done by self-declared witches or wizards. The methods of magic are everywhere the same. Only the names of the higher powers called upon to perform the healing differ. As students of magic, we should not allow ourselves to become distracted by religious beliefs or prejudices against religion—we should always look at the methods being used, because a method of magic has no loyalty. It can be used just as effectively by a witch as by a Catholic priest.

The healing methods of the Pennsylvania pow-wows are those used around the world by magical practitioners, both in past centuries and in the present day. They involve the occult power of the breath and spoken incantations, as well as hand gestures. The healer quoted above asserted that she could "always blow the fire out" of those who had suffered a burn. By this she meant that she could take away the pain and heat of the burn. The folklorist Wrenshall added,

> The practice of treating burns by words, blowing, and movements of the hands, is very general in the mountains, and I have always been able to trace it to German origin.
>
> Not long since a visitor in a house where I was staying was very anxious "to try for it" on an inmate of the house, who had been badly burned, but in this case the family physician had forestalled him. Words often used are these:—

---

144. Letitia Humphreys Wrenshall, "Incantations and Popular Healing in Maryland and Pennsylvania," *Journal of American Folk-Lore* 15 (October–December 1902): 269.

"Clear out, brand, but never in. Be thou cold or hot, thou must cease to burn. May God guard thy blood, thy flesh, thy marrow, and thy bones, and every artery, great and small. They all shall be guarded and protected in the name of the Father, the Son, and the Holy Ghost." [145]

The significant features noted by Wrenshall as she watched the healings of the pow-wow were "how to use the words, how to speak them, how to move her hands (much value is attached to the movements of the hands)." [146] Added to this list must be the use of the breath for such functions as the blowing away of the heat in burns. Notice that words are mentioned twice— how to use them and how to speak them. The first is the understanding of the words of power and their application in works of magic, and the second is the correct manner of vibrating the words upon the air when speaking them aloud and the number of times they should be repeated.

The Long Lost Friend

In 1819 a German immigrant to Pennsylvania named John George Hohman (c. 1780–c. 1846) wrote a book of magic spells titled *Der Lang Verborgene Freund* (*The Long Lost Friend*), which was published in the German language in 1820. Hohman was himself the German version of a cunning man, able to heal with words and touches of his hands. His book was an immediate success and continued to be held in high regard by rural American healers during the nineteenth and early twentieth centuries. The first English edition was published in 1846, but it was filled with grammatical errors. The second English edition, published in 1850, had a wider success and became a kind of bible for folk healers, who refused to part with it.

When the folklorist Wrenshall, quoted above, tried to buy the copy in the possession of the pow-wow she was studying, the healer refused to sell it for any price. Wrenshall's annoyance at not obtaining the book is evident in her choice of wording.

---

145. Wrenshall, "Incantations and Popular Healing in Maryland and Pennsylvania," 269.
146. Wrenshall, "Incantations and Popular Healing in Maryland and Pennsylvania," 271.

My witch would not part with her book. No, she must leave it to her daughter. She *could* not sell it; money could not buy it. If she had no daughter, she would give it to me, but could not sell it. I might study it all I wanted, but she could not part with it. All blandishments failed, and I came away without the book, but she told me of an old man who had another copy. A long drive to his home yielded the same result. Since then I have instituted a search, but no other copy has yet been found. I am still looking for it.[147]

We are more fortunate than this folklorist because copies of Hohman's *Long Lost Friend* are easy to obtain today. Beginning with the edition circa 1900, the term "pow-wows," referring to the spells in the book, was added to the title, which became *John George Hohman's pow-wows, or Long lost friend*.[148] Concerning the origins of his book, Hohman wrote in his introduction, "This Book is partly derived from a work published by a Gipsey, and partly from secret writings, and collected with much pain and trouble, from all parts of the world, at different periods, by the author, John George Hohman. I did not wish to publish it; my wife, also, was opposed to its publication; but my compassion for my suffering fellow men was too strong." [149]

It is unlikely that Hohman originated many of his spells. They were gathered by him primarily from several German sources, among them the anonymously authored *Romanusbüchleinn* (*Romanus Book*) and the *Aegyptische Geheimnisse* (*Egyptian Secrets*), a book apocryphally attributed to Albertus Magnus.[150] The book Hohman describes as "published by a Gipsey" is unidentified.

The folk remedies in *Long Lost Friend* consist of simple actions that are usually, but not always, coupled with a spoken charm. Often the charm makes reference to Jesus, the Virgin Mary, God the Father, or the Holy Spirit. Hohman was a firm believer in Christianity and did not see any heresy in

147. Wrenshall, "Incantations and Popular Healing in Maryland and Pennsylvania," 271.

148. Daniel Harms, ed., *The Long Lost Friend* (Woodbury, MN: Llewellyn Publications, 2012), 22.

149. Hohman, *Long Lost Friend*, 8.

150. Harms, ed., *Long Lost Friend*, 18.

asking Jesus to heal the injuries of other people: "Wo unto those who misconstrue these tidings at the moment of danger, or who follow the ill advise of any preacher who might teach them not to mind what the Lord says in the 50th Psalm: 'Call upon me in the day of trouble: I will deliver thee, and thou shalt glorify me.'"[151]

Since this book is the iconic text on folk healing in American history, I will give a few of its remedies that involve the use of spoken charms.

> ### A good remedy for bad Wounds and Burns.
> "The word of God, the milk of Jesus' Mother, and Christ's blood, is for all wounds and burnings good."
> † † †
>
> It is the safest way in all these cases to make the crosses with the hand or thumb three times over the affected parts; that is to say, over all those things to which the three crosses are attached.[152]

In this remedy the powers of three substances are invoked with the spoken words, which I have placed inside quotation marks. Those things are the living breath of God, in the form of the Logos; the milk of the Virgin Mary, which was fed to Jesus in infancy; and the blood of Jesus, which forms part of the holy Eucharist of the Roman Catholic Mass. None of these substances is obtainable in material form by the healer who uses the charm, but they are called into imaginary existence by the words of the charm and then symbolically applied to the cut or burn. The three small crosses after the charm indicate the sign of the cross made three times, once for each of the magical substances named.

Hohman gives directions about how the remedy is to be applied. His instruction is a bit ambiguous, but based on what is described for other remedies, I believe he intends that a cross be made in the air with the hand or thumb over the injury for each substance named, and that this should be done three times, so that the charm is spoken three times and a total of nine crosses are made.

---

151. Hohman, *Long Lost Friend*, 4.
152. Hohman, *Long Lost Friend*, 13–14. The quotation marks are mine.

Charms to stop bleeding are common in folk healing. They arose in ages past when an injured person could bleed to death on the ground where he fell if the flow from a wound was not checked. The Greek poet Homer (born c. 800 BCE) mentioned such a charm in the *Odyssey*, when Odysseus is treated for a wound in the thigh suffered during a boar hunt: "The wound of noble, god-like Odysseus they bound up skilfully, and checked the black blood with a charm." [153]

In the following charm from Hohman's book, the Virgin Mary is again invoked. Something impossible is named as a condition that must be fulfilled before the blood will be allowed to flow—in this case, that Virgin Mary must bring forth another son. Since Mary's only virgin birth is Jesus, and by Catholic doctrine there will never be another virgin birth, the blood cannot flow.

A good remedy to stop Bleeding.

This is the day on which the injury happened. "Blood, thou must stop, until the Virgin Mary bring forth another son."—Repeat these words three times.[154]

By the first statement, Hohman means that the charm must be spoken on the same day the injury occurs. I would add, within the first hour if at all possible. The charm is spoken three times. Hohman did not explicitly state it, but I believe he intended that a cross gesture be made with the hand after each utterance of the charm. Three crosses are often indicated for other charms in his book. If I were to use this charm, I would inscribe these crosses on the air with my right thumb, then press the thumb near to the bleeding wound. If the thumb becomes stained with blood by this action, so much the better.

Why the thumb and not one of the fingers? Because the thumb symbolically represents the phallus, due to its rounded shape, and thus has greater potency in magic. Catholic priests apply the chrism, or holy anointing oil, to the forehead of worshippers during confirmation with their thumbs for the same reason.

---

153. Homer, *The Odyssey*, trans. A. T. Murray, vol. 2 (London: William Heinemann, 1919), 261.
154. Hohman, *Long Lost Friend*, 14. The quotation marks are mine.

Hohman had great faith in the number three, the number of the Holy Trinity. From a symbolic point of view, three is not the best number when you desire a manifest, material outcome. Four is the number of manifestation. However, three is an excellent number when calling upon the power of God. The way to solve this conflict is to speak the charms three times, using three crosses or three times three crosses, but to conclude the charm with a fourth statement and action to represent its manifestation. For example, a witch could lay her hand over the wound and speak the words "So mote it be" as the fourth, concluding element in the charm.

Witches and other pagans should not be dissuaded from using Hohman's charms merely because they are Christian. They should study the structure of the charm, learn from it, and then rewrite it in a form that better suits their pagan sensibilities. For example, in the charm quoted above, the spoken part could be rewritten like this: "Blood, thou must stop, until the Queen of Heaven bring forth another world." The Queen of Heaven is a pagan goddess with whom the Virgin Mary has been associated. A cross is a pagan symbol as much as a Christian symbol, so there is no reason not to seal each statement of the charm with a cross having equal arms. It is the basic function of a cross in magic to seal. It has much the same function as the word "Amen" in Christian prayer or the phrase "So mote it be" in Wicca.

A symbol I like to use for purposes of magical sealing is a variation on the Celtic cross—I draw a cross with equal arms, first the vertical pillar from top to bottom, then the horizontal arm from left to right, and finally a circle that cuts through the four arms of the cross at mid-length, beginning at the upper arm and proceeding clockwise.[155] As an alternative to a cross, you can use as a sealing gesture, the Golden Dawn gesture of silence, also known as the Sign of Hippocrates.[156] You stand with feet together, arms at your sides, then raise your left hand and touch the tip of your left index finger to your lips.

---

155. Something very similar to the circle-cross gesture I use for sealing is used in Golden Dawn magic. See Regardie, *The Golden Dawn*, 245 and 306.

156. Regardie, *The Golden Dawn*, 133.

Composing Original Healing Spells

Now that we understand how that greatly revered pow-wow John George Hohman employed his spells, we can create an original healing incantation based on the same general principles. First, let's reiterate those principles.

1. Touch the place on the body that is injured with the hands. Let the warmth of your hands (or coolness, in the case of injuries that are hot) transfer itself to the injury.

2. Allow your breath to flow over the injury as you recite the incantation. If it feels hot, blow gently to cool it with your breath.

3. Keep the wording of the incantation simple and brief. If the ends of the lines rhyme, so much the better, but rhyme is not essential.

4. Use repetitions of three in the incantation, such as three names of power, three actions, or three objects within the incantation. If desired, you may recite the incantation three times or even nine times, a number that has great power in magic, being three times three.

5. Seal the incantation with three crosses or other sealing symbols drawn upon the air or upon the body of the sufferer with the right hand, which is the hand of projection.

6. To seal the entire incantation verbally, speak the word "Amen" at the end of all or, if you are pagan, the phrase "So mote it be" or another concluding word or phrase of your own choice.

7. Do not be afraid to violate any of these rules if your intuition tells you to do so. Listen to your inner guide and follow it.

Touch is important, both the touch of your hands on the injured place, and the touch of your breath, particularly while you are speaking the incantation. The incantation need not be spoken loudly—you can emulate the biblical wizards who "peep and mutter"—but your lips should be held close to the injured place as you speak it so that the patient can feel the warmth of your breath on his skin. If the charm appears to have no effect, you can try vibrating the incantation more forcefully, so that not only your breath but also the vibrations of your voice touch the injury.

Something you may wish to try is to wet the three largest fingers of your right hand with your tongue and apply them to the injured place at the beginning of your healing, while focusing your mind and will strongly on the place of injury. Then remove your hand and speak your incantation. Your saliva on the skin of your patient will cool as your breath passes over it, heightening the effect of your breath. Do not do this for open wounds—you do not want bacteria from your mouth to cause an infection.

As you speak your healing incantation, hold the confidence in your mind that what you are doing will be completely effective. Do not allow even a shadow of doubt to intrude itself. One trick for achieving this state of mind is to tell yourself that it is inevitable, that you could not stop the working of the charm even if you wanted to, that it has already done its work even before you start to speak it. You must regard it with as much confidence as if it were something that had already happened and thus was impossible to change.

Spell Against Headache

If we were to compose an original incantation designed to cure a headache, it might look something like the following example, which I have just made up:

> Cool is water from a well,
> Cool is the wave of the sea,
> Cool is the welling from a spring,
> The Goddess's touch heals thee.

If you were to apply this charm to yourself, you would change the final line to read "The Goddess's touch heals me." Note the structure of the incantation: three lines that begin with "cool is" for the power of three, then a fourth concluding line for realization of the purpose.

To apply this incantation to another person—for example, to a woman who suffers from chronic headaches—you would instruct the person suffering to sit comfortably in an armchair with her eyes closed and to keep them closed no matter what happens. This both builds expectation and allows participation in the healing, because you have given her something to do. You should have a bowl of very cold water ready to use. It is best to have earlier blessed this water in the name of the Goddess, who is the living deity at the root of all the great goddesses of history who are linked to the moon and the sea, such as Astarte, Isis, Aphrodite, and the Virgin Mary.

As you lean close and vibrate the first line of the incantation so that your breath touches the forehead of the reclining woman, dip the fingertips of your right hand into the bowl of icy water and flick them at her face so that the droplets of water from your fingertips fall upon her forehead. Do the same thing for the second line and the third line. After you speak the fourth and final line, dip your right ring finger in the water, and use its tip to draw a circle-cross on the person's forehead—first the vertical line of the cross from top to bottom, then the horizontal line from left to right (from your own perspective), and finally a circle that begins midway down the upper arm of the cross and proceeds around the cross clockwise, cutting through each of the arms to return to its starting point. The ring finger is generally associated with love and with the moon.

Take a clean cloth and wet it in the water, then wring it out. Instruct the woman to keep her eyes closed and lean her head back against the back of the chair. This charm can also be worked on a person who is lying down. Press the folded cloth across her forehead. Hold it there gently for at least a minute, then remove the cloth with a closing word such as "Amen" or "So mote it be" or "Blessed be." The closing words in this instance signify the completion of the charm. Instruct the person to open her eyes and tell her that the Goddess has taken her pain away. If she protests that she is still in pain, tell her that the pain is leaving her head very rapidly and will soon be gone.

Eight
Love Spells

After fear, the two most powerful emotions in the human heart are love and hate. Incantations to procure the love of another person are of ancient use. We find them scattered throughout the literature of lost civilizations, and they are almost certainly older than writing itself. They were composed and spoken by shamans in caves before open fires when the human race was young. The following chant occurs in the *Atharva Veda*, an Indian text that dates from the tenth century BCE:

1. As the creeper embraces the tree on all sides, thus do thou embrace me, so that thou, woman, shalt love me, so that thou shalt not be averse to me!

2. As the eagle when he flies forth presses his wings against the earth, thus do I fasten down thy mind, so that thou, woman, shalt love me, so that thou shalt not be averse to me.

3. As the sun day by day goes about this heaven and earth, thus do I go about thy mind, so that

thou, woman, shalt love me, so that thou shalt not be
averse to me.[157]

Note the use of repetition. The magician makes statements about the natural world that are absolutely true and cannot be denied by anyone and then likens the thing described to the actions of the person he seeks to enchant. Each line finishes with the imperative command "thou shalt not be averse to me." Love magic is usually a form of dominance magic. The desired person is not reasoned with or attracted by flattering words or promises of gift but is commanded to obey the will of the magician.

When you make magic to attract the love of a person who otherwise would not be interested in you, it is a violation of that person's freedom to choose. I would go so far as to say that love magic of this kind may be classified as a type of black magic. Even so, there has never been a time in human history when it was not used. Those who consulted witches or wizards for help very often wanted a love charm. The literature of such charms is extensive.

In the Greek magical papyri there is a love charm that relies on the power of a secret name of Aphrodite, the goddess of love: "Aphrodite's name which becomes known to no one quickly is NEPHERIĒRI—this is the name. If you wish to win a woman who is beautiful, be pure for 3 days, make an offering of frankincense, and call upon this name over it. You approach the woman and say it seven times in your soul as you gaze at her, and in this way it will succeed. But do this for 7 days." [158]

The name Nepherieri is based on the Egyptian name *Nfr-iry t*, which means "the beautiful eye." [159] By "be pure for 3 days," the writer of the charm meant that the magician must refrain from sexual orgasm for three days. The purpose for retaining the seed is to heighten sexual energy in the magician. Frankincense is burned before an image of the goddess Aphrodite on her altar, and the goddess is called aloud to be present within her image by using her secret Egyptian name seven times. Once the goddess is present, which is indicated by slight movements in her statue, such as the blinking of her

157. Maurice Bloomfield, trans., *Hymns of the Atharva-Veda, Together with Extracts from the Ritual Books and the Commentaries* (Oxford: Clarendon Press, 1897), 100–101.

158. Betz, ed., *The Greek Magical Papyri in Translation*, PMG 4, 62.

159. Betz, ed., *The Greek Magical Papyri in Translation*, 62n171.

eyelids or twitching of the corners of her lips, the magician then expresses his purpose and asks the aid of the goddess in its fulfillment. If the goddess agrees to help, she will indicate this by a change in the expression of her image or the twitch of her finger. The image itself does not move, but it will be perceived to move by the person performing the invocation.

The actual working of the spell is accomplished by getting near to the woman, ideally so that there is direct eye contact between the magician and the woman, at least momentarily, and then reciting the secret name of the goddess seven times silently in the mind while looking intently at the woman. Contact of the eyes upon the woman must not be broken as this name is recited, although it is not necessary that the woman be looking back at the magician the whole time. This should be done for seven days. The charm does not specify, but we may assume that seven consecutive days are intended. Why seven? Because seven is the astrological number of the planet Venus, the planet associated with the Greek goddess of love, Aphrodite (the Roman goddess Venus).

Needless to say, if a woman notices that some man is hanging around near her and staring at her with lovelorn puppy-dog eyes for seven days running, she is going to pay attention to him. But whether or not her heart is moved with love for him is up to the goddess of love, Aphrodite. This spell is probably of Egyptian origin, and the original goddess to be invoked was probably Hathor of the Beautiful Eye. Note that in this spell it is the secret name itself that has power, not the occult manner of its voicing. However, vibrating the name silently while imagining that it echoes and resounds throughout the whole universe will heighten its efficacy.

Identifying a Future Lover

There is a huge number of spells in the folk literature of magic with the purpose of identifying a future lover and spouse. In past centuries, the first was naturally assumed to lead to the second. Most of these spells were worked by young women seeking some hint of whom they would marry—his name, appearance, and profession. Some of the chapbooks of the nineteenth century that concern divination and folk magic devote a large portion of their pages to this purpose.

For example, in *Mother Shipton's Gipsy Fortune Teller and Dream Book*, published in 1890, there is a spell titled "Love's Cordial." On the third night of the new moon, a young woman is to mingle a teaspoon each of brandy, rum, gin, wine, and the oil of amber with a tablespoon of cream and three tablespoons of spring water. This is drunk just before going to bed, and the following incantation recited:

> This mixture of love I take for my potion,
> That I of my destiny may have a notion;
> Cupid befriend me, new moon be kind,
> And show unto me that fate that's designed.[160]

When she falls asleep, she will "dream of drink," and the manner of the dream will forecast her fate and the character of her future husband—if she dreams of water, she will have a marriage of privation and poverty, but if she dreams of a drunken man, her husband will become a drunkard. If she dreams of herself drinking too much, it foreshadows her decline into alcoholism.[161]

Another spell to learn the identity of a future husband is referred to as "Charming the Moon." At the first appearance of the new moon after New Year's Day, a young woman seeking to know her future spouse by means of a dream oracle must go out into the night and stand over the pickets of a gate or stile. While staring at the new moon, she is to recite the following incantation:

> All hail to thee, moon! all hail to thee,
> I prithee, good moon, reveal to me
> This night who my husband must be.[162]

This spell has some interesting aspects. It is an almost religious adoration of the moon, and in that sense has a very pagan feel to it. The woman uttering it is essentially worshipping the goddess of the moon, called by the Greeks Selene and by the Romans Luna. The woman is to "stand over the spears of

---

160. Anonymous, *Mother Shipton's Gipsy Fortune Teller and Dream Book, with Napoleon's Oraculum* (New York: Henry J. Wehman, 1890), 55.

161. Anonymous, *Mother Shipton's Gipsy Fortune Teller and Dream Book*, 55.

162. Anonymous, *Mother Shipton's Gipsy Fortune Teller and Dream Book*, 62.

a gate or stile," which I take to mean that she is to straddle the sharp pickets of the gate with one foot on one side and the other foot on the other side.[163] The shape of the pickets, called "spears" in the *Mother Shipton* text, is phallic, and this posture will cause them to point upward toward her womb. The act of straddling the gate is a symbolic deflowering of her virginity in marriage. The gate itself represents a portal, the transition between one state of being and another—specifically, between her maiden condition and her married condition. By straddling the gate, she places herself between her past life as an innocent child and her future married life.

Notice that the incantation has three lines—three is a lunar number, because the moon has three faces—waxing, full, and waning. New Year's Day represents a new beginning since it is the beginning of the new year. The earliest visible crescent of the new moon, seen low in the western sky shortly after sunset, likewise represents the beginning of a cycle.

The anonymous little tract titled *Everybody's Book of Luck* gives the same spell, but with interesting variations. It states that the woman who stands on the stile must do so on the first new moon after Midsummer and that she must turn her back upon the moon, rather than face it. The incantation is more extensive, having five lines rather than three:

> All hail, new moon, all hail to thee.
> I prithee, good moon, reveal to me,
> This night, who shall my true love be.
> Who he is and what he wears,
> And what he does all months and years.[164]

Of the two versions of this spell, I prefer the first. It makes better magical sense to face the new moon while reciting the verse, and symbolically, three lines are more meaningful than five, which is not a number of the moon but of Mars. It might be argued that Mars is the most masculine and virile of the planets and so is appropriate to invoke when seeking the identity of a husband,

---

163. Anonymous, *Mother Shipton's Gipsy Fortune Teller and Dream Book*, 62.

164. Anonymous, *Everybody's Book of Luck* (Racine, WI: Whitman Publishing, [c. 1900]), 111. This paperback book was probably published around 1900, and is a grab bag of topics, among them dream interpretation, astrology, lucky numbers, lucky colors, crystal gazing, and fortune telling with playing cards.

but since the verse is directed at the moon, it is better if its number of lines is a number of the moon.

Four Kinds of Love Incantations

Although all love spells have as their purpose to bring about an amorous union, they differ in their manner of going about it. In his book *Ancient Greek Love Magic*, Christopher Faraone divides Greek love spells into *eros* magic (spells that induce passion) and *philia* magic (spells that induce affection). He suggests that *eros* magic is generally more aggressive or invasive, whereas *philia* magic seeks a state of shared respect and admiration. Within these two groups he defines a number of subgroups.[165] In the present work I will break down love spells into four broad categories based on the intended effect.

The first division is into spells designed to bring about a sexual union and spells intended to cause a romantic union. Carnal love spells are not really concerned with the happiness of the person at whom they are directed, only with bringing together the individuals for sex. Love spells that are worked to cause affection of the heart to kindle in another person are of quite a different type. This division roughly parallels Farone's division into *eros* and *philia*.

We can also divide love incantations into spells designed to attract and spells designed to compel. These functions are usually separate, although sometimes both aspects appear combined in a single incantation. An attraction spell makes the magician, or the person who commissioned the spell from a magician, irresistibly fascinating and attractive to the person targeted. A compulsion spell is of quite a different type, and causes discomfort, unrest, and actual pain until that individual targeted by the spell goes to the person for whom the spell was made in an effort to find relief. The difference can be summed up by saying that a compulsion spell pushes the targeted individual against his will, whereas an attraction spell pulls the target by arousing admiration and interest.

By combining these two general categories, we get four compound types of love spells, which I will describe:

---

165. Christopher A. Faraone, *Ancient Greek Love Magic* (Cambridge, MA: Harvard University Press, 1999), 28.

1. Carnal Attraction

This type of love spell is constructed in such a way that it makes the magician or witch who works it intensely arousing to the person targeted by the spell. The targeted person finds it impossible to stop thinking about the one for whom the spell is cast and will have potent erotic fantasies about that person. These fantasies will involve masturbation. Erotic dreams involving that desired person may also occur. The targeted individual may even see apparitions of the person who attracts them while awake. There will be a persistent dull ache in the sexual parts, which will be in a constant state of arousal—women will be moist, men erect for sustained periods. The intensity of this attraction will continue to increase until the targeted person cannot help but seek ways to cross the path or be in the company of the desired individual.

An example of a spell of carnal attraction is found in a nineteenth-century chapbook titled *Mother Bunch's Closet Newly Broke Open.* A young woman seeking to know who her future husband will be is told to peel a St. Thomas onion, wrap it in a clean handkerchief, and lay it under her pillow. Then she is to lie on her back in bed with her arms spread wide to each side of her body and recite the following spell of attraction:

> Good St. Thomas do me right,
> And bring my love to me this night,
> That I may look him in the face,
> And in my arms may him embrace.[166]

When the woman falls asleep in this unnatural and uncomfortable posture, she will dream of her future husband, who will come to her bed and try to kiss her. She must not hinder him, but rather must try to catch him in her arms and clasp him to her breast. If she succeeds in embracing him, she is told to hold him fast and that he will surely be her future mate. The author writes, "This I have try'd, and it has prov'd true." [167]

---

166. George Laurence Gomme, ed., *Mother Bunch's Closet Newly Broke Open* (London: Villon Society, 1885), 7. The first edition of this work is dated 1685. See the entry "St. Thomas's Eve," Jacqueline Simpson and Steve Roud, eds., *A Dictionary of English Folklore* (Oxford: University Press, 2000), 312.

167. Gomme, *Mother Bunch's,* 7.

There is much unsaid about this spell. The very fact that it involves induc-ing the spirit of a man to visit the bed of a young woman at night suggests its carnal nature. She is advised to catch the spirit in her arms and hold him close so that he cannot get away. The sexual aspect of this embrace is obvi-ous. What will probably come to the woman who works this spell is an incu-bus, a spirit of sexual love who has not been sent by a Christian saint, but the woman using this spell would be blissfully ignorant of the spirit's true ori-gin. It is very possible that she would succeed in attaining climax during this union and that she would feel the spirit lying at full length upon her body and penetrating her sexually. It is, however, very unlikely that the spirit who made love to her would be that of her future husband. There are countless incubi and succubi ever eager to unite with young men and woman and only waiting for an invitation to do so.

St. Thomas the Apostle was known as Doubting Thomas, because when Jesus returned to life after his crucifixion, Thomas did not believe he was real, and put his hand into the wound in Christ's side. St. Thomas onions were a variety of onion imported from France and sold on the streets of London in long strings by street vendors. The connection with the saint appears to be accidental rather than mythical. St. Thomas's Eve was December 20, and in some texts it is stated this spell should be worked on this night. It was the eve of the Day of St. Thomas, December 21, typically the shortest day of the year (the winter solstice falls on December 21–22), and as such marks a transition or portal from one condition to another.

In a Victorian version of the spell, the onion is to be stuck with nine pins, a single pin with eight others surrounding it, then placed under the pillow.[168] Onions are the herb of Mars, the most virile and masculine of the planets. The onion represents the future husband, who is tormented by the pins until he appears. When the pins are used, this spell of attraction becomes a spell of compulsion.

2. Carnal Compulsion

This is a much darker class of spell. The targeted person will feel compelled against their will to fantasize about the one for whom the spell was cast. These

---

168. Donald C. Watts, *Dictionary of Plant Lore* (Amsterdam: Elsevier, 2007), 342.

fantasies will often involve fetishes, dominance and submission, or even sado-masochism. A sensation not only of arousal toward the person for whom the spell was cast but also discomfort at being apart from that person will grow in strength until it becomes agonizing and impossible to resist. Against all judgment and prudence, the tormented target of the spell will be compelled to go to the individual who is the object of their dark obsession and submit to that person sexually in whatever manner the other person desires. There will often be a need for self-degradation or humiliation in this total submission.

The following verses appear in the second idyll of Theocritus, titled "The Incantation." They are chanted by the lovelorn Simaetha to compel the sexual desire of the young man she loves, Delphis:

> Delphis hath wronged me, and I burn this bay
> In Delphis' name; e'en as it wastes away
> Crackling and swift-consumed, no ashes seen,
> So be his flesh to fiery flames a prey!
> *Turn, magic wheel, and lure my lover home.*
>
> Lo, as I melt this wax, and heaven implore,
> So may Love melt the Myndian to the core;
> And as this brazen wheel goes whirling round,
> May he love-maddened eddy round my door!
> *Turn, magic wheel, and lure my lover home.*[169]

The flaming sprig of bay, the melting wax, represent the heat of the erotic passion the charm is intended to produce in Delphis. This is not only the heat of ardor but also a fiery burning that is unendurable and can only be cooled by going to Simaetha and making love to her.

The magic wheel referred to is a device used to actualize the power of the incantation, in a way somewhat similar to a Tibetan prayer wheel, which, when turned, carries the prayer written on it to the heavens. It was called an iynx wheel, or jynx wheel, and named after the wryneck, or jynx (*Jynx torquilla*), a kind of woodpecker native to Greece. In Greek mythology the deity Jynx was transformed into a bird by Hera and bound to a wheel as punishment. Jynx

---

169. Theocritus, *The Idylls of Theocritus*, trans. James Henry Hallard (London: Longmans, Green and Co., 1894), 9. See also the "Eighth Eclogue" of Virgil.

wheels were ritual instruments sacred to the lunar goddess Hecate that were used for divination and the casting of love spells. They were thin, light disks several inches in diameter usually made of metal, ceramic, or wood. Originally, they were decorated with the image of a jynx bird having its wings and tail spread out in four directions, but later examples do not bear a bird design.

The magical use of these wheels was quite simple. They had two holes through their center, very much like a large button. A string was passed through these holes and its ends tied to make a continuous loop. The ends of this loop of string were held in the hands about eighteen inches apart, with the wheel suspended from the center. The wheel was then spun around to rotate it, causing it to wind up the string. When the string was pulled gently apart, it spun the wheel in the opposite direction. The momentum of the wheel caused it to wind the string up the opposite way, and when the string was pulled apart again, it spun the wheel backward. By gently pulling the ends of the loop of string, the wheel could be made to continuously wind and unwind the loop as it rotated first one way, then the other way. As it did so, it made a rhythmic whirring noise, like a miniature bullroarer. The person casting the spell focused his or her intention on the sound while reciting or chanting the incantation.

Another somewhat larger version of this wheel may have been hung at the end of multiple threads attached around its circumference that supported the wheel parallel with the ground. By rotating the wheel to wind the threads, then pulling gently up at the appropriate moments, the threads could be made to wind up in one direction, then unwind and wind up in the opposite direction. In this way the wheel was made to rotate first clockwise, then counterclockwise, rhythmically by turns.

3. Romantic Attraction

Persons subjected to this class of love spell will find their thoughts dominated day and night by the one for whom the spell was cast. This will not be unpleasant for them—on the contrary, they will regard it as the most delightful thing in the world to think of that person, to say their name aloud, to gaze on the person's photograph, to imagine being with the person. The one who casts the charm, or for whom the charm is cast, becomes in the mind of the bewitched lover the most perfect, the most wonderful, the most fascinating human being in the world. They develop a highly inflated opinion of the person's physical appearance and abilities that has no basis in reality. Their devotion is absolute. They would sacrifice anything for that person just to demonstrate their love and admiration.

Here is the incantation of a Cherokee medicine man to attract the love of a woman:

> Now! Listen!
> You and I are truly set apart!
>
> It was Decided that you think of me.
> You think of my entire body.
> You think of me from your very soul.
> You think of me, never to forget that I walk about.
>
> This is my name _____,
> I am a man!
>
> The mourning doves will be calling: *"Gu:le! Hu:! Hu:!*
> *Hu:! Hu:!"*
> You say, you woman, that your name is _____,
> that your people are _____.[170]

The words are to be recited while sending the breath in the direction of the one whose love it is desired to attract. The breath can be sent on tobacco smoke that is exhaled. Or you can breathe through a rising column of incense smoke to achieve a similar effect. The same incantation can be adjusted for gender simply by changing the words "I am a man" and "you woman." In place of the clan name, the last name may be used, since it is the name of the family bloodline.

4. Romantic Compulsion

The effect of this kind of spell is that the person targeted by it cannot stop thinking about the one for whom it has been cast. They feel restless, uneasy, and increasingly uncomfortable to be separated from that individual. Their heart will actually ache, and they will feel that they must go to that person

---

170. Jack Frederick Kilpatrick and Anna Gritts Kilpatrick, *Walk in Your Soul* (Dallas, TX: Southern Methodist University Press, 1965), 44.

no matter what the social or personal cost in their lives. This is done against their better judgment and against their will. They will give up their career, their marriage, and even their children to be with the loved person. They will travel over vast distances if necessary to be with them and will devote great energy conceiving ways to gain the adored person's attention or company. The motivation in this class of spell is not sexual but is an aching need for spiritual union, a deep need to be in the presence of the adored person, a feeling of emptiness and lack of worth when apart from that person. It will defy all common sense and reason.

An example of romantic compulsion is the following dark spell that is presented in a deceptively lighthearted way in a nineteenth-century chap-book on fortune telling as a way for a woman to learn if her sweetheart will marry her. It is actually a spell for compelling a lover to come and declare his love. An unmarried woman is to take the shoulder bone of a lamb to bed with her for nine consecutive nights. Using a borrowed penknife, she must pierce the bone each night while reciting the following verse:

> 'Tis not this bone I mean to stick,
> But my lover's heart I mean to prick,
> Wishing him neither rest or sleep,
> 'Till he comes to me to speak.[171]

It is important that she not tell the person from whom she has borrowed the knife what she intends to do with it. At the end of nine days, it is said, the young man will come to the woman and ask for something to put on a wound he has received at some point during those days. This is obviously a spell to compel the presence of a man so that he will be forced to make a declaration of love to the woman who has worked the magic. He will find no relief until he has come to her.

Feeding the Lover

A common feature of traditional love spells, which is not found in other forms of folk magic, was the practice of secretly giving the target of the spell something to eat or drink that came from the body of the person for whom

---

171. Anonymous, *The Universal Fortune Teller*, 3 (unpaginated).

the charm is worked. When taken from women, it might be saliva, sweat, urine, or menstrual blood. When derived from a man, it might be saliva, sweat, urine, or semen. In both cases, blood drawn from a small cut in the skin might be used.

I advise against the use of bodily fluids in love magic because it is a deception to secretly put such fluids into food or drink fed to another person without that person's knowledge or consent. It is also considered assault in some jurisdictions. Such bodily substances are not needed to work magic. Love spells can be effective without them.

However, for educational purposes, in this method, the person targeted by the love spell is tricked into consuming a tiny amount of one of these substances. This acts as an occult link between the person for whom the spell is cast and the one who is its target. If the targeted individual becomes aware of the deception, the power of the bodily fluid they have consumed is broken. Young women might bake their lovers cakes or pies and put into them a small amount of menstrual blood for their lovers to consume. This was usually accompanied by a spoken or chanted charm that was recited over the food as it was prepared.

The smallest drop of these fluids is sufficient to create a psychic occult link. If the flavor of the food is spoiled by it, the effect will also be spoiled. It must be completely undetected. The lover who works this magic must remain silent about it forever after and must never tell his or her lover what was done. A sweet tart or cake containing sugar or honey was often used, both because the sweetness hid the taste of the bodily fluid and because sweetness on the tongue is associated with the sweetness of love.

Saliva is linked with the intellect, since it comes from the head, which is the region of mind, and from the mouth, the part of the body that expresses articulate speech.[172] Sweat symbolizes physical realization, a material work accomplished. Fluids that come from the sexual parts are naturally more sexual in their nature. The most potent are semen and menstrual fluid. Urine is more appropriate for types of carnal love that are forbidden or not intended to produce children, since urine is a sterile substance and is voided in concealment. A girl would not use urine if she wished to attract a man for marriage,

---

172. Saliva is frequently mentioned in the love magic of the Cherokees. See Kilpatrick and Kilpatrick, *Walk in Your Soul*, 23, 46, 105, 114, and elsewhere.

for example. Blood from a wound has a general potency that, when ingested, enables a link to be created for any type of love spell.

As the food was prepared, a spoken incantation would be recited over it in such a way that the breath of the one saying the incantation touched the food. A spell similar to the one I have just composed below as an example might have been employed by a woman to attract the romantic love of a man:

> This cake I bake for _____,
> And place upon it kisses three;
> When he tastes it with his lips,
> Let him return a kiss to me.

Historically, love potions and love incantations were often used together in traditional love magic. One especially potent substance for inducing love in another person is the fabled *hippomanes* (horse madness), which is said by the Roman historian Pliny the Elder to have been a small fleshy lump found on the forehead of a newly foaled colt. He wrote in his *Natural History* that unless it was immediately eaten by the mother horse, she would not give milk to her offspring: "If anybody takes it before she gets it, and keeps it, the scent drives him into madness of the kind specified." [173] Aelian expanded on this point in his work *On Animals*, writing that if a man is made to taste the hippomanes, he immediately runs mad with lust and seeks to have sex with everyone he meets: "And his body pines and wastes away and his mind is agitated by erotic frenzy." [174]

For this reason the hippomanes was regarded as a powerful love compound. Bits of it were put in secret into the food or drink of the person whose love was desired, in conjunction with the utterance of appropriate incantations containing the name of the person to be loved. The hippomanes by itself was supposed to generate uncontrolled lust in the one who tasted it, but it was the incantations accompanying it that directed that love at a specific individual. A woman who simply hid the aphrodisiac in the food of a man whose sexual

---

173. Pliny the Elder, *Natural History*, vol. 3, trans. H. Rackham (Cambridge, MA: Harvard University Press, 1940), 115.

174. Aelian, *On the Characteristics of Animals*, vol. 3, trans. A. F. Scholfield (Cambridge, MA: Harvard University Press, 1959), 165.

embrace she sought might gain nothing by it, because the man would lust after anyone he chanced to meet in the street.

In the matter of love magic, the secretions of the body of the person seeking love were more effective when hidden in the food or drink of the targeted individual than a general aphrodisiac, which, although it may have appeared to be more powerful, was undirected. The Greeks called such targeting substances *ousia* (magical material). Along with *ousia* composed of hair or bits of clothing from the person, such secretions were used "to target the spell most precisely." [175] Magic is all about focus. Great effects can be achieved with little effort if the focus is explicit and precise. The purpose of incantations is to limit the scope of magic and thereby heighten its efficacy. A dull knife will not cut, but a sharp knife cuts without effort.

---

175. Faraone, *Ancient Greek Love Magic*, 8.

Nine

Spells of Protection

Whereas healing spells are designed to restore people to health after they are injured or fall sick, spells of protection are intended to prevent injuries or sickness from occurring in the first place. Incantations to turn aside evil are as ancient as those designed to cause evil to others, and they are even more numerous since it is human nature to suppose malice where none really exists. In past ages and in our present time in many parts of the world, it is believed that sorcerers are constantly at work, making magic to sicken, injure, or kill others. It was this belief that fueled the witch craze in Europe during the sixteenth and seventeenth centuries. But where magic is made that is intended to do harm, magic can also be made to counter that harm and protect those against whom it may be directed.

Everyone is familiar with the prayer that is taught to young Christian children to say at the side of their beds before going to sleep each night. It was taught to me at an early age in these words:

> Now I lay me down to sleep,
> I pray the Lord my soul to keep;
> If I should die before I wake,
> I pray the Lord my soul to take.

This prayer is older and more venerable than most people realize. It occurs in the *Carmina Gadelica*, a collection of Gaelic folk hymns and incantations gathered during the latter half of the nineteenth century in the Highlands and northern islands of Scotland. The first verse of the hymn titled "An Urnuigh Chadail" ("The Sleep Prayer") reads in English translation:

> I am now going into the sleep,
> Be it that I in health shall waken,
> If death be to me in the death-sleep,
> Be it that on Thine own arm,
> O God of Grace, I in peace shall waken,
> > Be it on Thine own beloved arm,
> > O God of Grace, that I in peace shall waken.[176]

The version of this verse from my childhood is very much a prayer. Indeed, the words "I pray" occur in it twice. However, the Gaelic version, which calls upon the power of God to shield the person who utters it from harm during sleep, is an incantation rather than a prayer. It is purely magical in nature. The general distinction between incantations and prayers is that incantations command and prayers request. The person speaking the verse is not asking for protection from God; he is demanding it. If he had used language such as "if it be thy will, O Lord" or "thy will and not mine be done," it would be a prayer, but there is no such proviso in the verse.

This being understood, there is often considerable overlap between prayers and incantations. Prayers are frequently used in magic, and incantations often occur embedded in prayers. Sometimes an incantation is worded in such a way as to suggest that a favor is being asked of a spirit, but then the spirit is threatened with punishment if it fails to fulfill the favor—which makes it not really a request at all, but a demand.

Types of Protective Spells

Spells of protection fall into two general classes: those that *request* protection by prayers and offerings and those that *compel* protection through acts of ritual magic. The first kind humbly ask the aid of gods, angels, or other

---

176. Alexander Carmichael, ed., *Carmina Gadelica*, vol. 1 (Edinburgh, Scotland, 1900), 85.

higher spirits. Often these prayers are accompanied by offerings, sacrifices, and promises to fulfill certain actions if the prayer is answered. The second kind use the natural properties of objects, materials, and symbols to provide protection, or command the help of spiritual beings, often with threats of punishment if that help is not provided.

Protection spells can also be divided into *passive* and *active*. Passive spells work in the background, without needing to be voiced at the time their protection is required. They are set up to prevent harm to a person, place, or thing, and they continue to function in this way by themselves even if the person who created them is absent and unaware of the danger. They may be written down on a scroll that is carried on the body, inscribed on the wall of a building, or spoken over an object to empower it. Active spells, on the other hand, are voiced at the time of their use, to protect against an immediate perceived threat such as a malign spiritual presence.

This results in four classes of protection spell:

Request, Passive: Prayers are recited, usually on a continuing regular basis, asking a higher spiritual being for general protection for oneself, another person, an enterprise, a dwelling, and so on.

Request, Active: A prayer is spoken at a moment of danger to safeguard oneself or another. For example, the spontaneous prayers uttered by soldiers when they come under fire on the battlefield.

Demand, Passive: A ritual incantation is performed to create a spell of protection that is usually bound up with an object or a place so that a person carrying that object or entering that place at any time in the future is safeguarded. It can be used to make a protective amulet or to safeguard a house, for example. In this type of spell, the protection is not requested from a higher being; it is expected as a natural consequence of the act of magic.

Demand, Active: Words of power and incantations are voiced to ward off or shield against an immediate perceived threat or the possibility of imminent danger. An example would be words spoken to turn aside the harmful effect of the evil eye.

Each of these four classes has a number of subclassifications based on the manner of their intended working—avertive, reflexive, binding, warding, and guarding.

Avertive: Turns the malice or harm away from the person, place, or thing protected by the spell by deflecting it like a kind of magic shield.

Reflexive: The malicious intention of a person who intends harm is reflected back upon that individual the way light is reflected from a mirror.

Binding: With a binding spell, malicious magic can be symbolically bound or contained by means of such things as knots, windings, or suspension so that it is incapable of doing any mischief.

Warding: A magical ward is a kind of barrier made on a threshold that prevents the passage of malicious magic or beings with harmful intentions.

Guarding: This type of spell relies on a guardian spirit that uses its own judgment in protecting a thing, place, or person from harm. This guardian may be attached to some convenient object such as a ring or a pendant.

The Evil Eye

The most common way harm is believed to be sent to others through occult means is the evil eye. Belief in the evil eye seems to be universal across all cultures and time periods. It is the conviction that certain individuals, often through no fault of their own, possess or acquire the power to project injury from their eyes merely by looking at a person or thing. The evil effect was thought to be heightened if the eye that cast it was bloodshot and if the glance came askance, from the corner of the eye, rather than directly. The danger was greatest still when the evil glance was met by the glance of another person, although it was thought possible for those with the evil eye to cause damage to crops or cattle merely by "over-looking" them.

The most harmless and inoffensive human beings acquired the reputation of casting the evil eye and were on this account shunned by their neighbors or even driven away from their homes. They regarded the power of the evil eye as a curse upon themselves. In a Polish folktale, a man cursed with the evil eye blinds himself by cutting out his own eyes rather than cause harm to his newborn son by looking upon him. Before doing so, he utters these dread words to his loving wife, who is about to give birth: "Upon our child these eyes shall never look. Him they shall never harm, and he shall not have reason to curse his father." [177] The man's servant buried his master's eyes in the garden. Six years later the servant grew curious wondering what had happened to them, so he dug them up. When he looked at the eyes, they seemed to glare at up him. He gave a cry and fell down dead.

A Scottish clergyman of the seventeenth century wrote about a man who once lived within his own parish, who merely by looking at animals could cause their deaths: "Tho also some are of so venemous a Constitution, by being radicated in Envy and Malice, that they pierce and kill (like a Cockatrice) whatever Creature they first set their Eye on in the Morning; so was it with Walter Grahame, some Time living in the Paroch wherein now I am, who killed his own Cow after commending its Fatness, and shot a Hair with his Eyes, having praised its swiftness, (such was the Infection of ane evill Eye;)." [178]

A cockatrice is a mythical creature with the body of a snake and the head of a cock that was fabled to possess the power to kill with a glance. By "hair" Kirk meant a hare, a beast resembling a large rabbit.

Skeptics would discount the ability of any person to cause harm merely with a glance, but the prevalence of this belief across all cultures and all history gives pause for thought. No one can deny that there is a sensation of a connection or union when eye contact is made with another person. There is power in the simultaneous awareness of two people when they gaze upon each other. A psychic link of some kind is formed that can be felt, sometimes in a physical way. The folklore of "love at first sight" is based on this power.

Francis Bacon ascribed the baneful effects of the evil eye to envy. In his ninth essay he wrote,

---

177. Charles John Tibbets, ed., *Folk-Lore and Legends: Russian and Polish* (London: W. W. Gibbings, 1890), 133. This story was initially recorded by the folklorist Kazimierz W. Wójcicki (1807–1879).

178. Robert Kirk, *The Secret Commonwealth of Elves, Fauns & Fairies* (London: David Nutt, 1893), 54–55.

There be none of the affections which have been noted to fascinate or to bewitch, but love and envy; they both have vehement wishes, they frame themselves readily into imaginations and suggestions, and they come easily into the eye, especially upon the presence of the objects which are the points that conduce to fascination, if any such there be. We see likewise the Scripture calleth envy an evil eye; and the astrologers call the evil influences of the stars evil aspects, so that still there seemeth to be acknowledged, in the act of envy, an ejaculation or irradiation of the eye; nay, some have been so curious as to note, that the times when the stroke or percussion of an envious eye doth most hurt, are when the party envied is beheld in glory or triumph, for that sets an edge upon envy; and besides, at such times, the spirits of the person envied do come forth most into the outward parts, and so meet the blow.[179]

That envy rather than malice was the underlying cause of the harm done by the evil eye was a common belief around the world. An article in the August 1857 issue of the *North British Review* quotes a native of Cairo, Egypt, concerning the evil eye: "An intention to harm may render more virulent the poison of the glance; but envy, or the desire to appropriate a thing, or even excessive admiration, may render it hurtful without the consciousness, or even against the will, of the offender."[180] Those with the evil eye may even unintentionally inflict it upon themselves. Plutarch relates the story of Eutelidas, a beautiful youth who paused to admire his face and hair reflected in the water of a stream and inflicted on himself a "dread fascination" that caused him to waste away with disease.[181]

---

179. Francis Bacon, *Bacon's Essays with Annotations* (Boston: Lee and Shepard, 1875), 90.

180. Anonymous, "*Bacon's Essays, with Annotations*. By Richard Whately, D.D., Archbishop of Dublin. London, 1856," *North British Review*, August 1857, article 1, page 10.

181. Plutarch, *Symposiacs*, in vol. 3, *Plutarch's Morals* (Boston: Little, Brown, and Company, 1878), 331.

Those seeking to avoid the ill-effects of the evil eye avert their gaze from those who are reputed to possess it, since its power is strongest when there is eye contact. They may also spit on the ground or into their shirts on their own chest. It was a proverbial saying in Somorset, England, "nif you do meet wi' anybody wi' a north eye, spat dree times."[182] Here we see the occult power of spittle, a product of the mouth and, by association, the mind. Hand gestures were believed to be able to turn aside the force of the evil eye. One such gesture is the hand held in a fist with the thumb inserted between the first and second fingers. Another avertive gesture is the horns, made by projecting the index and small finger while holding the other fingers closed.

A defensive tactic is to put something bright or shiny near the person or thing that may become the object of envy, and in this way distract the harmful gaze away from it. This is why some cultures, such as that of the Romani, decked their horses in colorful ribbons and bright brass or silver bangles. Of course these adornments have a decorative function as well, but their primary practical purpose was to distract the evil eye.

It was the custom of the ancient Romans to sing lewd songs at weddings, in the belief that they would avert from the happy couple the baneful effects of the envious evil eye. The protection of the gods Nemesis, Cunina, and Priapus was invoked in the lyrics of these songs, which were a kind of incantation.[183] Nemesis is the goddess of divine retribution for evil deeds. Cunina is the Roman goddess who protects babes in their cradle (*cunae*) from evil enchantment. Priapus is a god of masculine fertility who is usually depicted with a very large, erect penis. These deities addressed the natural concerns of the newly married couple that they should not suffer from the malicious envy of others, that their union should never be plagued by infertility or impotence, and that their children should not die in their cradles, which was as inexplicable an event in ancient Rome as it is today. The Italian writer Niccola Valletta (1750–1814) mentions the invocation of the goddess Nemesis in a list of remedies he gives against the evil eye.[184]

---

182. Frederick Thomas Elworthy, *The Evil Eye* (London: John Murray, 1895), 417. Three was considered a holy number.

183. Elworthy, *The Evil Eye*, 16n35.

184. Niccola Valletta, *Cicalata sul fascino volgarmente detto jettatura* (1777; Naples: Dalla Stamperia Della Societa' Tipografica, 1814), 91. See Elworthy, *The Evil Eye*, 21.

I will compose an original invocation to the goddess Nemesis as an example of the kind of wording you might use if you wished to employ this ancient Roman remedy against being ill-looked.

> Fell goddess of awe and dread,
> Nemesis, dark as midnight,
> Your black wings shade my head,
> Your sharp glance shields my sight;
> Judge to both the quick and dead,
> No wrong escapes your light;
> The deed is done, the words are said,
> To render justice is your right.

If you believe that someone has cast the evil eye upon you, visualize that person in your mind with your eyes closed and recite this incantation while making the sign of the horns with both hands with your forearms crossed over your heart. If the person in your mind is guilty, Nemesis will surely punish them and right the wrong they did to you by removing the curse of their evil glance. But if they are innocent, nothing will happen to them since this goddess is always just.

Mezuzah

It is the custom of Jews to fix an oblong or cylindrical box to the right side of the doorframe of their houses or apartments. These boxes are of many designs, but inside them is a handwritten parchment scroll containing the words in Hebrew of Deuteronomy 6:4–9 and 11:13–21. The words must be written with a special pen that is made from either a bird's feather or a reed and in waterproof black ink that will not fade, and the writer of the words must be a qualified scribe who has trained in the writing of these scrolls and in the detection of imperfections in them that would invalidate them and cause them to have no magical effect.

The purpose of the *mezuzah*, as it is called, is to turn aside evil from the household and from those who dwell within it, as is indicated by the wording of Deuteronomy 11:20–1: "And thou shalt write them upon the door posts of thine house, and upon thy gates; That your days may be multiplied, and the days of your children, in the land which the LORD sware unto your fathers to give them, as the days of heaven upon the earth." [185]

This is a purely magical function. The occult power inherent in the words of the Torah calls down divine protection from enemies and misfortunes. The mezuzah is fixed in its box to the doorframe at shoulder level. The Jew who places it there presses it to the doorframe and recites the words "Blessed are you, Lord our God, King of the Universe, who sanctified us with his *mitzvot* [biblical commandment] and commanded us to affix a mezuzah." The box is then nailed into place, care being taken not to pierce or tear the scroll inside it, because if the sacred scroll is damaged in any way, its avertive power is lost. The integrity of the scroll is verified periodically by a scribe, and if it has become damaged, it is replaced with a new scroll.

It is the scroll itself that is the mezuzah, not the box, which can be of many designs and various colors and can be crafted by anyone. On the empty back of the scroll the scribe writes the ancient name of God, *Shaddai* (Almighty). Some scroll boxes are transparent so that this Hebrew word can be seen through their fronts, but when the box does not have a window, oftentimes the name Shaddai is painted or carved into the front, or only the first letter of the name, Shin, is used to represent the name as a whole. This name is three letters in Hebrew (Sh-D-I) and the Hebrew letter Shin (Sh) has three branches. By this name or letter, the power of three is invoked.

When a Jew passes into the house through the door, it is the general custom to touch the box with the fingers and to kiss the fingertips. This is a way of transferring the verses written on the scroll to the lips, thereby symbolically reciting them, although they are not actually spoken aloud. The great Torah scholar Maimonides (1138–1204) cautioned against writing any names of angels, other sacred names or verses, or other symbols on the scroll, particularly on the front of it where the sacred text was inscribed, because that would transform "the unity of the name of the Holy One" and turn the scroll into a mere talisman for personal benefit. In the second book of his *Mishneh Torah*, titled *Sefer Ahavah* (*The Book of Love*) he wrote:

> There is no harm in writing שרי on the outside; but those who write on the inside the names of angels, or

---

185. Deuteronomy 11:20–21 (KJV).

holy names, or verses, or other formula, are of those who will have no share in the future world. For these fools not only defeat in this manner the fulfilment of a great commandment which has for its end the remembrance of the unity of God, and the love of Him and worship of Him, but turn it into an amulet for their selfish interest, believing in their foolish hearts that it can be made to serve the preservation of transitory worldly goods.[186]

No doubt Maimonides was completely sincere when he wrote this, but what is the mezuzah if it is not a magic talisman for the benefit of the person or persons residing in the house where it is placed? Jews do not place it on their doorframes for the benefit of others but for their own benefit. It is a completely magical practice, and it is both a prayer and an invocation since the words of the scroll are symbolically recited each time the case is touched and the fingers that touched it are kissed. The *Jewish Encyclopedia*, from which the quote above was taken, acknowledged, "In Talmudic times a protective power, especially in warding off evil spirits, was attributed to the mezuzah."[187]

An even more overtly magical amulet of protection against the evil eye, and against the Evil that Flies by Night (the demoness, Lilith), is the scroll that pregnant Jewish mothers had written on the walls of their bedchambers, or hung over the cribs of their newborn infants to protect them against crib death and other misfortunes. This bore the names in Hebrew characters of three angels, Senoi, Sansenoi, and Samangeloph, who were known to be the protectors of the health of pregnant women and babies. E. A. Wallis Budge wrote about these charms: "And if they were to be really effective, the texts had to be written in ink in which holy incense had been mixed, and even the

186. Isidore Singer, ed., *Jewish Encyclopedia*, vol. 8 (London: Funk and Wagnalls Company, 1904), 532. Refer to Maimonides, Mishneh Torah, Sefer Ahavah, *Tefillin, Mezuzah and Sefer Torah*, ch. 5, sec. 4.

187. Singer, ed., *Jewish Encyclopedia*, vol. 8, 532.

copyist had to be a man ceremonially pure and a believer." [188] These requirements are very similar to those for making the mezuzah.

These angels had the power to drive off Lilith when she came in the guise of the screech owl to suck the breath from an infant. The charms took the form of a tightly rolled scroll and often contained crude symbolic drawings of these angels, the very thing that Maimonides cautioned against placing on the mezuzah scroll. Images were considered a debasement of Jewish magic by the rabbis, since all the power was believed to stem from the words of the Torah, the sacred words of God, written or spoken in Hebrew, the sacred tongue of the angels. Almost all Jewish magic is word magic.

It may be that an incantation containing the names of the three angels was uttered by the pregnant woman or the mother of the newborn baby who possessed this charm. There is no record of such incantations, but the general practice was common. Jewish amulets and talismans that were accompanied by a spoken incantation were known as *lehasham*. Budge wrote, "The singular of this word *lahash* was applied to any object or ornament which was associated with the whispering of incantations, spells, charms, prayers, etc., and which was used as an amulet. The plural is found in Isa. iii. 20 f, when the jewellery and ornaments and attire of the daughters of Jerusalem is criticized and condemned. Among the objects enumerated are ear-rings, arm-chains, stepping-chains, girdles, finger-rings, bracelets, armlets, scent tubes, mirrors, etc." [189]

During morning prayers, Jewish men wear on their arms or head *tefillin* (phylacteries) in the form of small black cubes made of leather that contain scrolls of parchment inscribed in a ritual manner with texts in Hebrew from the Torah. The cube is the symbol of matter and thus of materialization or realization in this world. Note the similarity in shape and color between these tefillin and the Kaaba at Mecca, a roughly cubic structure that is shrouded in black and is the ultimate earthly focus of Muslim prayers.

---

188. E. A. Wallis Budge, *Amulets and Superstition* (London: Humphrey Milford, 1930), 224.

189. Budge, *Amulets and Superstitions*, 215.

Hoodoo Charms

The practice of using verses from the Bible as magic charms and incantations is by no means confined to the Jews. It is also used in the American branch of folk magic known as hoodoo, practiced predominantly by Black Americans. It found its way into hoodoo via such influential magical texts as the 1849 German edition of the *Sixth and Seventh Books of Moses*, edited by Johann Scheible, which was translated into English in 1880, and the *Long Lost Friend*, a book by the Pennsylvanian Dutch cunning man and healer John George Hohman, first published in the German language in 1820 and in English translation in 1846 and 1850.

The *Sixth and Seventh Books of Moses* is an anonymous grimoire that gained popularity in the middle of the nineteenth century. It is filled with seals and symbols containing Hebrew words and names of God that are to be used in conjunction with incantations to produce various magical effects. The Hebrew letters are hopelessly corrupted, making it impossible in most cases to determine what the original Hebrew words on the charms may have been. Concerning this book, the modern hoodoo practitioner Miss Michaele, coauthor of *Hoodoo Bible Magic*, wrote, "As soon as the text was translated into English, it was picked up by African-American root doctors in the South as well as Afro-West-Indian obeah practitioners."[190] Those using the charms in hoodoo have no idea what the Hebrew writing may mean, but they have implicit faith in the power of biblical words, names, and text, in the same way the magicians of the ancient world had faith in the barbarous words.

The authors of this hoodoo text advise that when a verse of the Bible is written down, it becomes a potent magical charm.[191] Below the verse the practitioner writes his or her name and, if necessary, a brief command or instruction for how the magic of the verse is to be applied. This can be retained as a talisman or burned in the flame of a candle to create empowered ashes, which may then be used in various ways. For example, the ashes can be mixed in with food and consumed by a sick person if the purpose is to heal.

---

190. Miss Michaele and Professor Charles Porterfield, *Hoodoo Bible Magic* (Forestville, CA: Missionary Independent Spiritual Church, 2014), 10.

191. Michaele and Porterfield, *Hoodoo Bible Magic*, 22.

Since the time of the psalms' composer, the Hebrew King David, Jews have used them as potent magical incantations of protection. Christians have used them in the same way for the past two thousand years. The manner of their use appears in the 1880 edition of the *Sixth and Seventh Book of Moses*, in the section entitled "Sepher Schimmusch Tehillim; or, Use of the Psalms, For the Physical Welfare of Man," which was translated by Godfrey Selig from a Hebrew Kabbalistic text in 1788.[192] This section was extracted and more recently published as a separate book under Selig's name with the title *Secrets of the Psalms*.[193]

Selig wrote that for magical purposes, the psalms may be recited while burning incense and anointing oneself with holy oil. He quoted the Kabbalist "Isaac Loriga" (Isaac Luria), who asserted that the psalms may be recited in any language provided the holy names of God and of the angels are written down or held in the mind in the Hebrew language. These sacred names are never to be spoken aloud lest they be profaned and their occult power lost.[194] After quoting this admonition from Luria, Selig stated that he is giving all the Hebrew sacred names in English transliteration—however, they do not appear in Hebrew letters in the English text of either the *Sixth and Seventh Book of Moses* or in *Secrets of the Psalms*, thus posing a vexing task for non-Jewish readers, who must research their Hebrew original forms if they wish to follow Luria's advice.

A large portion of the psalms have protective or preventive efficacy, according to Selig's source. For example, psalm 11 is used to overcome fear and persecution; psalm 13 to protect against physical suffering and death; psalm 14 to liberate oneself from slanderous accusations; psalm 15 to protect against insanity; and so on.[195] Various holy names are given with each psalm. The reciting of the psalm, or key verses from it, empowers these holy Hebrew names, or rather, awakens their latent occult power. Some of the psalms are accompanied by specific prayers directed at the purpose for which the psalm is recited.

---

192. Johann Scheible, ed., *The Sixth and Seventh Books of Moses*, pt. 2 (New York, 1880), 77–109.

193. Godfrey Selig, *Secrets of the Psalms* (Arlington, TX: Dorene Publishing Co., 1982).

194. Selig, *Secrets of the Psalms*, 9.

195. Selig, *Secrets of the Psalms*, 14–15.

For psalm 2, which protects against dangers at sea, the practitioner is directed to recite the psalm, hold the holy name Shaddai (Almighty) in the mind, then recite a prayer asking that the storm may cease. The psalm, name, and prayer are to be written down on a potshard (which suggests the age of this bit of magic), and the potshard is thrown into the sea to still the storm. But this same psalm may also be used to banish a headache, by writing down the first eight verses, along with the holy name and a prayer, on virgin (new and unused) parchment, which is then rolled up and hung around the neck of the sufferer while the psalm and prayer are recited.[196]

These tiny scrolls inscribed with sacred verses were often inserted into small silver cylinders, which were capped and worn around the neck on chains as pendants. They can also be folded until they are small enough to fit into lockets. Clean, new paper may be substituted for parchment—the paper should not be made from recycled materials. If you make one of these charms for yourself, I suggest that you light incense of your choice and allow the rising smoke to play over the pen you will use for writing down the sacred text. Hold the blank paper over the smoke as well. As you do so, recite the incantation I have composed here as an example, in such a way that your breath touches the object and moves the rising incense smoke:

> By fire and fume devoted be
> Unto the task I set for thee.

Copy the chosen text, whether verses from the psalms or other verses from the Old or New Testament, in your own language. In my opinion, it is not necessary to use Hebrew letters for the charm to be effective, although you may use them if you wish. After you copy the verse onto the piece of paper, read it aloud to yourself, concentrating strongly on the words as you say them. Kiss the paper, then roll it into a scroll or fold it as many times as necessary to fit into your locket or into your wallet. If you fold it twice, making one fold cross the other, the result will be four layers. Four is an auspicious number since it signifies realization or fulfillment on the material plane.

---

196. Scheible, ed., *Sixth and Seventh Books of Moses*, vol. 2, 82.

Under no circumstances should you cut the verses you intend to use in your charm out of a Bible. To do so would show disrespect for the sacred text and would destroy any hope that your magic will be successful.

Obeah

Obeah, also known as obi (see the quote below), is the magic that was brought to Jamaica by enslaved Africans. It is not a full religion, as is Voudoun, which was also carried to the New World by enslaved peoples, but a kind of spell work or conjuring. The term "obeah" is conjectured to descend from the Egyptian word for serpent: "The term '*Obeah*' is most probably derived from the substantive '*Obi*,' a word used on the East coast of Africa to denote witchcraft, sorcery and fetishism in general. The etymology of Obi has been traced to a very antique source, stretching far back into Egyptian mythology. A serpent in the Egyptian language was called '*Ob*' or '*Aub*'—'*Obion*' is still the Egyptian name for a serpent." [197]

Herbert T. Thomas, a police inspector in Jamaica during the late nineteenth century who interacted with obeah on a daily basis in his police work, wrote that the term had been traced "to the same root as the Greek word signifying 'a serpent.'" He added, "A snake of some sort has always been, and is even now, held to be indispensable to the equipment of a practitioner of any pretensions to distinction, and a stick surrounded by a carved serpent embracing it in its folds is a frequent emblem of the calling." [198] The prominence of the serpent in obeah is not surprising when we consider that the greatest and oldest of the gods worshipped in the kindred black African magic of the West Indies, Voudoun, is Damballa, a giant serpent.

The worldview of the practitioner of obeah was somewhat similar to that of the magicians of ancient Sumer, in that everything was believed to be inhabited by spirits. Some were malicious and sought to do harm to human beings. Others could be harnessed for that purpose by evil magicians. These spirits caused not only misfortunes but also disease and madness. One of the primary functions of the obeah practitioner was to make charms that would turn aside these hurtful spirits. These charms were crafted for specific purposes.

197. Hesketh J. Bell, *Obeah*, 2nd ed. (London: Sampson Low, Marston & Company, 1893), 6.

198. Herbert T. Thomas, *Something About Obeah* (Kingston, Jamaica: Mortimer C. DeSouza, 1891), 2.

Within each charm was placed a spirit that empowered the charm. As long as the charm held the spirit, it was active, but when the spirit departed from it, the charm was called "dead." These charms are termed fetishes. Obeah is a magic of fetishism.

Thomas wrote that the homes of practitioners of obeah in Jamaica were raided by the police if the police had reason to believe that they had used fraud or tried to poison someone. The police would find odd collections of small objects having no intrinsic value, such as bits of horn, pebbles, pieces of charcoal, and scraps of clothing.[199] These seemingly worthless objects and substances are puzzling, until one realizes that in obeah, it is not the material of the charm or fetish itself that is important but the spirit that has been made to reside within it. These substances were to be used to compose various charms, into which spirits would be induced by various means.

In his 1904 book, *Fetichism In West Africa*, Robert Hamill Nassau wrote concerning the spirits of the fetish practitioners of the Western African peoples, "Beyond the regularly recognized habitats of the spirits that may be called 'natural' to them, any other location may be *acquired* by them temporarily, for longer or shorter periods, under the power of the incantations of the native doctor (uganga). By his magic arts any spirit may be localized in any object whatever, however small or insignificant; and, while thus limited, is under the control of the doctor and subservient to the wishes of the possessor or wearer of the material object in which it is thus confined."[200]

He added elsewhere in his work, "The thing itself, the material itself, is not worshipped. The fetich worshipper makes a clear distinction between the reverence with which he regards a certain material object and the worship he renders to the spirit for the time being inhabiting it. For this reason nothing is too mean or too small or too ridiculous to be considered fit for a spirit's *locum tenens*; for when for any reason the spirit is supposed to have gone out of that thing and definitely abandoned it, the thing itself is no longer reverenced, and is thrown away as useless."[201] What was done in West Africa by the *uganga* is pertinent when examining the practices of the obeah man of

---

199. Thomas, *Something About Obeah*, 10.

200. Robert Hamill Nassau, *Fetichism in West Africa* (New York: Charles Scribner's Sons, 1904), 62.

201. Nassau, *Fetichism in West Africa*, 75–76.

Jamaica, because a large portion of the enslaved people brought to the West Indies came from West Africa. It is here that obeah had its roots.

Of those means of empowering these charms, incantation played a key role, but the obeah practitioners of Jamaica were extremely careful that their incantations should not be overheard. Joseph J. Williams wrote, "A veil of mystery is studiously thrown over their incantations, to which the midnight hours are allotted, and every precaution is taken to conceal them from the knowledge and discovery of the white people." [202] Even when the incantations could be overheard, they could not be understood. The obeah practitioner used words of power that were incomprehensible to all who might hear them. This caused Williams to incorrectly conclude, "The incantations with which he accompanies his operations are merely a mumble of improvised jargon." [203]

It seems to me there is no reason to assume that the mumbled words of power used by Jamaican obeah practitioners were any less meaningful than the words of power uttered by the sorcerers of ancient Greece and Egypt. They were incomprehensible, but that is not the same thing as meaningless. Some of the words were probably secret names of gods, used to compel the obedience of spirits. Unfortunately, these incantations do not appear to have come down to us, or at least I have not run across them in the literature. Concerning the similar incantations used by the West African uganga, Nassau wrote, "The vocal [charms] are the utterance of cabalistic words deprecatory of evil or supplicatory of favor, which are supposed in a vague way to have power over the local spirits. These words or phrases, though sometimes coined by a person for himself or herself (and therefore like our slang having a known meaning), are often archaisms, handed down from ancestors and believed to possess efficiency, but whose meaning is forgotten. In this list would be included long incantations by the magic doctors and the Ibâtâ-blown blessing." [204]

The Ibâtâ-blessing to which Nassau referred in the quotation above is a specific kind of blessing that Nassau himself witnessed in 1875 while traveling aboard a river steamer on the Ogooué River in Western Africa. An Ogooué

202. Joseph J. Williams, *Voodoos and Obeahs* (New York: Dial Press, 1932), 111.

203. Williams, *Voodoos and Obeahs*, 120.

204. Nassau, *Fetichism in West Africa*, 78.

chief took a glass of liquor with the captain of the boat, then, "having taken a mouthful, wet his finger in his mouth, drew the wet finger across his throat, and then blew on a fetich which he wore as a ring on a finger of the other hand. I do not know the significance of his motion across his throat. The blowing was the Ibâtâ-blessing,—an ejaculatory prayer for a blessing on his plans, probably of trade."[205] Notice here the use of spittle and breath in this work of magic. The chief did not wet his finger in the glass, he wet it in his mouth. He blew across his ring to energize the spirit dwelling within it. The motion of crossing the throat, another part of the body associated with the breath, may have been to symbolically open it.

The primary purpose of the fetishes made by the obeah practitioner of Jamaica and the uganga of West Africa is protection. Nassau wrote, "Africans believe largely in preventive measures, and their fetich charms are chiefly of that order."[206] They are designed to turn away harm before it occurs. Concerning their making, he wrote:

> In preparing a fetich the oganga selects substances such as he deems appropriate to the end in view,—the ashes of certain medicinal plants, pieces of calcined bones, gums, spices, resins, and even filth, portions of organs of the bodies of animals, and especially of human beings....These are compounded in secret, with the accompaniment of drums, dancing, invocations, looking into mirrors or limpid water to see faces (human or spiritual, as may be desired), and are stuffed into the hollow of the shell or bone, or smeared over the stick or stone.[207]

Some of these practices can be explained by the general principles of magic. The drums and dancing are intended to achieve an exalted state of consciousness. The invocations are commands to the spirits. The uganga stares into a mirror or the reflective surface of water in order to see the spirit

---

205. Nassau, *Fetichism in West Africa*, 80.

206. Nassau, *Fetichism in West Africa*, 83.

207. Nassau, *Fetichism in West Africa*, 82.

he wishes to induce into the charm he is making. The mirror has the same function as the crystal ball in European crystal gazing or the drop of black ink on the palm that is gazed into by Egyptian seers.

Over time the spirit inhabiting the fetish object may leave it, and then the uganga will declare that it is "dead" and thus worthless. It will be thrown away or sometimes sold to tourists as an authentic native fetish. Some of the substances that went into the composition of these charms were necromantic in nature and differ little from the materials used by Greek witches in the dawn of the Christian era. Pieces of human bone, the brain, the heart, and the gall bladder were dug from graves in the dead of night. Nassau wrote that human eyeballs, particularly those of a white person, were especially prized by the uganga as objects of power and were rifled from newly made graves.[208]

---

208. Nassau, *Fetichism in West Africa*, 82.

Ten
Maledictions

In past centuries, and even in the present in many regions of the world, magic has been used to cause misfortune. Such uses involved inducing sickness, blindness, paralysis, loss of the voice, apparent loss of the penis for men, miscarriages in women, madness, accidents of various kinds, disputes, the blighting of crops or their destruction by fire or hail, the souring of milk, the sickening or killing of livestock or pets, raising storms at sea to wreck ships, or even death. Any misfortune that befell a human being was likely to be ascribed to malicious magic.

This kind of magic is commonly termed black magic, and most of it involves the use of incantations and enchantments, which is why we are examining it in this book. It's important to understand the distinction that black magic is not a type of magic that is evil—it is the use of magic for evil purposes.

The German philosopher and theologian Albertus Magnus (c. 1200–1280), who after his death acquired the reputation as a great magician, had this to say on the subject of whether magic can be evil in itself:

> Aristotle, the Prince of Philosophers, saith in many places, that every Science is of the kind of good things: But notwithstanding, the Operation

sometime is good and sometimes evil; as the Science is changed unto a good, or to an evil end, to the which it worketh. Of the which saying, two things are concluded: The first is, that the Science of Magick is not evil, for by the knowledge of it, evil may be eschewed, and good by means thereof, may be followed.

The second thing is also concluded, in so much as the effect is praised and is highly esteemed for the end, and also the end of Science is dispraised, when it is not ordained to good, or to vertue. It followeth then, that every Science or Faculty or Operation is sometimes good, and sometimes evil.[209]

Symbolically, the color black has always been the color of evil because it is associated with night, shadows, deception, what is hidden, the dark phase of the moon, what lies beyond the light. The color white is the color of good because it is linked with clarity, what is revealed, openness, daylight, the sun, purity, cleanness. White magic is associated with brightness, black magic with darkness. It should be unnecessary to add that the color black also has other symbolic associations that are not connected with evil or darkness, but in the historical use of the term "black magic," it is the association of the color black with the night, the dark, shadows, the concealed, and hidden dangers that is intended.

Prior to the twentieth century, most of the working of black magic around the world was assigned to witches. It is part and parcel of the traditional definition of a witch that appears in dictionaries. A witch is defined not just as a worker of magic but as a worker of evil magic—and sometimes just as a worker of evil. Dr. Samuel Johnson, in his 1755 *Dictionary of the English Language*, defined a witch broadly as "a woman given to unlawful arts."[210] He made no mention of magic, because for him the key understanding of a witch was unlawfulness.

---

209. Albertus Magnus, *The Secrets of Albertus Magnus* (London: Printed for M. H. and J. M, [1691]), leaf A-3 recto-verso.

210. Samuel Johnson, *A Dictionary of the English Language*, vol. 2 (London: W. Strahan, 1755), unpaginated, under "witch."

The traditional concept of witchcraft as invariably malicious arouses the ire of modern witches, and justifiably so, because they do not consider what they do evil. Modern witchcraft has redefined the word "witch" to mean a worshipper of the Goddess, and perhaps the Horned God as well, who uses natural magic primarily to help and heal others. The modern witch is very near in nature to the traditional cunning men and wise women of past centuries in Europe and America, who were often disparagingly called witches by neighbors fearful and suspicious of their abilities. These were rural healers who used natural remedies and natural magic for the benefit of those in their communities. Modern dictionaries may reflect this change in attitude. However, the older traditional definitions are invariably negative.

This understanding of a witch as someone who works malicious magic against others was worldwide. The anthropologist Evans-Pritchard wrote concerning the nature of witchcraft among the Azande, a people of Central Africa: "The Zande phrase 'It is witchcraft' may often be translated simply as 'It is bad.' For, as we have seen, witchcraft does not act haphazardly or without intent but is a planned assault by one man on another whom he hates. A witch acts with malice aforethought. Azande say that hatred, jealousy, envy, backbiting, slander, and so forth go ahead and witchcraft follows after. A man must first hate his enemy and will then bewitch him." [211] The Azande concept of witch was very similar in this regard to that of sixteenth century European witch-burners.

Evans-Pritchard wrote that the Azande made a distinction between a witch, in whom the power of black magic was innate, and a sorcerer, who had deliberately studied black magic so as to work evil. A witch might sometimes be forgiven by the people, because in a sense the evil was beyond a witch's control, but a sorcerer was never forgiven, because his evil magic was always deliberate and intentional: "Azande have always told me that in the past those who killed men with witchcraft were generally allowed to pay compensation, but that those who killed men by sorcery were invariably put to death, and probably their kinsmen also." [212]

---

211. E. E. Evans-Pritchard, *Witchcraft, Oracles and Magic among the Azande* (Oxford: Clarendon Press, 1937), 107.

212. Evans-Pritchard, *Witchcraft, Oracles and Magic among the Azande*, 392.

The Azande fought the evil power of witches, which was thought to be innate in them and hereditary, with ritual magic. They cursed the witch they wished to punish for their crimes by unleashing vengeance magic upon them. The same curse was used against criminals to punish them. Witchcraft was understood to be a criminal act. These are the words of one such curse:

> May misfortune come upon you, thunder roar, seize
> you, and kill you. May a snake bite you so that you die.
> May death come upon you from ulcers. May you die
> if you drink water. May every kind of sickness trouble
> you. May the magic hand you over to the Europeans so
> that they will imprison you and you will perish in their
> prison. May you not survive this year. May every kind
> of trouble fall upon you. If you eat cooked foods may
> you die. When you stand in the center of the net, hunt-
> ing animals, may your friend spear you in mistake.[213]

The worker of this magic, having spoken this curse, then took off his clothing and puts on a skirt of leaves. He covered his face and shoulders with ashes. Then he uttered an incantation over his magic whistle and blew a long, shrill blast. This sound was thought to unleash the spirits of vengeance against the evildoer. In effect, the sound of the whistle, produced by the living breath of the shaman, carried the curse to those spirits who would execute it and achieve justice. The power of the whistle came from the breath, which was expressed as sound.

The name of a person was also used for malediction among the Azande. Evans-Pritchard quoted the text of a native spell that illustrates this point: "A sorcerer gathers up the medicine he has ground into flour and pours it on the path and he addresses it to the name of that man whom he wishes to kill, and when he has finished addressing it he departs and returns to his homestead. However many other people walk over this medicine it will not seize them. But only that man to whose name the sorcerer addressed the medicine,

---

213. Evans-Pritchard, *Witchcraft, Oracles and Magic among the Azande,* 389–90. Evans-Pritchard is here translating directly from C. R. Lagae and V. H. Van den Plas, *La Langue des Azande,* vol 1., Grammaire, Exercices, Légendes (1921), 75.

only he, as he steps over the medicine, will it adhere to him so that when he returnes to his home it prostrates him and his gullet closes." [214]

When the Bible was translated into English, the words "witch" and "witchcraft" were used to replace Hebrew words for enchanter, sorcerer, diviner, necromancer—all activities prohibited by religious law and punishable by death. The "witch of Endor" was a necromancer. One of the Hebrew words replaced by "witch" in early English Bibles is *mekashshepah* (M-K-Sh-P-H), from the Hebrew root *kashaph* (mutterings). *Mekashshepah* means an enchanter, "one who practices magic by using occult formulas, incantations, and mystic mutterings." [215] It indicates the importance of the voice in the working of prohibited magic. It is the voice that is used to curse.

The powers ascribed to European witches from the time of the ancient Greeks until the middle of the seventeenth century are vast and miraculous. Among them is the power to use incantations to cause disasters, blights, and storms through magic. The Roman writer Lucan asserted, "The world, on hearing an incantation, would instantly be arrested in its course." [216] Christianus Pazig wrote concerning the fell power of Greek witches: "Here it is to be observed that, in the opinion of simple-minded persons, the moon could by incantations be actually drawn down from heaven, and when drawn down could be compelled to discharge upon herbs the froth of her influences, by reason whereof authors allege that the women of Thessaly acquired a great proficiency in this art." [217]

This practice, which in ancient times was done during lunar eclipses, so that the moon seemed to disappear for a time from the night sky, has come to be known by modern witches as "drawing down the moon." The liquid that appeared to issue from the moon when it was drawn down in this way by the incantations of witches was called the sweat of the moon. It was believed to be generated from the moon due to her suffering caused by the incantations, which were regarded as a form of torture. The lunar sweat was thought to be poisonous and to render the herbs on which it fell deadly poison. It may be

---

214. Evans-Pritchard, *Witchcraft, Oracles and Magic among the Azande*, 393. Translated directly from C. R. Lagae and V. H. Van den Plas, *La Langue des Azande*, vol 1., 114.

215. Merrill F. Unger, *Biblical Demonology* (Grand Rapids, MI: Kregel Publications, 1994), 153.

216. Lucan, *Pharsalia*, bk. 6, line 463. Quoted by Pazig, *A Treatyse of Magic Incantations*, 15.

217. Pazig, *A Treatyse of Magic Incantations*, 31.

conjectured that it was actually nighttime dew that collected in droplets on plants in a natural way during the open-air ritual.

The popular understanding of this rite and the actual purpose of the witches who conducted it were probably quite different. When the moon began to darken during an eclipse, the alarmed common people of Thessaly made as much noise as possible with brass trumpets, cymbals, and bells so as to drown out the sound of the witches' chanting and, in this way, preserve the brightness of the lunar orb. The idea was that if the moon could not hear the incantation, the words would have no power over her.

By their words, it was said, witches could draw the strength from fire so that it would go out, or they could make water flow backward in a stream so that it re-entered the spring from whence it had issued from the ground. Such incantations could make the ground tremble and volcanoes erupt or could carry standing crops ripe for harvest from one man's field and deposit them into the field of another man. The Roman poet Virgil makes mention of this last wonder in his "Eighth Eclogue."[218] There was a prohibition in the Twelve Tables of bronze that bore the laws of ancient Rome: "Entice not away the crop from another man's field."[219]

The Roman poet Ovid, writing in his *Amores* that he is upset with himself because he is unable to keep an erection when he wants to make love, wonders if he has been bewitched and mentions a number of common beliefs concerning the powers of witchcraft.

> Is Verse, or Herbs the Source of present Harms?
> Am I a Captive to *Thessalian* Charms?
> Has some Enchantress this Confusion brought,
> And in soft Wax my tortur'd Image wrought?
> Deep in the Liver is the Needle fix'd?
> Plagues she by Numbers, or by Juices mix'd?
> By Numbers, sudden the ripest Harvests die,
> And fruitful Urns no more their Streams supply:
> Oaks shed, unshook, their Acorns at the Call,
> And the Vine wonders why her clusters fall.

---

218. Virgil, Eclogue 8, verse 99.
219. Pazig, *A Treatyse of Magic Incantations*, 34.

Why may not Magick act on me the same,
Unstring the Nerves, and quite untune the Frame? [220]

It was commonly believed that witches used magic to render men impotent or to steal away entirely the penis and testicles, leaving only a bare, smooth patch of skin in their place. This is mentioned in the infamous *Malleus Maleficarum* (*Hammer of Witches*), first published in 1486, although the Inquisitors who were its authors, Heinrich Kramer and Jacob Sprenger, concluded that it was no more than a glamour of the senses.[221] Witches were also credited with the ability to make women barren. In the quote above, Ovid refers to the use of a wax image to project malice, which we will examine at greater length later in this chapter. By the term "numbers" is probably intended metrical verses that are rhythmically chanted or sung. Ovid claims that through their use, crops could be killed, springs dried up, and acorns made to fall from oaks and grapes from vines before they were ripe. The witches of Thessaly were particularly noted throughout the ancient world for these types of incantations.

Bone Pointing

One of the most ancient forms of malediction that is still practiced in Australia, South America, Africa, New Zealand, New Guinea, Haiti, and various Pacific islands is known by the somewhat absurd term "voodoo death," a name given to it by the psychologist and medical doctor Walter B. Cannon in his essay "Voodoo Death," which appeared in the April–June 1942 issue of *American Anthropologist*.[222] Cannon gathered examples from around the world of practitioners apparently causing the death of individuals solely by magical means.

Another more dignified name for this phenomenon is "psychogenic death" (death caused by the mind). That these deaths occur is not seriously doubted, but it is the opinion of scientists and medical doctors that they are

220. Ovid, *Ovid's Epistles: with His Amours* (London: T. Davies, W. Strahan, W. Clarke et al., 1776), bk. 3, elegy 7, 323.

221. Heinrich Kramer, *Malleus Maleficarum*, trans. Montague Summers (Suffolk, UK: John Rodker, 1928), 58.

222. Walter B. Cannon, "Voodoo Death," *American Anthropologist, New Series* 44, no. 2 (April–June 1942): 169–81.

caused not by the magic of the shamans, but by the belief of the victims. Writing about this kind of homicidal black magic as it was used in ancient Mesopotamia, the Assyriologist Tzvi Abusch observed, "It is the act of seeing the omen or object that causes the victim to fall ill and threatens to lead him to an untimely death. I suspect that fear is responsible for the effectiveness of this magic and its ability to bring on death."[223]

Retired British Major Arthur Glyn Leonard wrote in his 1906 book *The Lower Niger and Its Tribes*:

> Indeed I have seen more than one hardened old Haussa soldier dying steadily and by inches, because he believed himself to be bewitched; so that no nourishment or medicines that were given to him had the slightest effect either to check the mischief or to improve his condition in any way, and nothing was able to divert him from a fate which he considered inevitable.
>
> In the same way, and under very similar conditions, I have seen Kru-men and others die, in spite of every effort that was made to save them, simply because they had made up their minds, not (as we thought at the time) to die, but that being in the clutch of malignant demons they were bound to die.[224]

Another term for this kind of black magic is "bone-pointing syndrome," after the practice of Australian Aborigine magicians of "pointing the death-bone" at those they wish to kill. W. E. Roth, who served as government surgeon to the aborigines of North-West-Central Queensland, Australia, wrote concerning this practice: "So rooted sometimes is this belief on the part of the patient, that some enemy has 'pointed' the bone at him, that he will actually lie down to die, and succeed in the attempt, even at the expense of refus-

---

223. Tzvi Abusch, *Further Studies on Mesopotamian Witchcraft Beliefs and Literature* (Leiden: Brill, 2000), 200.

224. Arthur Glyn Leonard, *The Lower Niger and Its Tribes* (London: Macmillan and Co., 1906), 257–58.

ing food and succour within his reach: I have myself witnessed three or four such cases." [225]

The bone in question is a sharply tapered wand some three to five inches in length, usually fashioned from a human forearm bone, that is pointed at the victim by the shaman. It is part of a magical apparatus called the *munguni*, which consists of the pointing bone itself; a cylinder made from a piece of human arm or shin bone three to five inches long that has been hollowed out and sealed at one end with a kind of glue; and a woven thread or twine made from human hair, which varies in length from three or four feet up to fifteen feet or so. This twine connects the blunt end of the pointing bone with the bottom of the interior of the cylinder, where it is glued into place.[226] When these materials were not obtainable from a human body, the person making the apparatus would use substitutes.

The twine acts as a magical conduit between the sharpened bone and the hollow cylinder. The function of the munguni consists in using the pointing bone to draw through the air the esoteric lifeblood of the victim at whom the sharp end of the bone is pointed. This vital essence enters the bone, flows along the twine, and is collected in the cylinder, which is then sealed at its top to retain it with the pointer inside, its sharp end downward, along with the twine. The shaman uses physical blood to represent this occult lifeblood, which he puts into the cylinder before sealing it.

At the same time the practitioner is stealing the life essence from the victim, he projects an object into the body of the victim through the pointing bone so that it enters the victim's flesh and lodges there—or so the victim believes when he thinks he has been bewitched in this manner. This object is usually a small stone or piece of rock crystal. It steals away the health of the victim, who only regains his health when a shaman or other skilled person removes the object from his body by magical means. When he is shown the object by the person who treats him, he is relieved and begins to recover.

The death bone is used in various ways. The hollow cylinder into which the life essence is to flow must be supported in a stable upright position.

---

225. Walter Edmund Roth, *Ethnological Studies Among the North-West-Central Queensland Aborigines* (Brisbane: Edmund Gregory, 1897), 154.

226. See Roth, *Ethnological Studies Among the North-West-Central Queensland Aborigines*, the description on page 152 and plate 23, illustrations 392–95.

Sometimes it is bound to the trunk of a tree, or the shaman may hold it between his knees as he squats. The pointed bone is often supported in the Y of a stick, which may be held in the hand or fixed upright into the ground. The connecting string of woven human hair is never permitted to touch the ground, or the power of the apparatus is lost. One way of working the bone is to lay it in the cleft of the stick and then shove it forward in the direction of the victim with the palm of the hand, so that it falls through the cleft and dangles down on the other side of the stick. It is never allowed to touch the ground but is caught by the string as it is falling by the shaman's assistant and pulled back. This action is repeated as more and more of the life essence is drained from the victim, and as the deadly object is projected into his body.

While this is being done, the practitioner chants or sings barbarous words of power. Roth, who observed various forms of this procedure firsthand, did not provide the words, which probably varied according to the locality and the purpose of the magic. Of the method used in the Cloncurry District, he wrote, "The receptacle is clutched between the two knees, the string held in the hand, while the pointer, directed in the proper quarter, is made to rest upon a branch or stick.…In low tones, so as not to notify his presence, he sings a dirge (the meaning of which he does not know) while pointing." [227] It is this song, coupled with the malicious intention of the singer, that powers the death bone.

Papal Curses

The most common form of malediction is the spoken or written curse. The words of the curse define the evil that is to befall the person against whom it is directed. This information is usually conveyed to the victim, either directly face to face, or indirectly through third parties. As is true of the various forms of psychogenic death magic, the belief and expectation of the victim play a significant part in the working of curses, although it would be rash to presume that they are the whole of it. The assumption by anthropologists that voodoo deaths can be explained by natural psychological and physical processes alone seems to me arrogant in the extreme, since the mechanism of such deaths is still not understood.

---

227. Roth, *Ethnological Studies Among the North-West-Central Queensland Aborigines*, 156.

It is not widely known that it was, and perhaps still is, the practice of the Vatican to issue papal curses against the enemies of the Roman Catholic Church. These were formal curses framed in the most horrifying language, intended to strike fear into the hearts of those against whom they were directed. The Council of Lateran in 1215 declared excommunication and anathema against all heretics and all heresies. However, where heresy was suspected, not proven, it was considered sufficient only to pronounce anathema against the accused. Anathema is a formal curse delivered by a pope or a council of the Roman Church. When King Henry VIII of England separated from Rome in 1534, he and all the English people were cursed by Pope Paul III, and his daughter Elizabeth, after she became queen, was cursed along with her people by Pope Pius V.

A universal curse against all heretics was repeated once a year, on Holy Tuesday, by the pope. This was described by William Hurd in his work *A New Universal History of Religious Rites*:

> The next ceremony is that of excommunicating and giving over to the devil, all the Protestants in the world, who at Rome, and among Roman Catholics, are known by the name of Heretics. The Pope is then clothed in red, and stands on a high throne, the better to be seen by the people. The sub-deacons, who stand at the left hand of his holiness, read the bull, and in the mean time, the candles are lighted, and each of them takes one in his hand. When the excommunication is pronounced, the Pope and cardinals put out their candles and throw them among the crowd, after which the black cloth that covered the pulpit is taken away.[228]

The wording of these various papal curses is so extreme that it is difficult to reconcile it with Christianity, to say nothing of the act itself, which is magical rather than religious, and black magic at that. William Cooke wrote in a nineteenth-century penny pamphlet on this matter, "The curses of Rome are

---

228. William Hurd, *A New Universal History of the Religious Rites* (Manchester: J. Gleave, 1811), 248.

so numerous, that time and space would fail to enumerate them; and some parts of them are so disgustingly indecent, that modesty forbids us to place them before the general reader." [229] He went on to present the "form of anathema used on ordinary occasions":

> In the name of the Father, and of the Son, and of the Holy Ghost, and of our blessed and most Holy Mary; also by the power of the angels, archangels, &c. We separate M. and N. from the bosom of the holy Mother Church, and condemn them with the anathema of a perpetual malediction. And may they be cursed in the city, cursed in the field, cursed be their barn and cursed be their store, cursed be the fruit of their womb and the fruit of their land, cursed be their coming in and their going out. Let them be cursed in the house and fugitives in the field; and let all the curses come upon them which the Lord by Moses threatened to bring on the people who forsook the Divine law; and let them be Anathema Maranatha, that is, let them perish at the second coming of the Lord. Let no Christian say *Ave* to them. Let no priest presume to celebrate mass with them, or give them the holy communion. Let them be buried with the burial of an ass, and be dung upon the face of the earth. And as these lights are this day cast out of our hands and extinguished, so let their light be put out for ever, unless they repent, and by amendment and condign penance, make satisfaction to the church which they have injured. [230]

We see from the text, comparing it with Hurd's description of the Holy Tuesday curse against heretics, that the extinguishing and casting of candles held by the priests into the gathered worshippers must have been a common

---

229. William Cooke, *The Pope's Curse Turned into a Blessing* (London: H. Webber, [1868]), 1.

230. Cooke, *The Pope's Curse Turned into a Blessing*, 1–2. Cooke translated the text out of the original Latin, which appears in the article on "Excommunication" in the *Edinburgh Encyclopaedia*, vol. 9 (Edinburgh, Scotland: William Blackwood, 1830), 249–52.

feature of the papal curse. Note that these papal curses are designed to be spoken aloud, and in the living voice and breath of the pope lies the root of their occult power.

The sheer venomousness of these curses is scarcely to be believed. I will quote a small portion of the curse recorded by Ernulfus, Bishop of Rochester (1040–1124), which was reproduced in a late-seventeenth-century pamphlet titled the *Popes Dreadfull Curse*: "May him or them be Cursed in Living, in Dying, in Eating, in Drinking, in being Hungry, in being Thirsty, in Fasting, in Sleeping, in Slumbring, in Waking, in Walking, in Standing, in Sitting, in Lying, in Working, in Resting, in Pissing, in Shitting, in Blood-letting. May he or they be Cursed in all the Faculties of their Body." [231]

In these papal curses, the pope assumed the authority to command God the Father, Christ, Mary, the angels, and the saints to do his bidding. This is purely magical. Indeed, it is black magic and demonic. Cooke wrote:

> The Roman Pontiffs and priesthood, among other pre-rogatives, claim that of cursing mankind; and there are no anathemas so awful as theirs, none so consistently, systematically, and fiercely pronounced. Mahomet was a malignant curser, as well as a ferocious persecutor, but in both Mahomet falls far short of the Roman Pontiffs. Pagan priests and potentates have thundered their anathemas against Christians, and ofttimes bathed their sword in blood; but Rome surpasses even them in the maledictions she utters, and the sanguinary cruelties she has inflicted. She has, indeed, no rival in these infernal arts. [232]

In the following extract from the papal curses collected by Bernard L. Quinn in his 1881 pamphlet *Papal Curses*, we can see this supreme arrogance of the pope, in presuming to instruct the Holy Trinity: "May the Father who created him curse him; may the Son who suffered for us curse him; may the Holy Ghost who suffered for us in Baptism curse him. May the Holy Cross

---

231. Ernulfus, *The Popes Dreadfull Curse* (London: L. C. on Ludgate-Hill, 1681), 2.

232. Cooke, *The Pope's Curse Turned into a Blessing*, 1.

which Christ for our salvation, triumphing over his enemies, ascended, curse him." [233]

No evil, cackling witch, no degenerate Satan worshipper, no necromancer who steals the bones of corpses from open graves, could pronounce more blood-curdling maledictions against other human beings than those that were routinely pronounced over a span of centuries by Christ's Vicars on Earth, the Holy Roman Pontiffs.

Family Curses

Many of the ancient noble bloodlines of Europe are noted for their weird— that is to say, for their involvement with the supernatural. Over the centuries, stories grew up and were passed down from generation to generation. Some of these noble families had a guardian spirit who watched over their houses or who came in the night and wailed in mourning when one of their members was about to die. Other families were burdened with a curse on their bloodline that persisted down through the centuries.

One of these latter was the Scottish family Erskine of Mar. In the latter half of the sixteenth century, John, Lord Erskine, the twentieth Earl of Mar, made the mistake of seizing the Abbey of Cambuskenneth. He expelled the abbot and the monks and had the abbey demolished so that he could use the stones to build himself a palace in Stirling. For this effrontery, the abbot cursed him in Gaelic verse, very much as an ancient Druid might have done. The curse is noteworthy for both its length and its complexity. It was as much a prophecy as a curse, since it foretold the misfortunes that would befall the Erskines. [234]

This curse is said to have begun to act almost immediately. The palace the Earl of Mar was constructing from the stones taken from the abbey was never completed and remained for centuries no more than a facade. One by one, the details of the curse realized themselves. In 1715 the then–Earl of Mar was defeated in battle by the English at Sheriff Muir and had his lands and title taken from him, thus fulfilling the prophecy that when the family's wealth and power were greatest, they should be brought low. The grandson

---

233. Bernard L. Quinn, *Papal Curses* (Cleveland, OH: Leader Printing Company, 1881), 3.

234. Elliott O'Donnell, *Famous Curses* (London: Skeffington & Son, 1929), 16–17.

of this unfortunate earl, John Francis Erskine, lived in a tower that remained in the possession of the Erskine family until a tragic fire there took the life of his wife. The daughter of John Francis, who escaped the fire, later gave birth to three children who were born blind. The tower was subsequently abandoned and allowed to go to ruin, all of which was foretold in the curse. It was not until 1822 that the Earldom of Mar was restored to a descendant of the family by King George IV.

Another cursing of a noble English family occurred during the English Civil War to the Payne family on the Isle of Wight. The Paynes were staunchly loyal to the monarchy and on two occasions concealed King Charles II in their stronghold, keeping him safe from the forces of Oliver Cromwell. In gratitude for their service, the king's son, James, who then bore the title Duke of York but would later become James II, told Stephen Payne that he would be happy to stand as godfather to Stephen's first child, if it was a boy. Stephen eagerly agreed to this honor and looked forward to it with great anticipation, but when the midwife who attended on Stephen's wife during her labor informed him that she had given birth to a girl, his was unable to contain his disappointment and fury. He grabbed the midwife by the shoulders, shook her, and threw her across the room. He began to blaspheme and shouted, "I wish you, and my wife, and the brat, and everyone in the house to hell."[235]

That night, the midwife saw the apparition of a tall man in full shining armor. The spirit declared himself the ghost of the late Duke of Normandy and told the midwife that he had been sent by God to curse Stephen Payne and his descendants for the sin of his blasphemy. She was told to inform Stephen that his despised baby daughter would die soon and that for many generations no descendant of his would ever be "blessed with a daughter's love."[236] The next day the midwife went to Stephen and related this curse, as she had been ordered to do by the ghost. Within a few weeks, the baby girl died. Stephen would later have a son but he never sired another daughter, and for at least six generations thereafter, neither did any of his bloodline, thus fulfilling the curse of God, uttered by the lips of the midwife, upon his family.

---

235. O'Donnell, *Famous Curses*, 53.
236. O'Donnell, *Famous Curses*, 54–55.

Another family curse spoken by a woman involved the venerable farm-house of Calgarth, near Ambleside in the English Lake District. The owners of the house, Kraster Cook and his wife Dorothy, were asked by their wealthy and influential neighbor, the local magistrate Myles Phillipson, to sell a portion of their land. Kraster Cook flatly refused and continued to refuse on many successive occasions when Phillipson brought up the subject. This caused great enmity between the couples, as Phillipson's demands for the land became more and more blunt. At length Phillipson sent word to the Cooks that he had given up his desire to buy the parcel of land and wanted to make amends for his previous behavior by inviting them to a banquet. The Cooks accepted the offer. At the banquet they were shown a silver cup, which Kraster Cook was heard by all the guests to greatly admire.

The following morning, Kraster and his wife were arrested and charged with the theft of the silver cup. They were completely innocent. Phillipson had contrived the theft as a way to get the Cooks out of the way so that he could obtain the land he coveted. It made no difference how strenuously they protested their innocence: Phillipson was magistrate of the district and condemned them to death. Before they were taken from the courthouse, Dorothy Cook spoke her curse.

> "Guard thyself, Myles Phillipson. Thou thinkest thou hast contrived cleverly; but that very piece of land of ours thou covetest will prove the dearest a Phillipson has ever bought. Failure will attend thee in whatever thou undertakest; and a day will come when no Phillipson will own a tittle of land in all this county.
>
> More than that, Myles Phillipson, and mark this well—we'll haunt ye, ye and all your breed, so long as two walls of our old farm house—the house I know ye want to live in—are left standing. Never will ye be rid of us." [237]

The Cooks were executed a few weeks later. Myles Phillipson seized their house and land, on the pretext that they had owed him money. He moved his

---

237. O'Donnell, *Famous Curses*, 77–78.

family into their ancient farmhouse. Some months after they were settled, they began to hear screams coming from the upper part of the house during the night. Phillipson was too frightened to investigate, but the next morning his wife thought she heard one of her children weeping in the nursery and went upstairs to look. A noise attracted her attention to the attic, and when she started up the stair to learn its source, she saw two skulls side by side, still covered with their hair, grinning down at her from the landing. As she watched, the skulls opened their mouths and began to scream, causing her to faint.

When the rest of the household investigated the sounds, they found the woman unconscious and two skulls staring down at her with eyeless sockets through the rungs of the railing on the upper landing. They were not ghosts but physical skulls. Phillipson had the bodies of the Cooks dug up and discovered that they were headless. He reburied the skulls with their bodies, but again they appeared within the farmhouse and began to scream. This happened repeatedly. Phillipson had the skulls cast into a lake and then smashed with hammers, but they continued to reappear intact. The people of the district began to shun the Phillipsons once the story of the skulls became known. They were so badly treated by their neighbors that Phillipson lost his wealth and was forced to move his family elsewhere. The skulls continued to reappear in the farmhouse, so that no subsequent owner ever found peace there, until at last the house was left to fall to ruin.[238]

The three family curses I have described have an element of just retribution about them. Each family cursed in some measure deserved the punishment, which was aided by the righteous judgment of God. The curses were not motivated solely by malice. Of course all three of them are matters of folklore. How much of the tales that surround them are based on factual events is impossible to judge. But it was not uncommonly believed that a curse could fall not just upon an individual, but upon his entire family line. Such curses are almost biblical in nature.

---

238. O'Donnell, *Famous Curses*, 79–80.

Biblical Curses

The Bible is filled with maledictions of various kinds. The greatest of them is the curse that God laid upon Adam and Eve for defying his instructions not to eat the fruit from the Tree of Knowledge in the midst of the Garden of Eden. We all know what happened in this ancient story, which derives from Mesopotamia. Eve was tempted by the serpent, who promised her that if she ate the fruit, she would not die but would be like a god, knowing good and evil. Eve succumbed to temptation and then tempted Adam to do the same.

For its transgression, the serpent was cursed by God. Its curse was bound up with the fate of the woman it had tempted: "And the LORD God said unto the serpent, Because thou hast done this, thou art cursed above all cattle, and above every beast of the field; upon thy belly shalt thou go, and dust shalt thou eat all the days of thy life: And I will put enmity between thee and the woman, and between thy seed and her seed; it shall bruise thy head, and thou shalt bruise his heel." [239]

For Eve, God reserved a special curse, the pains of giving birth to children: "Unto the woman he said, I will greatly multiply thy sorrow and thy conception; in sorrow thou shalt bring forth children; and thy desire shall be to thy husband, and he shall rule over thee." [240]

Adam was cursed separately, and through him God laid the same curse upon the entire human race:

> And unto Adam he said, Because thou hast hearkened unto the voice of thy wife, and hast eaten of the tree, of which I commanded thee, saying, Thou shalt not eat of it: cursed is the ground for thy sake; in sorrow shalt thou eat of it all the days of thy life;
>
> Thorns also and thistles shall it bring forth to thee; and thou shalt eat the herb of the field;
>
> In the sweat of thy face shalt thou eat bread, till thou return unto the ground; for out of it wast thou taken: for dust thou art, and unto dust shalt thou return. [241]

---

239. Genesis 3:14–15 (KJV).
240. Genesis 3:16 (KJV).
241. Genesis 3:17–19 (KJV).

One of the most famous curses in the Old Testament is that visited upon Job by God at the hands of the Adversary, Satan. This is not motivated by malice on God's part, or even by a desire for justice, but merely to settle a wager proposed by the devil that he could tempt God's most faithful worshipper, Job, into cursing God. In order to test this proposition, God permitted the devil to afflict Job. First, Satan asked permission to curse Job's household, which God granted him. God said, "Behold, all that he hath is in thy power; only upon himself put not forth thy hand." [242] Satan proceeded to kill Job's livestock and his children. When Job remained steadfast in his faith, Satan asked God for permission to afflict Job's body. This, too, God granted. "Behold, he is in thine hand; but save his life." [243] Satan cursed Job with boils over his entire body. Job was in such great suffering that he cursed the day he was born:

> Let the day perish wherein I was born, and the night in which it was said, There is a man child conceived.
>
> Let that day be darkness; let not God regard it from above, neither let the light shine upon it.
>
> Let darkness and the shadow of death stain it; let a cloud dwell upon it; let the blackness of the day terrify it.
>
> As for that night, let darkness seize upon it; let it not be joined unto the days of the year, let it not come into the number of the months.
>
> Lo, let that night be solitary, let no joyful voice come therein.
>
> Let them curse it that curse the day, who are ready to raise up their mourning.
>
> Let the stars of the twilight thereof be dark; let it look for light, but have none; neither let it see the dawning of the day:
>
> Because it shut not up the doors of my mother's womb, nor hid sorrow from mine eyes. [244]

---

242. Job 1:12 (KJV).
243. Job 2:6 (KJV).
244. Job 3:3–10 (KJV).

Listening to this curse, Satan must have believed that Job was ready to break. But Job did not curse God. He remained steadfast in his faith, and in the end God restored many times over what had been taken from Job.

Lead Curse Tablets

As sites of ancient habitation are excavated for various reasons, periodically there are unearthed caches of small tablets, usually made of thinly cast or beaten lead that has been folded up, upon which are written curses against named individuals. Sometimes the curses are written on fragments of pottery. Occasionally, the lead is shaped into a humanoid figure. Over a thousand of these inscribed curse tablets have been collected by archaeologists from different parts of the world.

One of the most famous of these caches was discovered in 1979 in the English city of Bath beneath the floor of a Roman bathhouse that had been removed to repair water pipes. Under a thick layer of Victorian concrete that had formed the floor of the King's Bath, excavators unearthed the ribbing of the Roman structure that had collapsed inward and, under it, the Sacred Spring of the local Celtic goddess Sulis, from which the warm bath waters issued. The Romans ruling Britain in the early centuries of the Christian era called this spring *Aquae Sulis* and worshipped this goddess as Sulis Minerva. In her spring were found approximately 130 small folded tablets of a lead-tin alloy, most of which were inscribed with Latin in the reverse of the usual order of letters. That is to say, the texts were written right to left. Some were blank. Some had been pierced with nails.

One of the first tablets found inscribed in reversed Latin script bore this curse: "May the person who has stolen 'Vilbia' from me become as liquid as water." [245] This was followed by a list of ten names, probably the names of potential thieves. The word "Vilbia" is unknown but may perhaps be a corruption for a word signifying some portable valuable such as a broach. Many of the Bath curse tablets are against thieves. Those taking the waters in the Roman bathhouse must often have been prey to thievery by other bathers and by slaves serving the bathhouse. The curse seems to have been written in retaliation, rather than in an attempt to recover the stolen item.

---

245. Roger S. O. Tomlin, "Voices from the Sacred Spring," in *Bath History*, ed. Trevor Fawcett, vol. 4 (Bath, UK: Millstream Books, 1992), 9.

The phrase "become as liquid as water" is an interesting curse and one that is appropriate for the goddess Sulis, deity of the hot spring. It seems to suggest that the thief should be deprived of strength and made too weak to stand up. Another possibility is that it signified a fit of vomiting or diarrhea. Or, less probably, the author of the curse may have intended the thief to begin to babble and reveal his crime.

Other caches of these lead curse tablets have been discovered throughout the ancient world, wherever the Greeks and Romans traveled. Examples have been dated as early as the fifth century BCE, but the practice continued well into the Christian era. The curses inscribed on these lead tablets usually take the form of binding spells (Greek: *defixiones*) which are worded in such a way as to inhibit the action of the person cursed. The purpose is to make the person impotent, in the general sense of the term (although sometimes also in its specific sexual sense)—to deprive the person of power or effectiveness. They are not so much designed to cause suffering as they are to prevent something from happening. Early examples from the classical period are found buried with a corpse or placed in crypts. In later centuries it became the practice to throw such curse tablets into the depths of wells or fountains, where the water issued from beneath the earth, as was done at Bath. The association was the same—the curses were sent to the underworld, the realm of the dead.

One early example from the fourth century BCE, which was discovered at Carystus, on the island of Euboea, and is kept in the Bibliothèque Nationale in Paris, is shaped in a roughly humanoid outline. The two lines of Greek text inscribed on it read,

> I register Isias, the daughter of A(u)toclea, before Hermes the Restrainer. Restrain her by your side!

> I bind Isias before Hermes the Restrainer, the hands, the feet of Isias, the entire body.[246]

---

246. Christopher A. Faraone, "The Agonistic Context of Early Greek Binding Spells," in *Magika Hiera: Ancient Greek Magic and Religion*, ed. Christopher A. Faraone and Dirk Obbink (Oxford: Oxford University Press, 1991), 3.

Hermes was the Greek psychopomp, the god who escorted the newly dead into the underworld. He was thus responsible for restraining the dead and keeping them from wandering. He enforced their entry into the realm of Hades, and it is this quality of compulsion, of enforcement, that was desired by the persons who composed these types of binding incantations. One who is bound is weak, incapable of asserting the will or taking action. Note that there is a common form of statue of the god Hermes called a *herma* or *herm*, which depicts this god in the form of an oblong block of stone having a head but without arms or legs. It thus gives the general impression of one bound hand and foot, in the way of an Egyptian mummy.

A variation of the *defixion* is to form the lead into a humanoid shape and then enclose the little doll inside a miniature lead coffin on which the binding curse is inscribed. Four of these tiny coffins were recently discovered in graves in the Kerameikos, an area in Athens, Greece, northwest of the Acropolis. They are dated from around 400 BCE.[247]

When it is desired to specify an individual in magic, it can be done by using an image of the individual or by using that person's name. Both are employed in the curse tablet from Carystus. It is in a human shape, intended to represent the woman against whom the curse is directed, and it also bears the name of the woman, Isias, who is further particularized by the words "daughter of A(u)toclea."

The text of the curse that is written on these lead tablets was probably spoken aloud by the person casting the curse just prior to throwing the tablet into the spring or well that was intended to carry it to the underworld. Indeed, since some of these lead tablets bear no inscription at all, the spoken curse must have been more important than the inscription. The written word is not only a representation of the spoken word but is a way of sustaining it and making it permanent. The spoken curse probably developed in Greece long before curses were written down. Faraone wrote, "Some scholars, in fact, have argued that the *defixio* was originally a purely verbal curse, although I prefer to think that both the spoken formula and the attendant gesture (i.e.,

---

247. D. R. Jordan, "Two Inscribed Lead Tablets from a Well in the Athenian Kerameikos," *Mitteilungen des deutschen archaologischen Instituts, Atheirische Abteilung* 95 (1980): 225–39. Cited by Faraone, "The Agonistic Context of Early Greek Binding Spells," *Magika Hiera*, 4.

the distortion of lead, wax, or some other pliable material) developed simultaneously."[248] The reference in the quote to "distortion of lead" refers to the folding of the lead tablet, which was itself a form of binding. The name of the person cursed was folded, or sometimes rolled, into the lead and thus trapped there.

Some lead tablets have been found uninscribed but pierced with iron nails. The curse was recited over the lead, probably in such a way that the breath of the speaker touched the lead, which was then folded or pierced with the nail. In this way the spoken incantation was trapped in the lead. What is the primary function of a nail? It is to fix something into place. By piercing the lead tablet, the curse was fixed into it. In vampire lore an iron or wooden stake was driven through the corpse of a suspected vampire, not to kill the vampire as is erroneously supposed in modern vampire movies, but to fix the vampire into the grave so that it could not leave it. For this purpose the stake had to be driven into the ground, because the intention was to pin the vampire to the ground.

Faraone enumerates three different types of binding curse used by the ancient Greeks.[249] The first type he calls a direct binding formula, which takes the form of a command: "I bind so-and-so with this curse." The magician relies on their own authority and perhaps on the natural occult properties of various materials or objects. The second type he calls the prayer formula: "Let Hermes bind so-and-so with this curse." This is a request rather than a command. The third type, known as the *similia similibus* formula, Faraone terms persuasive analogy: "As I wind this lead tablet with wire, so let so-and-so be bound by this curse." This type of curse involves a dramatic symbolic enactment of the fulfilment of the purpose.

In a sense, all these curses involved dramatic enactment, since the lead tablets were placed in a well or spring or in a tomb of the dead. The placing of the tablet symbolically substitutes for the placing of the person whose name is inscribed on the tablet with the dead, or in the land of the dead, under the binding authority of the keepers of the dead.

---

248. Faraone, "The Agonistic Context of Early Greek Binding Spells," *Magika Hiera*, 4.
249. Faraone, "The Agonistic Context of Early Greek Binding Spells," *Magika Hiera*, 10.

The Witch's Poppet

In early medieval Europe the use of the lead curse tablet gradually declined and was replaced by the use of what is generally called a poppet. Also popularly known in modern times as a "Voodoo doll," it is a small image intended to represent the person who is cursed. The practitioners of Voudoun in Haiti did not use dolls in this way, so the name "Voodoo doll" is misleading. These poppets were made of a wide variety of materials, including clay, wood, wax, and cloth. In size they were usually quite small, seldom more than twelve inches in length.

As nearly as possible, the little figure was made to resemble the person it represented. An exact likeness was not necessary. To create a stronger link between the doll and the subject of the malediction, the name of the person might be inscribed on it or on a bit of parchment or paper, which was then rolled up and inserted into the doll. If possible, a bit of the victim's hair was procured and attached to the head of the doll with glue, or it was impressed into it if the doll was made of wet clay or wax. Where a rag that had once been part of a garment worn by the person to be cursed could be gained, the witch sometimes made a small coat or dress from it and fitted this onto the doll. Fingernail parings, if procured, were also inserted into the doll. All these materials helped create a sympathetic occult link between the doll and the person to be cursed.

The manners in which the curse was applied were various. A wax doll might be melted in the heat of a flame, or placed on the inner ledge of a fireplace, to heat slowly and cause a fever, or a burning sensation on the skin of the victim of the curse. King James I makes mention in his *Demonology* of "pictures" of clay or wax slowly roasted in a fire to cause continual sickness.[250] By pictures he meant images or likenesses. A doll made of wood could be burned in a fire like a log, if a more rapid death were sought.

A clay doll might be placed in water to slowly soften and dissolve it. Haddon wrote of the *corp chreadh* (clay body), a form of poppet used in England. The doll was pierced with pins, nails, or thorns over its entire body, then placed into water. If it was desired that the victim should suffer at length,

---

250. James I, *The Demonology of King James I*, ed. Donald Tyson (Woodbury, MN: Llewellyn Publications, 2011), 128–30. See also 133n2.

care was taken to avoid piercing the region of the heart; but if death was the intention, the heart region was stuck thick with pins.

As each pin was inserted, the witch performing the curse spoke this incantation, or one like it, to the doll as though it were alive, saying, "As you waste away, may [name of victim] waste away; as this wounds you, may it wound [name of victim]."[251] When the doll was studded with pins, it was placed into a stream so that the soft clay would be slowly dissolved by the action of the running water. Periodically, the witch might return to the stream to insert more nails or pins into the doll to increase the suffering of the person. There was risk involved in this practice, however, for should the doll be discovered in the stream by some chance passerby, the curse would be broken.

One of the most famous instances of witch poppets involved three dolls found in a dung heap in Lincoln's Inn Fields in the year 1578, during the reign of Queen Elizabeth I. At that time the fields were open grassland used for pasturing cattle. One of the dolls had the name "Elizabeth" inscribed on it, and the other two were thought to resemble two of the queen's advisors. They were pierced with pig's bristles.[252] The new queen was very unpopular with her Catholic subjects because she had returned England to staunch Protestantism, banning the Catholic Mass, after her predecessor, "Bloody" Mary Tudor, had encouraged Catholics to worship freely. There were Jesuits in England at the time eager to assassinate the new queen, but it is unknown who was responsible for the poppets. Elizabeth was so alarmed by the discovery of the dolls that she sent for her advisor, the alchemist and magician Dr. John Dee. He examined the dolls and was able to assure the queen that there was nothing for her to worry about, that the sickness she was experiencing at that time was due to bad teeth, not to black magic.

We may gather from a passage in his work *Compendious Rehearsal* that Dee performed an act of countermagic on the poppet that bore the queen's name: "My carefull and faithfull endeavours was with great speede required

251. Haddon, *Magic and Fetishism*, 21. Square brackets are mine.

252. Glyn Parry, *The Arch-Conjuror of England, John Dee* (New Haven, CT: Yale University Press, 2011), 132. See also the essay by Carole Levin, "Witchcraft in Shakespeare's England," British Library, March 15, 2016, https://www.bl.uk/shakespeare/articles/witch craft-in-shakespeares-england#sthash.8iw4kFos.fnmz.

(as by divers messages sent unto me one after another in one morning) to prevent the mischiefe, which divers of her Majesties Privy Councell suspected to be intended against her Majesties person, by meanes of a certaine image of wax, with a great pin stuck into it about the brest of it, found in Lincolnes Inn fields, &c., wherein I did satisfie her Magesties desire, and the Lords of the Honourable Privy Councell within few houres, in godly and artificiall manner." [253]

By "artificiall" Dee meant artful or skillful. The whole affair may have been no more than a misunderstanding. A Spanish visitor to England remarked in a letter that a local conjuror, Thomas Elkes, "confessed himself to have been the doer there of: yet not to destroy the Queene, but to obtaine the love of some Londoners wyf." [254] Certainly the name "Elizabeth" was common enough in England in the sixteenth century. The heat of the dung hill may have been intended by Elkes to arouse the heat of passion in the woman the poppet was made to represent, rather than to sicken and kill, and the pin mentioned by Dee may have been there to provoke heartache and lovesick yearning.

Various simple objects were often used in place of a poppet, which required a certain amount of craft skill to make. Onions, lemons, and the hearts of sheep or pigs all might represent the subject of the malediction. They were pierced with thorns, nails, or pins and placed inside a fireplace chimney to be slowly roasted. From time to time, over the passage of centuries, these curious objects have been found inside the chimneys of older English houses. Elworthy illustrated two hearts studded with pins and thorns, or nails, one of which had a great iron nail through its center, by which it was nailed up inside a chimney above a fireplace. [255]

There was malice involved in this practice, but at the same time it was defensive or protective. When a farmer suspected a pig to have been killed by the evil magic of a witch, he took the heart, studded it with nails, and roasted it over a fire. This was believed to torment the witch who had cast the spell

---

253. John Dee, *Compendious Rehearsal*, in *Autobiographical Tracts of Dr. John Dee*, ed. James Crossley (Chetham Society, 1851), 21.

254. Richard Verstegan, trans., *The Copy of a Letter Lately Written by a Spanishe Gentleman* (Antwerp, 1589).

255. Elworthy, *The Evil Eye*, 53–58.

and also to prevent the witch from bespelling other livestock on the farm. If more livestock was sickened by magic, the pain caused by roasting the pig's heart would force the witch to lift the spell and restore the other animals to health.

This countermagic was accompanied by an incantation that was recited against the witch who was the target of the curse. Elworthy wrote about a "recent instance" (late nineteenth century) that had occurred in Somerset. The pig belonging to an elderly woman fell sick. She consulted a wise man, or "conjuror," as they were called, about what should be done. He told her that her pig was bewitched. A sheep's heart was procured (they could not use the pig's heart because the animal was still alive) and stuck all over with pins, then roasted before the open fire in the woman's fireplace. At intervals the old woman's son sprinkled salt into the fire, causing it to flare up with bright yellow flame.

While this was being done, the people assembled in the old woman's house chanted the following verse against the witch:

> It is not this heart I mean to burn,
> But the person's heart I wish to turn,
> Wishing them neither rest nor peace
> Till they are dead and gone.[256]

If the person who had worked the evil magic was known or suspected, the name of that person would be inserted into this incantation. If the person was not known, the verse would be recited without a specific name. Elworthy wrote that after a while, a black cat jumped out from where it had been hiding, frightening all those gathered around the fire, and the conjuror declared that the curse on the pig had been successful lifted.

The other illustration provided by Elworthy shows a lemon that had been studded all over its surface with twenty-four square iron nails and half a dozen smaller round wire nails. This was discovered in 1892 in a house in the Italian city of Naples, on top of a valence board above a window. Between the nails had been wound a piece of yarn or string, so that they were all linked together by it. Its color was too faded to be determined, but my guess is that

---

256. Elworthy, *The Evil Eye*, 56.

the string was originally bright red. When the owner of the house showed the object to his cook, the cook said that witches had made it, and that they put such things on braziers and danced around them naked in order to empower this ominous charm with their incantations. The Italians call such curse charms *fattura della morte* (deathmaker).[257]

---

257. Elworthy, *The Evil Eye*, 57–58.

Eleven
Enchantments

Enchantment is the imbuing of an object, place, or person with magic by uttering over it an incantation. The word "enchant" is from the Latin *incantare*: to "sing in." The thing is then said to be enchanted. The great Samuel Johnson came nearest to a correct definition in his *Dictionary of the English Language*, where he gave as the initial definition of the word, "To give efficacy to any thing by songs of sorcery."[258] For enchantment to be most effective, the incantation must be spoken, chanted, or sung aloud, and the breath must touch the thing enchanted as the words are uttered. For this purpose witches or magicians may hold an object close to their lips when they speak an incantation to it or murmur the incantation into the ear of the person they wish to enchant.

Cornelius Agrippa devoted a chapter of his 1530 apologetic work *De incertitudine et vanitate scientiarum* (*The Uncertainty and Vanity of the Sciences*) to this subject (chapter 44), and it was reprinted at the back of his *Occult Philosophy* in the 1651 English translation of that work. In the chapter, Agrippa stresses the importance of words and the voice in the use of enchantments: "So the Psylli and Marsi called together serpents,

---

258. Samuel Johnson, *A Dictionary of the English Language*, vol. 1 (London: Printed by W. Strahan, 1755), unpaginated, under "enchant."

and others by other things depressing them, put them to flight. So Orpheus repressed the tempest of the Argonauts with a hymn; and Homer relates of Ulysses that his blood was restrained with words. And in the law of the Twelve Tables punishment was ordained for them who enchanted the corn: that without all doubt the magicians did produce wonderful effects by words, affections, and such like, not only upon themselves, but also upon extraneous things."[259]

An aspect of enchantment usually overlooked in definitions is that of transformation. When something is enchanted, it is transformed either inwardly or outwardly. Enchantment can cause change in the essential nature of a thing. It is analogous in this sense to the alchemical transformation of base metal into gold. It can also cause change in the outward appearance of a thing, which may be either an actual transformation or the illusion of a transformation. Enchantments that produce the illusion of change without actually changing the essential nature of things are known as glamoury.

> For, according to S. Isidore (*Etym.* VIII, 9), a glamour is nothing but a certain delusion of the senses, and especially of the eyes. And for this reason it is also called a prestige, from *prestringo*, since the sight of the eyes is so fettered that things seem to be other than they are. And Alexander of Hales, Part 2, says that a prestige, properly understood, is an illusion of the devil, which is not caused by any change in matter, but only exists in the mind of him who is deluded, either as to his inner or outer perceptions.[260]

For example, it was commonly believed that magicians could mutter a charm over a handful of pebbles or twigs and make them appear to be gold coins to anyone who saw them, even though no real transformation of essence had taken place. Various magicians are supposed to have paid for goods with such enchanted pebbles or twigs, which would revert back to

---

259. Agrippa, *Three Books of Occult Philosophy*, 693.
260. Heinrich Kramer, *Malleus Maleficarum*, trans. Montague Summers (Suffolk: John Rodker, 1928), 59.

their original form after the passage of time: "It was also said by Martin Del Rio (in his *Disquisitionum magicarum libri sex*, first edition, Louvain, 1599–1600) and others that Agrippa paid his inn bills with bits of horn, casting a glamour over them so that they appeared to those who received them to be coins until Agrippa was safely away, at which time they changed back to their true appearance. But this fable is told of a number of magicians such as Faust and Simon Magus."[261]

European witches were supposed to possess the power to enchant men so that their penis and scrotum vanished, leaving only a smooth patch of skin.[262] This was a form of glamoury. The penis was not actually removed; it only appeared to the man that it was missing. Others who looked between his legs, if they were unaffected by the glamour, would see a penis, or they might share in the glamour and see only smooth skin. Elderly female witches are said to have used glamoury to change their appearance so that they looked like young women, for the purpose of lying with young men and stealing their semen.

Enchantment should not be confused with glamoury. A glamour is an illusion and involves an act of enchantment. But not all enchanted things are illusions. Enchantment confers magical power upon the thing enchanted. That power may take the form of an illusion, or it may take other forms that have a more material application, such as protection from injury. In the John Boorman movie *Excalibur*, the sorceress Morgana enchants the armor of her child Mordred to render it impenetrable to any weapon forged by men.[263] This enchantment is not an illusion but causes actual change in the armor.

Enchantments often have a hidden weakness in literature that renders them void. The heel of Achilles is a classic example—while still a baby, Achilles was made impervious to all weapons by his mother, Thetis, who dipped him into the River Styx. As she did so, she held the baby by one of his heels,

---

261. Tyson, ed., *Three Books of Occult Philosophy*, xxxiv–v. Refer to Del Rio, *Disquisitionum magicarum libri sex, lib. II, q. XII* (Louvain, 1599), 167. For the English translation, see Peter Maxwell-Stuart and Jose Manuel Garcia Valverde, eds. and trans., *Investigations into Magic, an Edition and Translation of Martin Del Rio's Disquisitionum magicarum libri sex*, vol. 2 (Leiden: Koninklijke Brill, 2023), 247.

262. See Kramer, *Malleus Maleficarum*, trans. Montague Summers, 58.

263. John Boorman, dir., *Excalibur* (Warner Brothers, 1981), Blu-ray disc, 1:45:35.

and that part of his body was the only part not touched by the water. Later in his life, Achilles was killed by an arrow shot into his heel. In Tolkien's *Lord of the Rings*, the enchanted Witch King of Angmar, who cannot be slain by any man, is killed in battle by the sword of a woman, with the aid of a hobbit, who is not of the human species.[264]

Another story related of the magician Faust is that he once used enchantment to create a horse, which he rode to a fair and sold for forty dollars, cautioning the buyer that he must never ride the horse over water. It was a common belief that things enchanted could not cross running water. "The Horse courser marvell'd with himself that Faustus bade him ride over no water: But, quoth he, I'll try, and forthwith he rid him into the River; and presently the Horse vanish'd from under him, and he left on a Bottle of Straw, insomuch that he was almost drown'd."[265] By "bottle of straw" I would guess a straw-covered glass bottle is intended. It was, and still is, the custom in some parts of Europe to protect bottles of wine from breaking with woven wrappers of straw.

We see in this tale that the enchanted horse was real enough for its new owner to ride, but when it was ridden over running water, it reverted to the items from which it had been formed, just as the coach that carried Cinderella to the royal ball reverted to a pumpkin at the stroke of midnight. The girl's fairy godmother cautioned her that she must leave the ball before this hour struck, but the girl lost track of time and suffered the consequence. There is quite often in these tales a condition that must be upheld in order for the enchantment to endure. When that condition is violated, the enchantment fails.

Fairy Enchantments

Fairy tales, folktales, and nursery rhymes are filled with enchanted objects, places, and persons. Cinderella's fairy godmother enchanted not only a pumpkin into a gilded coach but mice into the horses that would pull it. A rat became the coachman and lizards the footmen. The enchanted beans that Jack the future giant killer traded for a cow grew into a gigantic vine that stretched

---

264. J. R. R. Tolkien, *The Lord of the Rings* (London: George Allen and Unwin, 1969), 874–75.

265. Anonymous, *The Surprizing Life and Death of Doctor John Faustus* (London: Printed and sold by the booksellers, 1727), 51.

up into the heavens. The enchanted mirror of the wicked stepmother of Snow White was able to predict future events.

Real fairy tales, which involve actual eye-witness encounters between fairies and human beings, are much darker than the fairy tales told to young children. To the people who met them in past centuries, the fairies, who were sometimes referred to as elves, were terrifying: "These *Siths*, or Fairies, they call *Sleagh Maith*, or the Good People, it would seem, to prevent the Dint of their ill Attempts, (for the Irish use to bless all they fear Harme of;) and are said to be of a midle Nature betuixt Man and Angel, as were Daemons thought to be of old; of intelligent studious Spirits, and light changable Bodies, (lyke those called Astral,) somewhat of the Nature of a condensed Cloud, and best seen in Twilight." [266]

There is another class of beings said to be of a middle nature between humans and angels. They are the djinn of Arabs and Persians, who are believed to dwell in the wastelands of the deserts and to travel in the form of whirlwinds across the sand. Whereas fairies are of the earth and of the air, the djinn were "created of subtle fire." [267] Their lord is Eblis, who fell out of favor with God because he refused to kneel before Adam, the first man. When God demanded to know why he would not kneel, Eblis said, "Nobler…am I than he; me hast Thou created of fire; of clay hast Thou created him." [268]

The parallels between fairies and djinn are worth noting. Both have a general antipathy toward human beings. Both are said to harm those humans they encounter in an almost capricious manner, without real justification or even any deep malice. Both can work powerful glamours and other enchantments. Both were feared and avoided by humanity.

Everything possible was done to avoid meeting fairies in the gloaming, as the Scots call the transition between day and night, and above all to avoid displeasing them, since fairies did not hesitate to punish any humans who angered them. This they often did with enchantment, if the old stories are to be believed. One common way was through what was known as a fairy stroke, which crippled or caused death.

---

266. Kirk, *The Secret Commonwealth*, 5.

267. Robert Durie Osborn, *Islam under the Arabs* (London: Longmans, Green, and Co., 1876), 28.

268. Osborn, *Islam under the Arabs*, 29.

I was moved to this by what I had learned at the funeral of a man who had died from a fairy stroke a few days before, and by meeting two men who had been injured by similar strokes. One of the two was a farmer's son who had fallen asleep incautiously while near a fairy fort and was made a cripple for life; the other was a man of fairly good education, who, besides his English knowledge, read and wrote Gaelic. I was unable to obtain the details relating to his case, but the man who died had interfered with a fairy fort and hurt his hand in the act. The deceased was only thirty-three years old, a strong, healthy person, but after he had meddled with the fort his hand began to swell, and grew very painful. The best doctors were summoned, but gave no relief, and the man died from a fairy stroke, according to the statement of all, or nearly all, the people.[269]

Fairy forts are the mounds or hills believed in olden times to be the gateways to fairyland. Those who disturbed a fairy mound, or even trespassed upon it, were subject to the wrath of the Good People.

The fairy stroke of folktales was a stroke of death, quite often literally a stroke in the medical sense or a heart attack. It did not always kill. Sometimes it paralyzed the part of the body on which it fell or caused that part to become swollen or infected. At other times it caused a mental breakdown or other alteration in the working of the mind, so that the person fairy-struck spoke and acted in an otherworldly manner or fell into a coma.

The blow was delivered most commonly by what were known as elf-shot. These were stone arrowheads that were shot or thrown at individuals who had earned the ire of the fairies. The flint arrowheads of Stone Age peoples, when found on the ground by Celts or Saxons, were said to be elf-shot crafted by the fairies. But elf-shot might take the form of common pebbles that came seemingly from an empty sky and struck against the person to be harmed. Wherever the pebble struck, a pain or injury would develop. Sometimes the

---

269. Jeremiah Curtin, *Tales of the Fairies and of the Ghost World* (Boston: Little, Brown & Company, 1895), 4.

impact was fatal. The fairy chronicler Robert Kirk called such stones "these Arrows that fly in the Dark." [270]

The witch Isobel Gowdie described how these elf-shot were made and used when she was interrogated prior to her trial for witchcraft. Her accent is a bit thick, but I will explain her words below the quotation.

> As for Elf-arrow-heidis, the Divell shapes them with his awin hand, [and syne deliueris thame] to Elf-boys, who whyttis and dightis them with a sharp thing lyk a paking neidle; bot [quhan I wes in Elf-land?] I saw them whytting and dighting them....Thes that dightis thaim ar litle ones, hollow, and boss-baked! They speak ghowstie lyk. Quhen the Divell giwes them to ws, he sayes,
>   "Shoot thes in my name,
>   And they sall not goe heall hame!"
>   And quhan ve shoot these arrowes (we say)—
>   "I shoot yon man in the Divellis name,
>   He sall nott win heall hame!
>   And this salbe alswa trw;
>   Thair sall not be an bitt of him on lieiw!"
> We haw no bow to shoot with, but spang them from the naillis of our thowmbes. Som tymes we will misse; bot if thay twitch, be it beast, or man, or woman, it will kill, tho' they haid an jack wpon them. [271]

According to the witch, the Devil selected the stones for the elf-shot, but they were shaped and made sharp by "elf-boys" in "Elfland," which is to say, by fairy boys in fairyland, who picked at their edges with a kind of needle. These little fairies were hollowed out in the back and spoke with a gruff voice. When the Devil passed the stones over, he used this incantation:

---

270. Kirk, *The Secret Commonwealth*, 8. See also page xxv of Andrew Lang's introduction, and the note (a) on page 86.

271. Robert Pitcairn, *Ancient Criminal Trials in Scotland*, vol. 3 (Edinburgh, Scotland: Bannatyne Club, 1833), 607. Pitcairn's brackets.

> Shoot these in my name,
> And they shall not go whole home.[272]

The reference is to the persons who will be the targets of the elf-shot. When the witch cast the stones, she spoke this incantation:

> I shoot yonder man in the Devil's name,
> He shall not win whole home!
> And this shall be also true;
> There shall not be a bit of him alive.[273]

As to the manner of casting the stones, the witch meant that the enchanted arrowheads were not shot from a bow but were flicked with the thumb, in the same way that children flick marbles. This would require being at close range to the target, but since fairies were known to move through the world invisible, this would not be difficult for them. Witches might find it harder to approach, unless they had the secret of invisibility from their fairy friends. If the stones so much as touched beast, man, or woman, they would kill them, even if they were wearing a coat of armor ("haid an jack wpon them"). A man might be walking alone on an open heath, with no cover to hide behind for hundreds of yards, and suddenly feel the sting of the elf-shot hitting him. He would look around angrily, searching for the thrower of the stone, but would find no trace or sign of anyone.

Another way fairies used enchantment was by the casting of a fairy sleep. The story is told that John Conners, who lived near Killarney, in Ireland, lost his way on the road and spent the night in the castle of a stranger. Instead of staying one night, he was put into an enchanted sleep and slept for three weeks. When at last he was awakened and left the house, he turned to look behind, and all he saw was "fields and ditches."[274] A farmer's boy who dwelt near Ebeltoft, in Denmark, encountered a beautiful maiden who asked him if he was thirsty. He was put on his guard when he noticed that she would not turn her back to him, because fairies are known to be hollow in the back. Even so, when she offered him her breast to suck on, he accepted and was

---

272. My modernization of these lines from the quotation.
273. My modernization of these lines from the quotation.
274. Curtin, *Tales of the Fairies and of the Ghost World*, 8.

instantly enchanted by her milk. He was away from home for three days, and when he returned, he refused to eat what his mother set on the table for him, saying he knew a place that served much better food. His father grew angry and forced him to eat. The moment he took a bite, he fell into a deep sleep that lasted three days, and when he awoke, his mind was gone and he never recovered his reason.[275]

The land of fairy is an enchanted land always described as shining with lights and rich in gold and silver. Sometimes it is placed in a cavern beneath the earth, which is reached by a door that opens in a fairy hill, then closes again without a trace. Other times it is very near to the Summerland described by European witches in testimony they gave during their interrogations prior to their trials and executions. One such description occurs in the romance of Orfeo and Heurodis, who were said in the tale to be king and queen of Winchester, in England. After the queen is abducted by fairies, the king rides off to search for her and enters the land of fairy.

> He came into a fair country
> As bright as sun on summer's day;
> Smooth and flat and all was green,
> No hill nor dale was to be seen;
> Amid this land a keep he spies,
> Rich and proud and wondrous high;
> All the outermost wall,
> Was clear and shone of crystal;
> A hundred towers there were about,
> Fortified with battlements stout;
> The buttresses rose from the ditch,
> Of red gold they arched up rich;
> The gate was carved overall
> With every kind of animal;
> Within, there were wide zones
> All paved with precious stones;
> The meanest pillar to behold

275. Thomas Keightley, *The Fairy Mythology*, vol. 1 (London: William Harrison Ainsworth, 1828), 152–54.

Was made of burnished gold:
All that land was ever bright,
For when it should be dark as night,
The light of those rich stones shone
Bright as does at noon the sun:
No man may tell, nor think in thought
The wondrous work that there was wrought.[276]

Orfeo rides into the castle and so enchants the king of fairy with his singing and playing on the lute, that the fairy king gives back the woman he abducted. The power of his voice overcomes the fairy magic. Note here the resemblance of the name Orfeo to Orpheus. The poem is a retelling of the Greek myth of Orpheus and Eurydice.

The Summerland is always composed of green lawns and fruit trees laden with ripe fruit. It is forever summer, and the sun never sets. At its center is located the hall of the fairies, which varies in its description depending on who is telling the tale. Both fairies and witches have access to it. In folklore there is a close connection between them. Witches were supposed to be able to see fairies and converse with them. The Summerland was their meeting place.

It is common in myth and sagas for swords to be enchanted, and the most famous of all enchanted blades is undoubtedly Excalibur, the sword used by Arthur to unite the Britons. It was given to him by the Lady of the Lake, a fairy, in this account by Sir Thomas Malory:

> So they rode till they came to a lake, the which was
> a fair water and broad, and in the midst of the lake
> Arthur was ware of an arm clothed in white samite,
> that held a fair sword in that hand. Lo! said Merlin,
> yonder is that sword that I spake of. With that they

276. My version of this poetic description, which I have modified for clarity, is based primarily on that given in Keightley, *The Fairy Mythology*, vol. 1, 75–76. For something closer to the original Middle English text, see Sir Walter Scott, "Of the Fairies of Popular Superstition," in *Minstrelsy of the Scottish Border*, vol. 2 (Kelso, Scotland: James Ballantyne, 1802), 197–98. For an alternative modern translation, see Edward Eyre Hunt, ed., *Sir Orfeo* (Cambridge: Harvard Coöperative Society, 1909), 19–20.

saw a damosel going upon the lake. What damosel is that? said Arthur. That is the Lady of the Lake, said Merlin; and within that lake is a rock, and therein is as fair a place as any on earth, and richly beseen; and this damosel will come to you anon, and then speak ye fair to her that she will give you that sword.[277]

The fair place within the rock beneath the lake is the Summerland of fairy, and the lake itself yet another entrance to that enchanted realm.[278] The Lady of the Lake offers to give the sword to Arthur, if he will give her a gift in return when she asks it of him. This he hastily agrees to do. Arthur rows across the lake and takes the sword from the arm that holds it above the water, and a scabbard along with it. Merlin asks Arthur which he likes better, the sword or its scabbard, and Arthur chooses the sword. "Ye are more unwise, said Merlin, for the scabbard is worth ten of the swords, for whiles ye have the scabbard upon you, ye shall never lose no blood be ye never so sore wounded, therefore keep well the scabbard always with you."[279]

The sword and the scabbard make Arthur invulnerable in battle, and with them he is able to conquer all the kingdoms of England and unite them. The Lady of the Lake tells him the name of the sword when they meet at a later time. "The name of it, said the lady, is Excalibur, that is as much to say as Cut-steel."[280] From the name it is evident that the magic power of the sword is to cut through steel, both the steel of other blades and the steel of armor. When, near the end of his life, Arthur fights Mordred, his greatest foe, he is without his scabbard because Morgan le Fay (Morgan of Fairy) has stolen it from him. Morgan has at the same time given Mordred armor that is invincible to all weapons forged by man, but Arthur has retained Excalibur, which was forged by fairy magic, and it pierces Mordred's enchanted armor and kills him.

---

277. Thomas Malory, *Le Morte d'Arthur*, vol. 1 (London: J. M. Dent & Sons, 1906), 43.

278. "It is a very common occurrence for the heroes of popular tales to plunge boldly into a lake or fountain, and lo! they are in fairyland." W. A. Clouston, *Popular Tales and Fictions*, vol. 1 (Edinburg and London: William Blackwood and Sons, 1887), 193.

279. Malory, *Le Morte d'Arthur*, 44.

280. Malory, *Le Morte d'Arthur*, 49.

As he lies dying, Arthur orders one of his knights to cast Excalibur back into the lake, and as this is done, a hand rises from the waters to receive it. The sword is thus preserved by the Lady of the Lake for the arising of a future king of England who is worthy to wield it.

Merlin

The enchanter of greatest fame is Merlin. It is not known if he was an historical figure, although it has been speculated that he was a Druid. The name "Merlinus Ambrosius" first appears from the pen of Geoffery of Monmouth (c. 1095–c.1155), who wrote the highly popular Latin work *Historia Regum Britanniae* (*History of the Kings of Britain*). Geoffery referred to him as "Merlin, who was also called Ambrose."[281] He may have based his account on tales of two separate semi-legendary British sages, one named Myrddin and the other named Ambrosius. According to Geoffery, Merlin was the offspring of a royal princess and an incubus. His mother was questioned by King Vortegirn about the origins of the boy:

> "My Sovereign Lord," said she, "by the Life of your Soul and mine, I know no Body that begot him of me. Only this I know, that as I was one Time with my Companions in our Chambers, there appeared to me a Person in the Shape of a most beautiful young Man, who often and most eagerly embraced me in his Arms, and kissed me; and when he had stay'd a little Time, he suddenly vanished out of my Sight. But many Times after this he would be talking with me when I sat alone, without making any visible Appearance. When he had a long Time haunted me in this manner, he at last laid with me several Times in Shape of a Man, and left me with Child. And I do affirm to you, my Sovereign Lord, that excepting that young Man, I know no Body that begot him of me."[282]

---

281. Geoffrey of Monmouth, *The British History*, trans. Aaron Thompson (London: J. Bowyer, 1718), 202.

282. Geoffrey of Monmouth, *The British History*, 199–200.

Accounts of children born from the union of mortal women and spiritual beings are common throughout ancient literature, going all the way back to the biblical book Genesis and even earlier.[283] Since his mother was flesh and blood, Merlin was also flesh, the issue of her womb, but he was infused with the spiritual essence of his nonhuman father, which made him different from other boys.

Several chapters of Geoffrey's history are taken up with Merlin's prophecy, which he pronounced to King Vortegirn concerning the future of Britain. The prophecy is convoluted and obscure to an extreme degree, but it is on this that the later fame of Merlin was largely based. Geoffrey also credited Merlin with building Stonehenge (the "Giants' Dance") by magic, "a manifest Proof of the Prevalence of Art above Strength."[284]

When Merlin offers a prophecy concerning a new comet that appears in the night heavens, Uther Pendragon is emboldened by him to conquer England. While laying siege to the castle belonging to Gorlois, the Duke of Cornwall, Uther is captivated by the beauty of his wife, Igerna, and determines to seduce her. Merlin is able to accomplish this by his arts of glamoury, as he informs Uther.

> To accomplish your Desire, you must make use of such Arts as have not been heard of in your Time. I know how by the Force of my Medicines, to give you the exact likeness of *Gorlois*, so that in all Respects you shall seem to be no other than himself. If you will therefore obey my Prescriptions, I will metamorphize you into the true Semblance of *Gorlois*, and *Ulfin* into *Jordan* of *Tintagol*, his familiar Friend; and I myself being transformed into another Shape, will make the third in the Adventure; and in this Disguise you may go safely to the Town where *Igerna* is, and have Admittance to her.[285]

---

283. Genesis 6:4 (KJV).
284. Geoffrey of Monmouth, *The British History*, 250.
285. Geoffrey of Monmouth, *The British History*, 264–65. Geoffrey's italics.

It is thus by the enchantments of Merlin that Uther Pendragon is enabled to lie with Igerna, and upon her he engenders Arthur. After Uther's death, Arthur makes war against the Saxons and subdues them. The sword he uses is not called Excalibur in Geoffrey's account, but Caliburn, which Geoffrey described as "an excellent Sword made in the Isle of *Avallon*." [286] It must indeed have been excellent, for with it in a single battle Arthur kills 470 Saxons. To empower this enchanted weapon Arthur calls upon the Virgin Mary. At this period of history, the Britons were Christians but the Saxons were pagans.

Around the time Arthur is born, Merlin slips away and is no more seen in Geoffrey's history, but there are various accounts in the Arthurian romances, written by the French, in which Merlin becomes the mentor and advisor of Arthur. In these poetry and prose romances the downfall of Merlin is described in numerous different ways, but they have in common that it was brought about by Merlin's fatal attraction to a beautiful woman who was his apprentice in the magical arts. She is often a woman of fairy, or connected with fairy, such as Morgan le Fay or the Lady of the Lake. Other names given to her are Viviane or Nimue. After learning all she can from Merlin, his lover traps the enchanter in a prison where he remains forever. In various accounts the prison is said to have walls of air or to be a tower of crystal or a house of glass. Other accounts say it is deep in a cave or beneath a great stone.

---

286. Geoffrey of Monmouth, *The British History*, 283–84. Geoffrey's italics.

Twelve
Enchanting Herbs, Potions, and Wands

A common use for incantation in ancient times was the enchantment of herbs and potions that were intended to be used to heal the body, induce love, or for other purposes. This was done by uttering the incantation over the potion shortly before it was administered. For example, an enchantress among the Iban people of the island of Borneo (formerly known as the Sea-Dayak people) who prepared a love potion, or *jayan*, would enchant it in the following manner before employing it:

> The *jayan* must be kept in a place where people are not likely to pass or sit over it, otherwise its potency will be impaired. Just before the charm is applied the owner retires to some secluded spot, makes a small fire, into which scented flowers and pieces of aromatic bark and wood are put, and waves the potion over the smoke, reciting at the same time an incantation.… The potion is rubbed on the bedding or clothes of the person whose affection is desired, or smeared on his or her body

during sleep, or else mixed with the ingredients of a
betel-nut quid and sent by hand to the desired one.[287]

The prepared potion is kept apart from other people to retain its purity so
that it does not pick up the occult energies of random thoughts and desires
from those who pass near it. Scented flowers and aromatic bark are used to
create a pleasant incense over which the love potion is purified just prior to its
empowerment. Then the enchantress utters an incantation designed to acti-
vate the potion, in such a way that her breath touches the potion. The incantation given in the original text is uncommonly long and convoluted, with the
name of obscure deities, but I will extract and adapt a more general, somewhat condensed version that will serve the same purpose:

> You are no common or useless potion.
> You are a potion I obtained in my dream.
> I asked to have you and gave an offering for you.
> Now I fume you with coconut milk,
> With flowers, with scented things.
> Be not false or ineffective.
> Be not barren or impotent.
> I ask you to settle on and to sink into [name].
> Cause him to be anxious, cause him to be restless.
> Cause him to be mad, cause him to be enamored.
> Cause him not to sit down, cause him not to sleep.
> Cause him not to eat, cause him not to cook.
> Cause him to be vexed, cause him to blame himself.
> Cause him to weep, cause him to cry out loud.
> Now seven days from this cause him to come to my
>   room and lie with me.[288]

---

287. W. Howell and R. Shelford, "A Sea-Dyak Love Philtre," *Journal of the Anthropological Institute of Great Britain and Ireland* 34 (1904): 207.

288. Howell and Shelford, "A Sea-Dyak Love Philtre," 209–10. I have not quoted here directly but have used the original incantation as the basis for this truncated version.

The magic is in the breath and the sound and the meaning of the enchantress's voice. To be effective in its working, the potion must then be consumed by, or at least touch the skin of, the person to be enchanted by it.

Jane Wilde, the mother of the writer Oscar Wilde, described the way in which a cunning man of Ireland, whom she called a fairy-doctor, brewed and empowered a healing potion against the three malign influences of the fairies which were prone to afflict children and young women—the fairy strike, the fairy wind, and the evil eye of the fairy. First, the fairy doctor had to determine which of these three types of affliction was causing the sickness. He did this by cutting three small slips of witch hazel and marking each for one of the causes. An eyewitness related what followed to Lady Wilde. I will give the account here:

> He then takes off his coat, shoes, and stockings; rolls up his shirt sleeves, and stands with his face to the sun in earnest prayer. After prayer he takes a dish of pure water and sets it by the fire, then kneeling down, he puts the three hazel rods he had marked into the fire, and leaves them there till they are burned black as charcoal. All the time his prayers are unceasing; and when the sticks are burned, he rises, and again faces the sun in silent prayer, standing with his eyes uplifted and hands crossed. After this he draws a circle on the floor with the end of one of the burned sticks, within which circle he stands, the dish of pure water beside him. Into this he flings the three hazel rods, and watches the result earnestly. The moment one sinks he addresses a prayer to the sun, and taking the rod out of the water he declares by what agency the patient is afflicted. Then he grinds the rod to powder, puts it in a bottle which he fills up with water from the dish, and utters an incantation or prayer over it, in a low voice, with clasped hands held over the bottle. But what the words of the prayer are no one knows, they are kept as solemn mysteries, and have been handed down from father to

son through many generations, from the most ancient times. The potion is then given to be carried home, and drunk that night at midnight in silence and alone. Great care must be taken that the bottle never touches the ground; and the person carrying it must speak no word, and never look round till home is reached. The other two sticks he buries in the earth in some place unseen and unknown. If none of the three sticks sink in the water, then he uses herbs as a cure. Vervain, eyebright, and yarrow are favourite remedies, and all have powerful properties known to the adept; but the words and prayers he utters over them are kept secret, and whether they are good or bad, or addressed to Deity or to a demon, none but himself can tell.[289]

Lady Wilde added the following comment: "If a potion is made up of herbs it must be paid for in silver; but charms and incantations are never paid for, or they would lose their power. A present, however, may be accepted as an offering of gratitude."[290]

From this interesting and illuminating account we learn that the fairy-doctor used fire to cleanse the slips of wood, then water to select the one that must be employed in the potion. Fire is of the sun; water is of the moon. Magically, they are opposites. A prayer is offered to the sun because the sun is cleansing and energy-giving. Water also cleanses, but whereas the sun vigorously burns away corruption and sickness, the water washes it away more gently. The stick that selects itself by sinking first, thereby indicating which of the three classes of fairy affliction is involved, is ground into dust and put into a bottle of the same water in which the three sticks were floated. After its burning, it would be mostly charcoal, so this grinding procedure would not be difficult.

The incantation that is spoken over the bottle of water after the charcoal powder has been added to it empowers and enchants the potion. Lady Wilde

289. Jane Francesca Elgee Wilde, *Ancient Legends, Mystic Charms, and Superstitions of Ireland* (London: Ward and Downey, 1888), 232.

290. Wilde, *Ancient Legends, Mystic Charms, and Superstitions of Ireland*, 232.

gives no clue about which specific words were spoken, but this is not a problem. I will compose here an incantation that will serve as well as whatever words the fairy-doctor of Ireland may have muttered over the bottle:

> Heat of hearth, light of day,
> Wash this sickness clean away;
> Purge and cleanse this chosen one
> By water, wood, and fiery sun.

Speak the charm in a low voice so that your words will not be overheard by others, but with your lips close to the open bottle so that your breath touches it and the surface of the water it holds. Then seal up the bottle and give it to the person who will drink it.

In addition to speaking an incantation over a finished potion to enchant it, incantations may also be uttered over the herbs that will go into a potion at the time they are gathered, and even at the time they are prepared. It can be useful to call upon the power of appropriate spirits, angels, or deities by their names in these incantations, if the qualities associated with the deities or spirits will aid in the working of the potion. The incantation intensifies the virtues inherent in the chosen herbs.

Mistletoe Potion of the Druids

The Druids harvested the parasitic plant mistletoe from oak trees in their sacred groves. Mistletoe is green in winter, a characteristic that was believed to express its vitalizing power. The Roman writer Pliny the Elder (23–79 CE) described how it was harvested in his *Natural History*. He wrote that they cut it on the fifth day of the lunar cycle.

> This day they select because the moon, though not yet in the middle of her course, has already considerable power and influence; and they call her by a name which signifies, in their language, the all-healing. Having made all due preparation for the sacrifice and a banquet beneath the trees, they bring thither two white bulls, the horns of which are bound then for the first time. Clad in a white robe the priest ascends the tree, and cuts the

mistletoe with a golden sickle, which is received by others in a white cloak. They then immolate the victims, offering up their prayers that God will render this gift of his propitious to those to whom he has so granted it. It is the belief with them that the mistletoe, taken in drink, will impart fecundity to all animals that are barren, and that it is an antidote for all poisons.[291]

There can be little doubt that incantations were spoken as the plant was cut from the oak tree upon which it grew, but Pliny did not record them, probably because he knew nothing about them. Pliny's account of the harvesting of mistletoe by the Druids is the only account provided by the ancient Roman writers. Scant though it is, what can we gain from it?

The moon was in her waxing phase, growing stronger and brighter night by night. The mistletoe, a lunar plant due in part to its white berries, but also solar because it remained green in the winter, partook of that increase of strength and was therefore cut when its occult virtues were rising, yet not at their height. Why not cut it when the moon was full? Perhaps because immediately following the peak of virtue is its decline, and the Druids wanted the plant to retain its power after its cutting. They took it with a golden sickle. The sickle shape is lunar, but the metal gold is solar. The power of the sun has authority over the power of the moon. They were protected by this solar authority when they harvested this lunar plant.

Note that the priest who climbed the oak took care not to touch the mistletoe with his hands. He cut it and let it fall free onto a white cloak that his fellow Druids held spread out below to catch it upon. In this way, they also avoided touching it directly. Two Druids held the cloak open so that they could compensate if the plant did not fall straight down and could catch it before it hit the ground, for if the mistletoe struck the ground, its occult vir-

---

291. Pliny the Elder, *The Natural History*, vol. 3, trans. Bostock and Riley (London: Henry G. Bohn, 1855), 436. The H. Rackham translation, published in volume 4 of the Loeb Classical Library edition, says the mistletoe was harvested on the sixth day of the moon, rather than on the fifth day. See Pliny, *Natural History*, vol. 4, trans. H. Rackham (London: William Heinemann, 1945), 549. The discrepancy in days results from when the count is started, whether on the day itself or on the next day.

tue would be drawn out of it and it would become worthless. To keep an enchanted object from touching the ground is a common theme in magic.

White is a color of the moon. Why sacrifice two white bulls? The bull is a lunar animal due to the crescent shape of its horns. Two were sacrificed because the moon has both a waxing and a waning phase, and therefore is dual by nature, in contrast to the sun, which is ever and always the same, and therefore in a magical sense singular. The sacrifice of the bulls was probably made by cutting the throats of the animals with a crescent-shaped blade. The hot blood, falling down into a bowl that was probably made of silver, was then offered to the moon. The carcasses of the beasts were roasted over a sacred fire and formed the celebratory feast of gathering of Druids.

As he performed the sacrifice, the Druid priest would have made invocations, which Pliny called prayers to God (*deus*). Pliny was a pagan, so he meant prayers to the Druid equivalent of a Greek or Roman sun god, such as Apollo. I believe it is more likely that the invocation, spoken to the sacrificed beasts themselves, was intended for a Celtic lunar goddess. It's quite clear that the sacrifice was lunar in nature—two white bulls. The Druids would not have made a dual sacrifice to the sun; white is the lunar color, and the bull is a lunar beast. Pliny's Latin text reads, "*suum donum deus prosperum faciat iis quibus dederit* (may god make his gift prosperous to those on whom he bestows it)." But Pliny had no way of knowing to which god or goddess the invocation of the Druids was addressed.

The mistletoe was made into a potion which, when it was drunk, was thought to give fertility. During its making, incantations would have been spoken over it and into it. The potion was also held to be an antidote to all forms of poison. The Druids would have administered this potion only to those who were thought to merit this great gift from the goddess of the moon. In later centuries, mistletoe was also supposed by some to possess the power to open all locks, a virtue it shares with mandrake and vervain.[292]

Homeopathy

On this same matter, mention must be made of the practice of homeopathy, which has largely been rejected by modern medicine in spite of reports

---

292. Richard Folkard, *Plant Lore, Legends and Lyrics* (London: Sampson Low, Marston, Searle, and Rivington, 1884), 113.

of remarkable cures effected by its means. It was invented by the German physician Christian Friedrich Samuel Hahnemann (1755–1843), who discovered that a substance that produced a negative effect on a healthy body would cure a disease the symptoms of which were similar to the effect of the substance. This principle was summarized in the aphorism *similia similibus curantur* (like cures like).

George Lennox Moore, writing on homeopathy in 1858, rejected the customary practice of physicians to indiscriminately give patients large doses of potent medicines to cure disease. He expounded on the central principle of homeopathy:

> The homoeopathist…is enabled to oppose the disease of his patient in accordance with the great and essential characteristic of homoeopathy, viz., that *those medicines which produce certain effects in health are the best curative agents for similar symptoms of disease.* Every medicine produces phenomena peculiar in some respects to itself, and the changes which its presence occasion are manifested by symptoms or sufferings. Thus, when the berries of Belladonna, or deadly nightshade, are eaten, the sufferings produced are, general fever, headache, sore throat, and scarlet rash. Now, similar symptoms very frequently accrue from the operation of natural causes, and the disease is known as scarlet fever. The medicinal and the natural diseases are not the *same* but *like*, and, following out the principle of homoeopathy, Belladonna is the most appropriate remedy to give, not when the child has eaten the berries, but when it has been exposed to contagion, or to some other cause of scarlet fever. According to experience, we know Belladonna to be the most successful means of restoring and of retaining health under such circumstances.[293]

---

293. George Lennox Moore, *Supplement to the Domestic Practice of Homoeopathy* (Manchester, UK: Henry Turner, 1858), 3–4.

It is probably unnecessary to point out to the reader that the central operative principle of homeopathy is a magical principle, not medical. The Three Initiates, as they chose to call themselves, coauthors of the 1908 esoteric work *The Kybalion*, set forth this magical principle in these terms: "This Principle embodies the truth that there is always a Correspondence between the laws and phenomena of the various planes of Being and Life. The old Hermetic axiom ran in these words: 'As above, so below; as below, so above.' And the grasping of this Principle gives one the means of solving many a dark paradox, and hidden secret of Nature." [294]

The quotation in the *Kybalion* is from the Emerald Tablet of Hermes Trismegistus, which is perhaps the best known of all alchemical texts. The complete quote in the Emerald Tablet reads: "What is below is like that which is above; and what is above is like that which is below: to accomplish the miracle of the one thing." [295]

It expresses a magic principle that I will call here the "principle of resonance." This is simply the observation by occultists that a thing that resembles another thing by appearance, function, or substance has a resonance with that other thing, and by affecting the first thing, the second thing can be affected. In magic this is an open principle, in that the nature of the effect produced is not limited—it may cause good or evil, may be used to heal or harm. This general principle forms the basis for what is known as natural magic, the magical use of herbs, stones, metals, and other natural substances to produce various effects.

An example of natural magic is the use of the bloodstone to stop bleeding. The bloodstone is a green stone with flecks of red in it that resemble droplets of blood. In natural magic, the stone is used to stop bleeding from a cut by holding the stone against the cut. Often a prayer or incantation is uttered as this is done. The stone, because it resembles blood, is assumed to have a resonance with blood, and therefore may be used to affect bleeding.

We see in this example the underlying principle of homeopathy. The stone itself appears to be bleeding. Bleeding is a disorder of the body. By holding the stone against a cut, the bleeding is stopped. Like cures like. The homeopath

---

294. Three Initiates, *The Kybalion* (Chicago, IL: The Yogi Publication Society, 1908), 28–29.

295. Agrippa, *Three Books of Occult Philosophy*, 711. This is my own wording of the Emerald Tablet in English, which varies slightly from other translations from the Arabic and Latin.

would argue that in his practice, real medicines are used that have a demonstrable physical effect on the human body, whereas the effect of the bloodstone on the body is occult and hypothetical. But is this true? Do the medicines administered by homeopaths have an actual physical effect on the body?

In homeopathic practice, a very small amount of a medicinal substance is diluted with a much larger amount of water, and the resulting liquid, which is almost entirely pure water with only the merest trace of medicinal substance in it, is administered to the patient as a medicine. The amount of active ingredient in these medicines is far too small, in and of itself, to have any noticeable chemical effect on the human body. This is the main reason modern medicine rejects homeopathy. Writes Moore, "In the practice of homoeopathy, the quantity of medicine administered in sickness is extremely small, in comparison with the considerable doses which it is the custom of the old method [of conventional medicine] to introduce into the body. Hence it has been inferred, that the cures and relief which are acknowledged to occur cannot be due to the action of minute doses, but rather to the influence of diet, faith, imagination, etc."[296]

However, if a ritual structure is used in the preparation of the homeopathic medicine, and if prayers are uttered over it, even if they are only expressed in the mind, which must often be the case, these prayers will act as an incantation to empower the medicine, magnifying the effect of the trace amounts of active agent it contains, and the process will become indistinguishable from enchantment.

My contention is that many of the practitioners of homeopathy are enchanting their potions, although most of them probably do not realize it. This explains how such a vanishingly small amount of an active ingredient, far too little to cause by itself a physical change, can sometimes have such a miraculous curative effect. This also explains why homeopathy has both miraculous successes and abject failures. If the medicine of homeopathy is rightly enchanted, it is imbued with curative power, but if there is no enchantment of the medicine, it is without efficacy.

The published works on homeopathy make little or no mention of the use of prayer. Indeed, they appear to strenuously avoid all references to reli-

---

296. Moore, *Supplement*, 5. The brackets are mine.

gion, presumably because their authors were sensitive to the possibility of their cures being dismissed as another brand of faith healing. Homeopaths in the nineteenth century were determined that their practices be recognized as science. This did not occur. Science has rejected homeopathy. Magic, on the other hand, holds no such prejudices. It is willing to embrace homeopathy as soon as homeopaths realize that what they have been doing is a kind of magic—specifically, the ancient art of enchantment.

Cutting and Enchanting Wands

It is the custom in magic to utter an incantation when cutting from a living tree a bough that will be used for magical purposes. By incantation it is set apart and made sacred. Such branches may be used for a variety of purposes. They may be inscribed with runes or other symbols; they may be burned in ritual fires and reduced to ash, and the ash used in magic operations; they may be made into wands through which magic force is focused; they may form that specialized type of wand, the divining rod.

In his biography of Pythagoras, Iamblichus makes mention of the enchanted arrow of the Hyperborean sage Abaris, a priest of Apollo, which the sage presented as a gift to Pythagoras:

> Passing therefore through Italy, and seeing Pythagoras, he especially assimilated him to the God of whom he was the priest. And believing that he was no other than the God himself, and that no man resembled him, but that he was truly Apollo...he gave Pythagoras a dart which he took with him when he left the [Hyperborean] temple, as a thing that would be useful to him in the difficulties that would befal him in so long a journey. For he was carried by it, in passing through inaccessible places, such as rivers, lakes, marshes, mountains, and the like, and performed through it, as it is said, lustrations, and expelled pestilence and winds [noxious airs] from the cities that requested him to liberate them from these evils.[297]

---

297. Iamblichus, *Life of Pythagoras*, 66–67. The square brackets are mine.

Abaris traveled to the far corners of the world with this arrow and, by some accounts, flew upon it.[298] The supposition that he was guided in his travels by the arrow has led to speculation that this may have been a crude magnetic compass, since a compass is a very easy thing to construct once the principles of its working are understood. It is only necessary to magnetize a needle, which can be done with a natural lodestone, and suspend the needle on the surface of water by coating it with grease so that it floats freely. The grease causes it to be supported on the water by surface tension. The needle will then rotate on the water and always point toward the magnetic north pole. However it seems more probable to me that the arrow was a wand in the shape of an arrow that had been enchanted. Iamblichus stated in the quote that Abaris used the arrow to expel pestilence. Indeed, Abaris was famed for having cured Sparta of the plague. Plato said of Abaris that he cured diseases by means of incantations.[299]

The magic wand, which is perhaps the best known of all the instruments of traditional European ritual magic, was cut from a living tree by the magician who would use it. The purpose of the wand was to project the will of the magician. There are various instructions for how it is to be cut and prepared. The procedure given in the *Key of Solomon*, one of the oldest of the grimoires, is surprisingly perfunctory. I will provide it from the translation of S. L. MacGregor Mathers, leader of the Hermetic Order of the Golden Dawn:

> The Staff...should be of elderwood, or cane, or rosewood; and the Wand...of hazel or nut tree, in all cases the wood being virgin, that is of one year's growth only. They should each be cut from the tree at a single stroke, on the day of Mercury, at sunrise. The characters shown should be written or engraved thereon in the day and hour of Mercury.
>
> This being done, thou shalt say:

---

298. "Abaris also you have heard of, whom Phoebos sped through the air perched on his winged roving arrow." Nonnos, *Dionysiaca* (11.132), trans. W. H. D. Rouse, vol. 1 (London: William Heinemann, 1911), 367.

299. Plato, *Charmides* (158c). Plato refers to the "charms of Zalmoxis or of Abaris the Hyperborean." *Plato in Twelve Volumes*, vol. 12, 25.

Adonai, Most Holy, deign to bless and to consecrate this Wand, and this Staff, that they may obtain the necessary virtue, through Thee, O Most Holy Adonai, whose kingdom endureth unto the Ages of the Ages. Amen.

After having perfumed and consecrated them, put them aside in a pure and clean place for use when required.[300]

The procedure for cutting and enchanting what is called the blasting rod (*verge foudroyante*) which is provided in the *Grand Grimoire* is considerably more elaborate. An illustration is given of the rod, which is shown to be forked on its end. In some editions of this work, the rod has the appearance of a dowsing rod. I will translate the procedure for cutting and enchanting this wand as it is given in the original French edition of this work. The quotation is a bit long, but it is instructive.

On the day before the great enterprise you will search out a wand or rod from a wild hazel tree that has not yet put forth fruit...the said rod having a fork at the top, which is to say, on the side with the two ends; its length should be nineteen and a half inches. After you find a wand of this shape, you will touch it only with your eyes, waiting until the following day of the action, when you will go and cut it exactly at the moment of sunrise. Then you will strip it of its leaves and small branches, if it has any, with the same steel blade that was used to cut the throat of the sacrifice, which will still be stained with its blood, assuming you have taken care not to wipe the blade. Start to cut the wand when the sun begins to appear above the horizon, while pronouncing the following incantation.

"I beseech you, O great Adonai, Elohim, Ariel, and Jehovah, to be favorable to me and to give to this wand

300. Mathers, trans., *The Key of Solomon the King*, 87.

that I cut the strength and the virtue of that of Jacob, of that of Moses, and that of the great Joshua; I also beseech you, O great Adonai, Elohim, Ariel, and Jehovah, to place into this wand all the strength of Samson, the righteous wrath of Emanuel, and the wrath of the great Zariatnatmik, who will avenge the injuries of men on the great day of judgment. Amen."

After having pronounced these great and terrible words, while continuing to look toward the rising sun, you will finish cutting your wand, and will take it into your chamber; then you will find a piece of wood the ends of which you will make the same thickness as the ends of the fork on the real wand, and you will take this to a blacksmith, for him to cap the ends of this rod with the steel from the blade you used to slit the throat of the sacrifice, taking care that he makes the caps a little pointed on their ends. The whole being thus executed, you will return home and you yourself fit the steel caps onto the forked end of the true wand. You will then take a lodestone and use it to magnetize the two caps on your wand, speaking the following words as you do so.

"By the power of great Adonai, Elohim, Ariel, and Jehovah, I command you to unite and attract all the things that I desire. By the power of great Adonai, Elohim, Ariel, and Jehovah, and by the incompatibility of fire and water, I command you to separate all things, as they were separated on the day of the creation of the world. Amen."

Then you will rejoice in the honor and glory of great Adonai, assured that you possess the greatest treasure of the Light.[301]

---

301. Antonio Venitiana del Rabina, *Le grand grimoire* (1202 [1750]), 14–18. My translation.

It is presumed by the author of this grimoire that the reader does not have the metalworking skills to fashion caps for the wand from the blade of the blood-stained sacrificial knife, so a substitute rod is taken to a blacksmith that has ends of a diameter similar to the forked ends of the wand. The blacksmith fits the sharp, or pointed, steel caps to this stick, and the magician then removes them and puts them on the forked end of his wand. The sacrifice referred to is the sacrifice of a "virgin kid"—a young goat, which is to be skinned with the knife, and the carcass wholly consumed by fire as a burnt offering to the spirits Adonai, Elohim, Ariel, and Jehovah.

The powers called upon are holy Hebrew names. Adonai and Elohim are names of God. Ariel is the name of an angel. Jehovah is probably intended to stand for the Tetragrammaton, IHVH, the greatest and most holy name of God. These names may have been associated by the anonymous author of the grimoire with the four quarters of the world—north, south, east, and west. It is not clear, however, how they should be assigned to the quarters from the text.

The Divining Rod

Traditionally the divining rod was a forked wand cut from a living tree that was used for various purposes, among them to locate fleeing criminals, lost or stolen items, hidden treasure, veins of metal ores, or water beneath the ground. It is for the last purpose that the divining rod is best known today, although five centuries ago it was used primarily by miners to find new lodes of gold, silver, copper, and tin. The rod was cut in a ritual way, and at the time of its cutting an incantation was spoken over it to set it apart and enchant it.

When the divining rod was adopted in Germany for the location of lodes and veins of metallic ore beneath the surface of the earth, its occult origins were shunned by the pious Christians who divined with it, and the manner of enchanting the rod was forgotten, or at least suppressed. Georgius Agricola (1494–1555) in his posthumously published 1556 Latin work *De re metallica* (*On the Nature of Metals*) made the following observation on this point:

> The wizards, who also make use of rings, mirrors and crystals, seek for veins with a divining rod shaped like a fork; but its shape makes no difference in the mat-

ter,—it might be straight or of some other form—for it is not the form of the twig that matters, but the wizard's incantations which it would not become me to repeat, neither do I wish to do so. The Ancients, by means of the divining rod, not only procured those things necessary for a livelihood or for luxury, but they were able also to alter the forms of things by it; as when the magicians changed the rods of the Egyptians into serpents, as the writings of the Hebrews relate; and as in Homer, Minerva with a divining rod turned the aged Ulysses suddenly into a youth and then restored him back again to old age; Circe also changed Ulysses' companions into beasts, but afterward gave them back again their human form; moreover, by his rod, which was called "Caduceus," Mercury gave sleep to watchmen and awoke slumberers. Therefore it seems that the divining rod passed to the mines from its impure origin with the magicians. Then when good men shrank with horror from incantations and rejected them, the twig was retained by the unsophisticated common miners, and in searching for new veins some traces of these ancient usages remain.[302]

Agricola was writing at a time when witches were being burned at the stake in Germany and surrounding European countries, so it is not surprising that those using the divining rod might want to distance themselves, at least publicly, from incantations and other magical arts. However, it is quite probable that incantations of various kinds were still being spoken over the rods at their cutting, if only secretly and under the breath. Arthur Jackson Ellis briefly observed on this matter, "Formerly incantations were used in connection with the divining rod."[303] John O'Neill wrote, "The divining-rod…was to be cut

302. Georgius Agricola, *De re metallica*, trans. Herbert Clark Hoover and Lou Henry Hoover (London: The Mining Magazine, 1912), 40–41.

303. Arthur Jackson Ellis, *The Divining Rod* (Washington, DC: Government Printing Office, 1917), 7.

with a single sweep of the knife on Mercury's day (Wednesday) at the planetary hour of Mercury. It was inscribed with certain characters and enchanted with a prayer, now lost to us."[304]

At least as old as the use of various rods and other devices to dowse for metal ores was their use for finding buried treasure. Samuel Sheppard wrote in his 1651 book of *Epigrams*:

> Some sorcerers do boast they have a Rod,
> Gather'd with Vowes and Sacrifice,
> And (borne about) will strangely nod
> To hidden treasure, where it lies;
> Mankind is (sure) that Rod Divine,
> For to the wealthiest (ever) they encline.[305]

The discovery of hidden treasure was arguably a more ancient use for the divining rod than the discovery of metallic ores. Divining for treasure was much practiced in England during the reign of Henry VIII. It was necessary to procure a license for this work, which was considered unsavory because it was understood that the treasure would be divined by occult means. In a note to appendix A of W. F. Barrett's extensive essay on the divining rod that appears in *Proceedings of the Society for Psychical Research* (volume 13, 1898), Barrett made mention of a man named Dowsing who was hired to find buried treasure by dowsing, and commented on the coincidence of the name.

> It is a curious coincidence that one *George Dowsing*, a
> schoolmaster of St. Faith's, near Norwich, used "magic"
> to find treasure in the early part of the reign of Henry
> VIII, (1521). A license had been given to Sir. R. Curzon
> to search for hidden treasure in Norfolk, and the aid of
> George Dowsing was sought, he being considered an
> expert "hill-digger," as those were called who searched
> for minerals and buried treasure, an uncanny occupation in those days. See Dr. Jessopp's *Random Roamings*,

---

304. John O'Neill, *The Night of the Gods*, vol. 1 (London: Bernard Quaritch, 1893), 53.

305. Samuel Sheppard, *Epigrams Theological, Philosophical, and Romantick* (London: Thomas Buckwell, 1651), 141.

> p. 103. Oddly enough, one of the very earliest uses of
> the divining rod was in the search for treasure.[306]

If we turn to Dr. Augustus Jessopp's *Random Roamings*, we find that Mr. Dowsing did not use a dowsing rod but a "glass," which is to say, a mirror, in which he perceived a spirit that guided him, but whether accurately or not is unrecorded. Another diviner who was present at this late-night undertaking, which took place at three in the morning and involved an occult ritual, raised a spirit in a "stone"—that is, a crystal.

> Before starting, a solemn council assembled and the
> necessary ceremonial was rehearsed "at Saunders' house
> in the market at Norwich," and then the schoolmaster
> "raised a spirit or two in a glass," and the parson of St.
> Gregory's "held the glass in his hand." Mr. Dowsing
> was not the only nor the most expeditious hierophant
> present, for the Rev. Robert Cromer "began and raised
> a spirit first." When the fellow Amylyon was examined
> on the subject he declared that when the Rev. Robert
> Cromer "held up a stone, he could not perceive any-
> thing thereby, but…that George Dowsing did areyse in
> a glass a little thing of *the length of an inch or thereabout*,
> but whether it was a spirit or a shadow he cannot tell,
> but…*George said it was a spirit*." [307]

It appears from this and other accounts from the period that the dowsing rod, although it was known at the time in various forms, was not as much employed for the finding of treasure as was the crystal globe or magic mirror, which were used to scry spirits. It was the spirits seen in these devices who pointed the way to the treasure.

---

306. W. F. Barrett, "On the So-Called Divining Rod, or Virgula Divina," in *Proceedings of the Society for Psychical Research*, vol. 13, part 32 (London: Kegan Paul, Trench, Trübner and Co., 1898), 261n2.

307. Augustus Jessopp, *Random Roaming and Other Papers* (London: T. Fisher Unwin, 1894), 106–7. Jessopp's italics. The quotations are from a judicial proceeding brought against the treasure hunters to investigate their practice, not of hunting for treasure, but of extorting money from others these rogues accused of treasure hunting without the proper license.

More than half a century after the events described in the quotation above, in October 1574, the Elizabethan astrologer and mathematician Dr. John Dee wrote to the Queen's counselor, Lord Burghley, seeking to obtain a license to explore for buried treasure, or as Dee put it, "Letters Patent to permit me to search for Threasor Throve and retain it for my use."[308] It appears between George Dowsing's day and that of John Dee, the use of the divining wand for treasure hunting had gained favor. Although Dee himself was not particularly psychic, he did have some talent in the use of the divining rod according to Dee's neighbor, Goodwife Faldo, whose mother cared for Dee at the end of his life. She told Dee's biographer John Aubrey, when he interviewed her in 1672, that Dee "did most miraculously have the divining power to find thynges that be missing and with his rod did bring back to manie persons silver and such objects which had been missing sometimes over yeres."[309]

According to Barrett, the first specific use in English of the term "dowsing rod" is in 1691, in the writings of the philosopher John Locke (who called it a "deusing rod").[310] Earlier references to the *virgula divina* may not have referred to the forked dowsing rod with which we are most familiar today but to other rods used in different forms of divination. But note that the modern dowsing rod has itself several different forms, is held in several different ways, and is even sometimes made of materials other than wood. The same was true in the sixteenth century. Agricola mentioned in the quotation from *De re metallica* given above that diviners also used "rings, mirrors and crystals" to dowse for ore, and said about the rod, "it is not the form of the twig that matters, but the wizard's incantations."

The preferred woods from which the divining rod was cut are the hazel, witch hazel (a different tree), the hawthorn, the blackthorn, the willow, and the pear tree. The rowan or mountain ash is also favored. "Among the many English names of the mountain ash, are witchen tree, witch elm, witch hazel, witch wood; quicken tree, quick beam (*quick* = alive, *beam* = German *baum*,

---

308. Richard Deacon, *John Dee* (London: Frederick Muller, 1968), 83.

309. Deacon, *John Dee*, 85.

310. W. F. Barrett, "On the So-Called Divining Rod, Book II," in *Proceedings of the Society for Psychical Research*, vol. 15, no. 38 (London: Kegan Paul, Trench, Trübner and Co., 1901), 135.

tree); roan tree, roun tree, rowan," writes Walter Kelly.[311] The rowan is said to have the power to turn aside the evil eye and ward off evil spirits. "It is dreaded by evil spirits; it renders null the spells of the witch, and has many other wondrous properties. The countryman will carry for years a piece of the wood in his pocket as a charm against *ill wish*, or as a remedy for his rheumatism."[312]

In Norway and Sweden, the first choice for a divining rod is the *flögrönn*, or fly-rowan. This is a rowan sapling that has grown from a seed dropped from the beak of a bird onto high place, where the plant has sprouted.

> When you find in the wood or elsewhere, on old walls or on high hills or rocks, a rowan which has grown out of a berry let fall from a bird's bill, you must go at twilight in the evening of the third day after our Lady's day, and either uproot or break off the said rod or tree; but you must take care that neither iron nor steel come nigh it, and that it do not fall to the ground on the way home. Then place the rod under the roof, at a spot under which you have laid sundry metals, and in a short time you will see with astonishment how the rod gradually bends under the roof towards the metals. When the rod has remained fourteen days or more in the same place, you take a knife or an awl which has been stroked with a magnet, and previously stuck through a great Frö-groda (?), slit the bark on all sides, and pour or drop in cock's blood, especially such as is drawn from the comb of a cock of one colour; and when this blood has dried, the rod is ready, and gives manifest proof of the efficacy of its wondrous nature.[313]

---

311. Walter K. Kelly, *Curiosities of Indo-European Tradition and Folk-Lore* (London: Chapman & Hall, 1863), 164–65.

312. Kelly, *Curiosities of Indo-European Tradition and Folk-Lore*, 163–64.

313. Kelly, *Curiosities of Indo-European Tradition and Folk-Lore*, 168–69. Quoted from Dybeck's *Runa* (Stockholm: P. A. Norstedt & Soner, 1842), 62.

The quotation above was translated by Walter Kelly from the Swedish of Richard Dybeck's *Runa*. Lady Day is the Feast of the Annunciation, March 25. Kelly did not know what a *frö-groda* might be and therefore did not translate the term but attached a question mark to it. Google Translate gives it as "seed frog." A reference in an 1873 book review by Felix Liebrecht is more enlightening. "Instead of *frögroda* it should be *frö* (*groda*): both words mean *frog* in Swedish, and the commoner expression *groda* is a parenthetical explanation of the rare form *frö*, which also means *seed*."[314] Therefore the awl is to be stuck through the body of a large frog before being magnetized, presumably with the frog's blood still upon it. A rod of the fly-rowan treated in this way is said to be potent for discovering hidden treasure. It is not clear from the passage whether the rod is to be forked. However, elsewhere Kelly makes the point that the wish rod or divining rod, which he treats as the same thing, is always to be forked on its end: "In every instance the divining or wish-rod has a forked end. This is an essential point, as all authorities agree in declaring."[315]

I am not nearly so sure that the wish rod and the divining rod were always the same thing. My impression is that the wish rod was a more general purpose instrument of magic used for protection and for blessing as well as for finding buried treasure. The divining rod had a narrower function, that of divining the whereabouts of things hidden or lost. I believe that the divining rod was more likely to be forked on its end than the wish rod, although there are examples of divining rods that are not forked and of wish-rods that are forked.

I will give one more general description of the cutting of the divining rod. Notice the similarities to the instructions in the *Grand Grimoire* for the cutting of the blasting rod, already quoted earlier in this chapter.

> "Ex quovis ligno non fit Mercurius:" it is not every
> forked hazel twig that is fit to make a divining-rod nor
> can so precious an instrument be manufactured at all

---

314. Felix Liebrecht, book review of Charles Hardwick's *Traditions, Superstitions and Folklore* (London: Simpkin, Marshall, and Co., 1872), in *The Academy* 4, no. 64 (January 15, 1873): 24.

315. Kelly, *Curiosities of Indo-European Tradition and Folk-Lore*, 171.

seasons and at a moment's notice....The success of such an operation is dependent upon many special conditions. It must always be performed after sunset and before sunrise, and only on certain nights, among which are specified those of Good Friday, Epiphany, Shrove Tuesday, St. John's day, the first night of a new moon or that preceding it. In cutting it one must face the east, so that the rod shall be one which catches the first rays of the morning sun; or, as some say, the eastern and western sun must shine through the fork of the rod, otherwise it will be good for nothing.[316]

Again in this description, nothing is said of the incantations that should be spoken when the divining rod is cut. Such incantations were kept secret or were spoken in a low tone or only whispered, and so have been lost. However, it is not too difficult to imagine what the general content should be. Sir James George Frazer gives one such incantation in his mammoth work *The Golden Bough*. It is highly Christianized, as was most of the magic used in Europe during the Middle Ages and Renaissance.

In Bavaria they say that the divining-rod should be cut from a hazel bush between eleven and twelve on St. John's Night, and that by means of it you can discover not only veins of metal and underground springs, but also thieves and murderers and unknown ways. In cutting it you should say, "God greet thee, thou noble twig! With God the Father I seek thee, with God the Son I find thee, and with the might of God the Holy Ghost I break thee. I adjure thee, rod and sprig, by the power of the Highest that thou show me what I order, and that as sure and clear as Mary the Mother of God was a pure virgin when she bare our Lord Jesus, in the

---

316. Kelly, *Curiosities of Indo-European Tradition and Folk-Lore*, 190–91.

name of God the Father, God the Son, and God the Holy Ghost, Amen!"[317]

St. John's Eve is June 23. From the text of this quotation we may gather that in Bavaria the rod was broken from the tree by hand, rather than cut with a knife. Frazer described another curious practice, that of baptizing the rod after it is taken from the tree. It is not overtly stated, but the name was applied, not to the twig of wood, but to the spirit assumed to reside within it that animated it.

> In the Tyrol the divining-rod ought to be cut at new moon, but may be cut either on St. John's Day or Twelfth Night. Having got it you baptize it in the name of one of the Three Holy Kings according to the purpose for which you intend to use it: if the rod is to discover gold, you name it Caspar; if it is to reveal silver, you call it Balthasar; and if it is to point out hidden springs of water, you dub it Melchior.[318]

Twelfth Night, also known as Epiphany Eve, is on January 5. I believe the practice of naming magic wands of all kinds was widespread, even though there is scant mention of it in texts on the subject. The names were not restricted to the three kings who came to the Christ child in Bethlehem but were as diverse as the names applied by witches to their familiar spirits, or imps, which resided in animals such as cats and dogs but also in inanimate objects such as mirrors and rings.

Below I will compose a set of incantations that may be used in the harvesting, preparation, and employment of a divining rod. These are intended as a general guide, to illustrate the points that should be addressed when cutting and shaping a rod or wand for any magical purpose.

---

317. James George Frazer, *The Golden Bough*, 3rd ed., vol. 11, "Part 7, Balder the Beautiful, Vol. 2" (London: Macmillan and Co., 1913), 67–68.

318. Frazer, *The Golden Bough*, vol. 11, 68.

Incantations for Enchanting a Divining Rod

The wand should be selected by eye during the day, prior to the night of its cutting, so that you know exactly which branch you will cut and how you will reach the branch in the darkness. Ideally, the wand will grow high on the tree, and the forked end will grow upright in such a way that when you stand facing the east, you can (if the angle is right) see the eastern sun through the fork of the wand. This means that the two upper branches of the wand will incline to the north and south.

The selection of the wand is a compromise. There is no point in selecting a branch that you cannot reach. It should be as high above the ground as possible, yet still within easy cutting distance. It should be as upright as possible, but it does not need to be perfectly upright. The wand should be around the thickness of a pencil. It must be springy when you use it to dowse, but if it is too thin it won't have sufficient spring. On the other hand, if it is too thick, a weak impulse may not be sufficient to turn the dowsing rod downward. Agricola wrote, "The force of the veins can not turn too large a stick." [319]

The best season of the year to cut a wand is said by some to be winter, but as you can see from the quotations above, opinion varied on this point. Different advice was also given in the literature regarding the best time of night and the ideal day of the lunar cycle to cut the wand. I suggest the wand be cut during the first half of the waxing phase of the moon, at the moment of sunrise, so that the rays of the sun shine through the cleft of the wand as you are cutting it. The base of the wand should be struck through using a single blow from a sword or long knife. By some accounts, it is better to break the wand off by hand so that steel does not touch it. The thinking behind this is that steel, which is derived from iron, is antagonistic to spirits and drives them away, and you do not wish to drive away the spirit that will reside in your wand.

As you cut or break away the forked branch from the tree, speak this incantation, or something like it:

> In the name of Apollo, god of the sun,
> In the name of Hecate, goddess of the moon,
> I receive this bough and the life within it

319. Agricola, *De re metallica*, 39.

From the living tree that bore it.
I dedicate this branch to the high arts
And swear before goddess and god
It shall never be dishonored or defiled.

I have used the Greek gods Apollo and Hecate as deities of the sun and moon, but you may wish to use other names of solar and lunar deities. In this incantation, we receive the living bough humbly as a gift from the tree that bore it, under the gaze of sun and moon, and dedicate it in a general way to the art of magic, swearing to use it rightly and protect it from defilement. Be aware when you speak these words that the wand you are cutting is now a sacred thing, imbued with the power of the sun and the moon.

Carry the wand to a private place where you can work to prepare it, taking care never to allow the wand to touch or rest on the ground. The end must be trimmed and the fork cut to equal length on both sides. In the preparation a knife may be used. The shape is roughly that of the wishbone of a turkey. The sides of the fork, which will be held in the hands, are usually (though not always) longer than the main stem, which will project forward while dowsing. Overall length is a matter of convenience and personal preference, but you will probably want a wand that is approximately eighteen to twenty inches (around forty-five to fifty centimeters) in length. After you cut a few wands, you will find the length that suits you best.

The leaves, if any, should be stripped from the sides, but I recommend leaving the bark in place, as it traps the fresh sap against the wood. A dowsing wand is not a permanent instrument. It was believed by some practitioners of this art that after a few days, the sap dried up and the occult virtue gradually left the wand. This required the dowser to regularly cut fresh wands. Some dowsers regard this as only a superstition and continue to use wands in which the sap has long since dried up. You will find what works best for you through trial and error. If your dowsing rod seems to be losing its effectiveness, cut a fresh rod.

You may wish to name your rod. Kelly wrote, "In the Oberpfalz, immediately after the wish-rod is cut, it is baptised and given a name, and three signs of the cross are made over it with the hand." [320] If you decide to baptize your

---

320. Kelly, *Curiosities of Indo-European Tradition and Folk-Lore*, 171.

rod, fill a pan with cool, clean water. Dip the forked end of the wand in the water and shake it dry with three shakes. Speak these words:

> Holy and most blessed rod,
> I cleanse and name thee _____.
> By this name I shall know thee,
> By this name you shall serve me.

The name is to be kept secret. Speak it to no other person. Do not write it down. When you wish to awaken the power of the divining rod and the spirit that dwells with it, speak its name by holding it close to your lips, so that no other person can hear what you have spoken.

Conclusion

We have reached the end of our journey of discovery, which began with the innate potency inherent in the breath that issues from the lips and progressed through the significance and power of vowel sounds, various methods for composing effective incantations, the use of barbarous words of power and the names of God, esoteric technique of vibrating the voice to magnify its force, ways to control the wind and to use of knots to bind and release it, healing incantations, love enchantments, charms of protection, maledictions, and finally enchantments of objects and human beings.

The scope of voice magic is so vast that no single book could hope to cover it all. What I have presented is an overview of the importance of the human breath and its articulation throughout the history of Western occultism. The paradox inherent in this effort is that no spoken incantation, no chant or song, has survived to us from ancient times. Until the late nineteenth century, the human voice could not be recorded, and recordings of incantations are still surprisingly scanty, because magicians guard their secrets with care. We have only written descriptions of the ways the voice was used in magic by the enchanters of ancient Sumer, Egypt, Greece, and Rome, along with occasional written records of the actual words used.

A large portion of modern magic is still based on the power of the breath. It is the living, vitalizing heart of magic, not only of the Western world but in the magic of the East as well. Magicians compose spells in their minds and record them in written form. The grimoires are filled with such rituals, prayers, invocations, and evocations. But it is only when these spells are enacted, and the words of power are vocalized on the living breath, that they awaken. The voice links mind to body. It carries what exists in potential in the imagination outward on the breath to the material world and projects it through the nesting levels of reality known as the astral planes.

It is highly significant that the first creative act of God recorded in the Bible is when God breathed upon the waters of chaos and made them ripple. You do not need to be Jewish or Christian to understand the significance of this symbolism for practical magic. When we work magic, we create from the stuff of our minds and then project our creation on our breath outward to realize the force of our creation in the material universe. In speaking incantations, we imitate the primary creative act of God. Reflect on this, and you will realize how vitally important the voice is for the effective practice of magic.

Bibliography

Abbott, John. *The Keys of Power: A Study of Indian Ritual and Belief.* London: Methuen & Co., 1932.

Abercromby, John. *The Pre- and Proto-historic Finns Both Eastern and Western, with the Magic Songs of the West Finns.* 2 vols. London: David Nutt, 1898.

Abusch, Tzvi. *Further Studies on Mesopotamian Witchcraft Beliefs and Literature.* Leiden: Brill, 2000.

Ady, Thomas. *A Perfect Discovery of Witches, Shewing the Divine Cause of the Distractions of this Kingdome, and Also of the Christian World.* London: R. I., 1661.

Aelian. *On the Characteristics of Animals.* Translated by A. F. Scholfield. 3 vols. Cambridge, MA: Harvard University Press, 1959.

Agricola, Georgius. *De re metallica.* Translated by Herbert Clark Hoover and Lou Henry Hoover. London: *The Mining Magazine,* 1912.

Agrippa, Henry Cornelius. *Three Books of Occult Philosophy.* Edited by Donald Tyson. St. Paul, MN: Llewellyn Publications, 1992.

Albertus. *The Secrets of Albertus Magnus: Of the Vertues of Herbs, Stones, and Certain Beasts.* London: M. H. and J. M, [1691].

Anonymous. *Everybody's Book of Luck*. Racine, WI: Whitman Publishing, [c. 1900].

Anonymous. *Extract from an Unpublished Manuscript on Shaker History*. Boston: E. K. Allen, 1850.

Anonymous. *Jack the Giant-Killer: Being the History of All His Wonderful Exploits Against the Giants*. Glasgow: J. Lumsden & Son, [c. 1815].

Anonymous. *Mother Shipton's Gipsy Fortune Teller and Dream Book, with Napoleon's Oraculum*. New York: Henry J. Wehman, 1890.

Anonymous. "*Bacon's Essays, with Annotations*. By Richard Whately, D.D., Archbishop of Dublin. London, 1856." *North British Review*, August 1857.

Anonymous. *The Surprizing Life and Death of Doctor John Faustus*. London: Printed and sold by the booksellers, 1727.

Anonymous. *The Universal Fortune Teller, Being Sure and Certain Directions for Discovering the Secrets of Futurity*. London: W. S. Fortey, [c. 1860].

Anonymous. *The Wonderful History of Virgilius, the Sorcerer of Rome*. London: David Nutt in the Strand, 1893.

Apollonius Rhodius. *The Argonautica*. Translated by R. C. Seaton. London: William Heinemann, 1912.

Ashby, W. H. Letter reprinted in *The Folk-Lore Journal* 5, no. 2 (April–June 1887).

Bacon, Francis. *Bacon's Essays with Annotations by Richard Whately, D. D. and Notes and a Glossarial Index by Franklin Fiske Heard*. Boston: Lee and Shepard, 1875.

Barker, E. H. *Lempriere's Classical Dictionary, Abridged for Public and Private Schools of Both Sexes*. Edited by Joseph Cauvin. London: Longman, Brown, Green, and Longmans, 1843.

Barnstone, Willis, and Marvin Meyer, eds. *The Gnostic Bible*. Boston: Shambhala, 2003.

Barrett, W. F. "On the So-Called Divining Rod, or Virgula Divina." In *Proceedings of the Society for Psychical Research*, vol. 13, no. 32. London: Kegan Paul, Trench, Trübner and Co., 1898.

———. "On the So-Called Divining Rod, Book II." In *Proceedings of the Society for Psychical Research*, vol. 15, no. 38. London: Kegan Paul, Trench, Trübner and Co., 1901.

Barthélemy, Jean Jacques. "Remarques sur les médailles d'Antonin frappées en Egypte." In *Oeuvres de J. J. Barthélemy*. Vol. 4. Paris: A. Berlin, Bossange Père et Fils, Bossange Frères, 1821.

Baudet, Louis. *Préceptes Médicaux de Serenus Sammonicus*. Paris: C. L. F. Panckoucke, 1845.

Bayle, Marc Antoine. *The Pearl of Antioch: A Picture of the East at the End of the Fourth Century*. Baltimore, MD: Kelly, Piet and Company, 1871.

Bell, Hesketh J. *Obeah: Witchcraft in the West Indies*. 2nd ed. London: Sampson Low, Marston & Company, 1893.

Betz, Hans Dieter, ed. *The Greek Magical Papyri in Translation, Including the Demotic Spells*. 2nd ed. Chicago: University of Chicago Press, 1992.

Bilimoria, Nasarvanji F. *Zoroastrianism in the Light of Theosophy*. Bombay: Blavatsky Lodge, Theosophical Society, 1898.

Bischoff, Erich. *Die Kabbalah: Einführung in die jüdische Mystik und Geheimwissenschaft*. Leipzig: Th. Grieben's Verlag (L. Fernau), 1903.

Black, George F. *Scottish Charms and Amulets*. Edinburgh, Scotland: Neill and Company, 1894.

Bloomfield, Maurice, trans. *Hymns of the Atharva-Veda, Together with Extracts from the Ritual Books and the Commentaries*. Oxford: Clarendon Press, 1897.

Boorman, John, dir. *Excalibur*. Warner Brothers, 1981. Blu-ray disc.

Bouisson, Maurice. *Magic: Its Rites and History*. Translated by G. Almayrac. London: Rider & Company, 1960.

Brooke, Stopford Augustus. *The History of Early English Literature: Being the History of English Poetry from Its Beginnings to the Accession of King Ælfred*. New York: Macmillan and Co., 1892.

Budge, E. A. Wallis. *Amulets and Superstitions*. London: Humphrey Milford, 1930.

———. *Egyptian Magic*. 2nd printing. London: Kegan Paul, Trench, Trübner & Co., 1901.

———. *The Gods of the Egyptians*. 2 vols. London: Methuen & Co., 1904.

———. *The History of Alexander the Great: Being the Syriac Version of the Pseudo-Callisthenes*. Cambridge: University Press, 1889.

——. *The Life and Exploits of Alexander the Great: Being A Series of Translations of the Ethiopic Histories of Alexander by the Pseudo-Callisthenes and Other Writers, with Introduction, Etc.* London: C. J. Clay and Sons, 1896.

Bulwer-Lytton, Edward. *The Coming Race*. Edinburgh, Scotland: William Blackwood and Sons, 1871.

Cannon, Walter B. "Voodoo Death." *American Anthropologist, New Series* 44, no. 2 (April–June 1942): 169–81.

Carmichael, Alexander, ed. *Carmina Gadelica: Hymns and Incantations*. 3 vols. Edinburgh, Scotland, 1900.

Carroll, Lewis [Charles Lutwidge Dodgson]. *The Hunting of the Snark: An Agony in Eight Fits*. Illustrated by Henry Holiday. London: Macmillan and Co., 1876.

——. *Through the Looking-Glass, and What Alice Found There*. London: Macmillan and Co., 1872.

Chambers, Robert. *Popular Rhymes of Scotland*. New ed. Edinburgh, Scotland: W. & R. Chambers, 1870.

Clodd, Edward. *Magic in Names and in Other Things*. New York: E. P. Dutton & Company, 1921.

Clouston, W. A. *Popular Tales and Fictions: Their Migrations and Transformations*. 2 vols. Edinburgh, Scotland: William Blackwood and Sons, 1887.

Colles, Abraham. "A Witches' Ladder." *The Folk-Lore Journal* 5, no. 1 (January–March 1887): 1–5.

The Compact Edition of the Oxford English Dictionary. Edited by J. A. Simpson and E. S. C Weiner. 2 vols. Oxford: Oxford University Press, 1971.

Cooke, William. *The Pope's Curse Turned into a Blessing: or, Popery Convicted by the Logic of Facts*. London: H. Webber, [1868].

Cornford, Francis Macdonald. *From Religion to Philosophy: A Study in the Origins of Western Speculation*. London: Edward Arnold, 1912.

Crowley, Aleister, ed. *The Lesser Key of Solomon. Goetia. The Book of Evil Spirits*. Chicago: De Laurence, 1916.

Crowley, Aleister. *Liber AL vel Legis: Sub Figura CCXX as Delivered by XCIII = 418 to DCLXVI [The Book of the Law]*. South Stukely, Quebec: 93 Publishing, 1975.

Curtin, Jeremiah. *Tales of the Fairies and of the Ghost World: Collected from Oral Tradition in South-West Munster*. Boston: Little, Brown & Company, 1895.

Daniels, Cora Linn, and Charles McClellan Stevans, eds. *Encyclopaedia of Superstitions, Folklore, and the Occult Sciences of the World*. 3 vols. Chicago: J. H. Yewdale & Sons Co., 1903.

Davies, Owen, ed. *The Oxford Illustrated History of Witchcraft and Magic*. Oxford: Oxford University Press, 2017.

Deacon, Richard. *John Dee: Scientist, Geographer, Astrologer and Secret Agent to Elizabeth I*. London: Frederick Muller, 1968.

Dee, John. *Compendious Rehearsal*. In *Autobiographical Tracts of Dr. John Dee*, edited by James Crossley. Chetham Society, 1851.

Defoe, Daniel. *A Journal of the Plague Year: Being Observations or Memorials, of the Most Remarkable Occurrences, as Well Publick as Private, Which Happened in London during the Last Great Visitation in 1665*. London: E. Nutt, J. Roberts, A. Dodd, & J. Graves, 1722.

Del Reo, Martin. *Disqvisitionvm Magicarvm Libri Sex, In Tres Tomos Partiti*. Lovanii: Ex Officina Gerardirivii, 1599.

Demetrius of Tarsus. *Demetrius on Style*. Translated by William Rhys Roberts. Cambridge: Cambridge University Press, 1902.

Dybeck, Richard. *Runa*. Stockholm: P. A. Norstedt & Soner, 1842.

Edinburgh Encyclopaedia. Vol. 9. Edinburgh, Scotland: William Blackwood, 1830.

Ellis, Arthur Jackson. *The Divining Rod: A History of Water Witching*. Washington, DC: Government Printing Office, 1917.

Elworthy, Frederick Thomas. *The Evil Eye: An Account of the Ancient & Widespread Superstition*. London: John Murray, 1895.

Ernulfus. *The Popes Dreadfull Curse: Being the Form of an Excommunication of the Church of Rome. Taken out of the Leger-Book of the Church of Rochester Now in the Custody of the Dean and Chapter There. Writ by Ernulfus the Bishop*. London: L. C. on Ludgate-Hill, 1681.

Evans-Pritchard, E. E. *Witchcraft, Oracles and Magic among the Azande.* Oxford: Clarendon Press, 1937.

Famin, Stanislas Marie César. *The Royal Museum at Naples: Being Some Account of the Erotic Paintings, Bronzes, and Statues Contained in That Famous "Cabinet Secret."* London: Privately printed, 1871.

Faraone, Christopher A. *Ancient Greek Love Magic.* Cambridge, MA: Harvard University Press, 1999.

Faraone, Christopher A., and Dirk Obbink, eds. *Magika Hiera: Ancient Greek Magic and Religion.* Oxford: Oxford University Press, 1991.

Folkard, Richard. *Plant Lore, Legends and Lyrics: Embracing the Myths, Traditions, Superstitions and Folk-Lore of the Plant Kingdom.* London: Sampson Low, Marston, Searle and Rivington, 1884.

Frazer, James George. *The Golden Bough.* 3rd ed. 12 volumes. London: Macmillan and Co., 1906–15.

Frazer, James George. "A Witches' Ladder." *The Folk-Lore Journal* 5, no. 2 (April–June 1887): 81–84.

Gager, John G., ed. *Curse Tablets and Binding Spells from the Ancient World.* Oxford: Oxford University Press, 1992.

Garrison, Fielding H. *An Introduction to the History of Medicine: With Medical Chronology.* 2nd ed. Philadelphia: W. B. Saunders Company, 1917.

Geoffrey of Monmouth. *The British History.* Translated by Aaron Thompson. London: J. Bowyer, 1718.

Gersh, Stephen. *From Iamblichus to Eriugena: An Investigation of the Prehistory and Evolution of the Pseudo-Dionysian Tradition.* Leiden: E. J. Brill, 1978.

Gilbert, Scott F., and Ziony Zevit. "Congenital Human Baculum Deficiency: The Generative Bone of Genesis 2:21–23." *American Journal of Medical Genetics* 101, no. 3 (May 2001): 284–85. doi:https://doi.org/10.1002/ajmg.1387.

Godwin, Joscelyn. *The Mystery of the Seven Vowels in Theory and Practice.* Grand Rapids, MI: Phanes Press, 1991.

Godwin, William. *Lives of the Necromancers: or, an Account of the Most Eminent Persons in Successive Ages, Who Have Claimed for Themselves, or to Whom Has Been Imputed by Others, the Exercise of Magical Power.* London: Frederick J. Mason, 1834.

Gomme, George Laurence, ed. *Mother Bunch's Closet Newly Broke Open, and the History of Mother Bunch of the West.* London: Printed for the Villon Society, 1885.

Greene, James B. "Approaches to Breath Support and Control." Master's thesis, Kansas State University, 1968.

Grendon, Felix. "The Anglo-Saxon Charms." *The Journal of American Folk-Lore* 22 (April–June 1909): 105–237.

Grimm, Jacob. *Deutsche Grammatik.* Vol. 1. Göttingen, Germany: Dieterich-schen Buchhandlung, 1819.

Haddon, Alfred Cort. *Magic and Fetishism.* London: Archibald Constable & Co., 1906.

Halliwell, James Orchard. *Popular Rhymes and Nursery Tales: A Sequel to the Nursery Rhymes of England.* London: John Russell Smith, 1849.

Harms, Daniel, ed. *The Long-Lost Friend: A 19th Century American Grimoire.* Woodbury, MN: Llewellyn Publications, 2012.

Heckethorn, Charles William. *Lincoln's Inn Fields and the Localities Adjacent: Their Historical and Topographical Associations.* London: Elliot Stock, 1896.

Hesiod. *Theogony.* In *Hesiod, the Homeric Hymns and Homerica.* Translated by Hugh G. Evelyn-White. London: William Heinemann, 1920.

Hohman, John George. *The Long Lost Friend: or, Faithful & Christian Instructions Containing Wonderous and Well-Tried Arts & Remedies, for Man as Well as Animals.* Harrisburg, PA, 1850.

Homer. *The Odyssey.* Translated by A. T. Murray. 2 vols. London: William Heinemann, 1919.

Howell, W., and R. Shelford. "A Sea-Dyak Love Philtre." *Journal of the Anthropological Institute of Great Britain and Ireland* 34 (1904): 207–10.

Hunt, Edward Eyre, ed. *Sir Orfeo.* Cambridge: Harvard Coöperative Society, 1909.

Hurd, William. *A New Universal History of the Religious Rites, Ceremonies and Customs of the Whole World*. Manchester: J. Gleave, 1811.

Iamblichus. *Iamblichus' Life of Pythagoras, or Pythagoric Life*. Translated by Thomas Taylor. London: A. J. Valpy, 1818.

———. *The Theology of Arithmetic: On the Mystical, Mathematical, and Cosmological Symbolism of the First Ten Numbers*. Translated by Robin Waterfield. Grand Rapids, MI: Phanes Press, 1988.

Irenaeus. *Against Heresies*. In vol. 1, *The Ante-Nicene Fathers*. Edited by Alexander Roberts and James Donaldson. New York: Charles Scribner's Sons, 1903.

James I. *The Demonology of King James I*. Edited by Donald Tyson. Woodbury, MN: Llewellyn Publications, 2011.

Jessopp, Augustus. *Random Roaming and Other Papers*. London: T. Fisher Unwin, 1894.

John Lydus. *On the Months*. Translated by Mischa Hooker. 2nd ed. Self-published, 2017.

Johnson, Samuel. *A Dictionary of the English Language*. 2 vols. London: W. Strahan, 1755.

Jones, John. *Medical, Philosophical and Vulgar Errors, of Various Kinds, Considered and Refuted*. London: T. Cadell Jun. and W. Davies, 1797.

Jordan, D. R. "Two Inscribed Lead Tablets from a Well in the Atheirian Kerameikos." *Mitteilungen des deutschen archaologischen Instituts, Atheirische Abteilung* 95 (1980): 225–39.

Keightley, Thomas. *The Fairy Mythology*. 2 vols. London: William Harrison Ainsworth, 1828.

Kelly, Walter K. *Curiosities of Indo-European Tradition and Folk-Lore*. London: Chapman & Hall, 1863.

Kieckhefer, Richard. *Forbidden Rites: A Necromancer's Manual of the Fifteenth Century*. University Park: Pennsylvania State University Press, 1998.

Kilpatrick, Jack Frederick, and Anna Gritts Kilpatrick. *Walk in Your Soul: Love Incantations of the Oklahoma Cherokees*. Dallas, TX: Southern Methodist University Press, 1965.

King, Francis. *Modern Ritual Magic: The Rise of Western Occultism.* London: Neville Spearman Limited, 1970. Reprint, Bridport, Dorset, England: Prism Press, 1989.

Kirk, Robert. *The Secret Commonwealth of Elves, Fauns & Fairies: A Study in Folk-Lore & Psychical Research.* London: David Nutt, 1893.

Kramer, Heinrich. *Malleus Maleficarum.* Translated by Montague Summers. Suffolk, UK: John Rodker, 1928.

Latimer, Charles. *The Divining Rod: Virgula Divina—Baculus Divinatorius (Water-Witching.).* Cleveland, OH: Fairbanks, Benedict and Co., 1876.

Leland, Charles Godfrey. *Etruscan Roman Remains in Popular Tradition.* London: T. Fisher Unwin, 1892.

———. *The Gypsies.* 5th ed. Boston: Houghton, Mifflin and Company, 1888.

Leonard, Arthur Glyn. *The Lower Niger and Its Tribes.* London: Macmillan and Co., 1906.

Liebrecht, Felix. Book review of Charles Hardwick's *Traditions, Superstitions and Folklore.* London: Simpkin, Marshall, and Co., 1872. In *The Academy* 4, no. 64, (January 15, 1873): 24.

Lovelock, James. *Gaia: A New Look at Life on Earth.* Oxford: Oxford University Press, 2000.

Lucan. *The Pharsalia of Lucan.* Translated by H. T. Riley. London: Henry G. Bohn, 1853.

———. *The Pharsalia of Lucan.* Translated by Edward Ridley. London: Longmans, Green, and Co., 1896.

Maitland, Samuel Roffey. *The Dark Ages.* London: J. G. F. & J. Rivington, 1844.

Malory, Thomas. *Le Morte d'Arthur.* 2 vols. London: J. M. Dent & Sons, 1906.

Mather, Cotton. *Magnalia Christi Americana: or, the Ecclesiastical History of New-England.* London: Thomas Parkhurst, 1702.

Mather, Increase. *Remarkable Providences Illustrative of the Earlier Days of American Colonisation.* London: John Russell Smith, 1856.

Mathers, Samuel Liddell MacGregor, trans. *The Key of Solomon the King (Clavicula Salomonis).* London: George Redway, 1889.

Maxwell-Stuart, Peter, and José Manuel Garcia Valverde, eds. and trans. *Investigations into Magic, an Edition and Translation of Martin Del Rio's Disquisitionum magicarum libri sex.* 6 vols. Vol. 2. Leiden: Koninklijke Brill, 2023.

Mead, George Robert Stow. "A Kabbalistic Catechism." *The Theosophical Review* 34 (April 15, 1904): 183–86.

Metzger, Bruce M. *Manuscripts of the Greek Bible: An Introduction to Greek Paleography.* Corrected ed. Oxford: Oxford University Press, 1991.

Michaele, Miss, and Professor Charles Porterfield. *Hoodoo Bible Magic: Sacred Secrets of Scriptural Sorcery.* Forestville, CA: Missionary Independent Spiritual Church, 2014.

Middleton, Erasmus. *Evangelical Biography: Being a Complete and Faithful Account of the Lives, Sufferings, Experiences & Happy Deaths of Eminent Christians.* 3 vols. London: J. Stratford, 1807.

Moore, George Lennox. *Supplement to the Domestic Practice of Homoeopathy.* Manchester, UK: Henry Turner, 1858.

Nassau, Robert Hamill. *Fetichism in West Africa: Forty Years' Observation of the Native Customs and Superstitions.* New York: Charles Scribner's Sons, 1904.

Nonnos. *Dionysiaca.* Translated by W. H. D. Rouse. Vol. 1. London: William Heinemann, 1911.

O'Donnell, Elliott. *Famous Curses.* London: Skeffington & Son, 1929.

Oliver, George. *The Pythagorean Triangle; or, The Science of Numbers.* London: John Hogg & Co., 1875.

O'Neill, John. *The Night of the Gods: An Inquiry into Cosmic and Cosmogonic Mythology and Symbolism.* Vol. 1. London: Bernard Quaritch, 1893.

———. *The Night of the Gods: An Inquiry into Cosmic and Cosmogonic Mythology and Symbolism.* Vol. 2. London: David Nutt, 1897.

Origen. *Origen Against Celsus.* In vol. 4, *The Ante-Nicene Fathers.* Edited by Alexander Roberts and James Donaldson. New York: Charles Scribner's Sons, 1907.

Osborn, Robert Durie. *Islam under the Arabs.* London: Longmans, Green, and Co., 1876.

Ovid. *Ovid's Epistles: with His Amours.* London: Printed for T. Davies, W. Strahan, W. Clarke et al., 1776.

Paget, Richard. *Babel: or, The Past, Present, and Future of Human Speech.* London: Kegan Paul, Trench, Trubner & Co., 1930.

———. *Human Speech: Some Observations, Experiments, and Conclusions as to the Nature, Origin, Purpose and Possible Improvement of Human Speech.* London: Kegan Paul, Trench, Trubner & Co., 1930.

Parry, Glyn. *The Arch-Conjuror of England, John Dee.* New Haven, CT: Yale University Press, 2011.

Pazig, Christianus. *A Treatyse of Magic Incantations.* Edited by Edmund Goldsmid. Edinburgh, Scotland, 1886.

Phelps, Guy Fitch. *The Black Prophet.* Cincinnati, OH: Standard Publishing Company, 1916.

Philostratus. *The Life of Apollonius of Tyana: The Epistles of Apollonius and the Treatise of Eusebius.* 2 vols. London: William Heinemann, 1912.

Pitcairn, Robert. *Ancient Criminal Trials in Scotland.* 3 vols. Edinburgh, Scotland: Bannatyne Club, 1833.

Plato. *Timaeus.* In *Plato in Twelve Volumes.* Vol. 9, *Timaeus, Critias, Cleitophon, Menexenus, Epistles.* Translated by R. G. Bury. London: William Heinemann, 1929.

Plato. *Charmides.* In *Plato in Twelve Volumes.* Vol. 12, *Charmides, Alcibiades I and II, Hipparchus, The Lovers, Theages, Minor, Epinomis.* Translated by W. R. M Lamb. London: William Heinemann, 1927.

Pliny the Elder. *The Natural History of Pliny.* Translated by John Bostock and H. T. Riley. 6 vols. London: Henry G. Bohn, 1855–57.

———. *Natural History, with an English Translation in Ten Volumes.* Vols. 3 and 4. Translated by H. Rackham. London: William Heinemann; Cambridge, MA: Harvard University Press, 1940–45.

Plutarch. *Plutarch's Morals.* Edited by William W. Goodwin. 5 vols. Boston: Little, Brown, and Company, 1878.

Potter, John. *Archaeologia Graeca: or, The Antiquities of Greece.* New ed. London: Thomas Tegg & Son, 1837.

Quinn, Bernard L. *Papal Curses: A Lecture by Father Quinn, Formerly Priest of the Roman Catholic Church, Delivered in New York City, April, 1880.* Cleveland: Leader Printing Company, 1881.

Regardie, Israel, ed. *Gems from the Equinox: Instructions by Aleister Crowley for His Own Magical Order.* Tempe, AZ: New Falcon Publications, 1974.

Regardie, Israel. *The Golden Dawn: The Original Account of the Teachings, Rites & Ceremonies of the Hermetic Order.* 6th ed. St. Paul, MN: Llewellyn Publications, 1989.

———. *The Tree of Life: A Study of Magic.* New York: Samuel Weiser, 1969.

Rhys, John. "Welsh Fairies." *The Nineteenth Century: A Monthly Review* 30 (October 1891): 564–74.

Roth, Walter Edmund. *Ethnological Studies Among the North-West-Central Queensland Aborigines.* Brisbane: Edmund Gregory, 1897.

Royal MS 12 E XXIII, British Library, London.

Sammonicus, Quintus Serenus. *De medicina praecepta saluberrima.* Leipzig: I. G. Mülleriano, 1786.

Sayce, Archibald Henry. "The Sacred Books of Chaldaea." In *Lectures on the Origin and Growth of Religion as Illustrated by the Religion of the Ancient Babylonians.* London: Williams and Norgate, 1887.

Schaff, Philip. *History of the Apostolic Church with a General Introduction to Church History.* Translated by Edward D. Yeomans. New York: Charles Scribner, 1857.

Scheible, Johann, ed. *The Sixth and Seventh Books of Moses; or, Moses' Magical Spirit-Art, Known as the Wonderful Arts of the Old Wise Hebrews, Taken from the Mosaic Books of the Cabala and the Talmud, for the Good of Mankind.* New York, 1880.

Scott, Walter. "Fairy Tales, or the Lilliputian Cabinet, Containing Twenty-Four Choice Pieces of Fancy and Fiction, Collected by Benjamin Tabart." *The Quarterly Review* 21 (January & April 1819): 91–112.

———. *Letters on Demonology and Witchcraft, Addressed to J. G. Lockhart, Esq.* London: John Murray, 1830.

———. "Of the Fairies of Popular Superstition." In *Minstrelsy of the Scottish Border.* 2 vols. Kelso, Scotland: James Ballantyne, 1802.

Selig, Godfrey. *Secrets of the Psalms*. Arlington, TX: Dorene Publishing Co., 1982.

Shah, Idries. *Oriental Magic*. New York: E. P. Dutton & Co., 1973.

Sheppard, Samuel. *Epigrams Theological, Philosophical, and Romantick*. London: Thomas Buckwell, 1651.

Simpson, Jacqueline, and Steve Roud, eds. *A Dictionary of English Folklore*. New York: Oxford University Press, 2000.

Simpson, W. Sparrow. "On a Seventeenth Century Roll Containing Prayers and Magical Signs, Preserved in the British Museum." *Journal of the British Archaeological Association* 40 (1884): 297–332.

Singer, Isidore, ed. *Jewish Encyclopedia*. 12 vols. London: Funk and Wagnalls Company, 1901–6.

Skehan, Patrick W. "The Divine Name at Qumran, in the Masada Scroll, and in the Septuagint." *Bulletin of the International Organization for Septuagint and Cognate Studies* 13 (Fall 1980): 14–44.

Skemer, Don C. *Binding Words: Textual Amulets in the Middle Ages*. University Park: Pennsylvania State University Press, 2006.

Taylor, Thomas. *The Mystical Hymns of Orpheus*. 2nd ed. Chiswick, UK: C. Whittingham, 1824.

Theocritus. *The Idylls of Theocritus*. Translated by James Henry Hallard. London: Longmans, Green and Co., 1894.

Theon of Smyrna. *Mathematics Useful for Understanding Plato*. Translated by Robert Lawlor and Deborah Lawlor. San Diego, CA: Wizards Bookshelf, 1979.

Thomas, Herbert T. *Something About Obeah*. Kingston, Jamaica: Mortimer C. DeSouza, 1891.

Three Initiates. *The Kybalion: A Study of the Hermetic Philosophy of Ancient Egypt and Greece*. Chicago, IL: The Yogi Publication Society, 1908.

Tibbets, Charles John, ed. *Folk-Lore and Legends: Russian and Polish*. London: W. W. Gibbings, 1890.

Thompson, R. Campbell. *The Devils and Evil Spirits of Babylonia*. 2 vols. London: Luzac and Co., 1903.

Tolkien, J. R. R. *The Lord of the Rings*. London: George Allen and Unwin, 1969.

Tomlin, Roger S. O. "Voices from the Sacred Spring." In *Bath History*, edited by Trevor Fawcett, vol. 4, 7–24. Bath, UK: Millstream Books, 1992.

Unger, Merrill F. *Biblical Demonology: A Study of Spiritual Forces at Work Today*. Grand Rapids, MI: Kregel Publications, 1994.

Valletta, Niccola. *Cicalata sul fascino volgarmente detto jettatura*. 1777. Naples: Nella Stamperia Della Societa' Tipografica, 1814.

Venitiana del Rabina, Antonio. *Le grand grimoire, avec la grande clavicule de Salomon, et la magie noire, où les forces infernales du grand Agrippa, pour découvrir tous les trésors cachés, et se faire obéir à tous les espirits; suivé de tous les arts magiques*. 1202 [1750].

Verstegan, Richard, trans. *The Copy of a Letter Lately Written by a Spanishe Gentleman*. Antwerp, 1589.

Virgil. *Virgil*. Translated by H. Rushton Fairclough. 2 vols. London: William Heinemann; New York: G. P. Putnam's Sons, 1916–1918.

Walsh, R. *An Essay on Ancient Coins, Medals, and Gems, as Illustrating the Progress of Christianity in the Early Ages*. London: Howell and Stewart, 1828.

Watts, Donald C. *Dictionary of Plant Lore*. Amsterdam: Elsevier, 2007.

Weber, Henry, ed. "Kyng Alisaunder." In *Metrical Romances of the Thirteenth, Fourteenth and Fifteenth Centuries: Published from Ancient Manuscripts*. Vol. 1. Edinburgh: Printed by George Ramsay and Company, 1810.

Westcott, W. Wynn, ed. *The Chaldean Oracles of Zoroaster*. Wellingborough, Northamptonshire, UK: The Aquarian Press, 1983.

———. *Numbers, Their Occult Power and Mystic Virtues*. Vol. 9, *Collectanea Hermetica*. 3rd ed. London: Theosophical Publishing Society, 1911.

Wilde, Jane Francesca Elgee. *Ancient Legends, Mystic Charms, and Superstitions of Ireland*. London: Ward and Downey, 1888.

Williams, Joseph J. *Voodoos and Obeahs: Phases of West India Witchcraft*. New York: Dial Press, 1932.

Wrenshall, Letitia Humphreys. "Incantations and Popular Healing in Maryland and Pennsylvania." *The Journal of American Folk-Lore* 15 (October–December 1902): 268–74.

Wright, Arthur Robinson. *English Folklore*. London: Ernest Benn, 1928.

Wright, G. Ernest. *Biblical Archaeology.* Philadelphia, PA: Westminster Press, 1962.

Yogi Ramacharaka [William Walker Atkinson]. *The Hindu-Yogi Science of Breath: A Complete Manual of the Oriental Breathing Philosophy of Physical, Mental, Psychic and Spiritual Development.* Chicago, IL: Yogi Publication Society, 1904.

Young, Jean I., trans. *The Prose Edda of Snorri Sturluson.* Cambridge, UK: Bowes & Bowes, 1954.

Index

H

Index

Priapus, 149

priests, Egyptian, 25, 26, 83

primum mobile, 26

principles, 4, 15, 26, 27, 112, 116, 124, 160, 216

Proceedings of the Society for Psychical Research, 221–23

prophecy, 176, 203

Prose Edda of Snorri Sturluson, The (Young), 77

protection, 4, 53–55, 57, 143–145, 149, 151, 152, 155, 160, 193, 225, 231

Protestant, 68, 93

psalms, 93, 121, 155, 156

psychè kósmou, 13

psychopomp, 184

Psylli, 191

Ptolemaic order, 19, 20, 22, 23, 101

protection, 4, 53–55, 57, 143–45, 149, 151, 152, 155, 160, 193, 225, 231

purpose, 2, 21, 34, 44, 50, 51, 53, 54, 65, 69, 70, 77–79, 81, 83, 84, 88, 91, 92, 94–96, 99, 100, 102, 106, 107, 125, 128, 129, 132, 141, 149, 150, 154, 155, 157, 160, 168, 172, 183, 185, 186, 191, 193, 206, 216, 219, 225, 227, 228

pyramid, 75

Pythagoras, 9, 215, 216

Pythagorean Triangle, The (Oliver), 98

Pythagoreans, 19, 20

Q

Queen of Heaven, 53–55, 123

Queensland, 170–172

Quinn, Bernard L., 175, 176

quintessence, 35, 36

R

Ra, 61

rabbis, 77, 79, 90, 153

Ramacharaka, Yogi, 14, 15

Random Roamings (Jessopp), 222

reflexive, 146

Regardie, Israel, 69, 85–88, 123

Reichenbach, Carl von, 14

Remarkable Providences (I. Mather), 75

"Remarques sur les médailles d'Antonin frappées en Egypte" (Barthélemy), 20

repetition, 30, 42–45, 47, 68, 74, 94, 108, 128

request, active, 145

request, passive, 145

resonance, principle of, 213

rings, 194, 220, 224, 227

rheumatism, 224

rhyme, 4, 41, 46–49, 69, 83, 108, 124

To Write to the Author

If you wish to contact the author or would like more information about this book, please write to the author in care of Llewellyn Worldwide Ltd. and we will forward your request. Both the author and the publisher appreciate hearing from you and learning of your enjoyment of this book and how it has helped you. Llewellyn Worldwide Ltd. cannot guarantee that every letter written to the author can be answered, but all will be forwarded. Please write to:

Donald Tyson
℅ Llewellyn Worldwide
2143 Wooddale Drive
Woodbury, MN 55125-2989

Please enclose a self-addressed stamped envelope for reply,
or $1.00 to cover costs. If outside the U.S.A., enclose
an international postal reply coupon.

Many of Llewellyn's authors have websites with additional
information and resources. For more information,
please visit our website at http://www.llewellyn.com.